THE EUROPEAN UNION

General Editors: Neill Nugent, William E. Paterson, Vincent Wright

The European Union series is designed to provide an authoritative library on the European Union ranging from general introductory texts to definitive assessments of key institutions and actors, policies and policy processes, and the role of member states.

Books in the series are written by leading scholars in their fields and reflect the most up-to-date research and debate. Particular attention is paid to accessibility and clear presentation for a wide audience of students, practitioners and interested general readers.

The series consists of four major strands:

- general textbooks
- the major institutions and actors
- the main areas of policy
- the member states and the Union

Published titles

Desmond Dinan
Ever Closer Union? An Introduction to the European Community

Wyn Grant
The Common Agricultural Policy

Justin Greenwood
Representing Interests in the European Union

Fiona Hayes-Renshaw and Helen Wallace
The Council of Ministers

Simon Hix and Christopher Lord
Political Parties in the European Union

Brigid Laffan
The Finances of the European Union

Janne Haaland Matláry
Energy Policy in the European Union

Neill Nugent
The Government and Politics of the European Union (Third Edition)

European Union Series
Series Standing Order ISBN 0–333–69352–3

You can receive future titles in this series as they are published by placing a standing order. Please contact your bookseller or, in the case of difficulty, write to us at the address below with your name and address, the title of the series and the ISBN quoted above.

Customer Services Department, Macmillan Distribution Ltd
Houndmills, Basingstoke, Hampshire RG21 6XS, England

Forthcoming

Simon Bulmer and Drew Scott
European Union: Economics, Policy and Politics

Simon Hix
The Political System of the European Union

David Millar, Neill Nugent and William E. Paterson (eds)
The European Union Source Book

John Peterson and Elizabeth Bomberg
Decision-Making in the European Union

Ben Rosamond
Theories of European Integration

Richard Sinnott
Understanding European Integration

● ● ● ●

Simon Bulmer and Wolfgang Wessels
The European Council (Second Edition)

Renaud Dehousse
The Court of Justice: A Brief Introduction

David Earnshaw and David Judge
The European Parliament

Neill Nugent
The European Commission

Anne Stevens
The Administration of the European Union

● ● ● ●

David Allen and Geoffrey Edwards
The External Economic Relations of the European Union

Michelle Cini and Lee McGowan
Competition Policy in the European Union

Laura Cram
Social Policy in the European Union

Martin Holland
The European Union and the Third World

Malcolm Levitt and Christopher Lord
The Political Economy of Monetary Union

Anand Menon
Defence Policy and the European Union

James Mitchell and Paul McAleavey
Regionalism and Regional Policy in the European Union

John Redmond, René Schwok and Lee Miles
Enlarging the European Union

Margaret Sharp and John Peterson
Technology Policy in the European Union

Hazel Smith
The Foreign Policy of the European Union

Mark Thatcher
The Politics of European High Technology

Rüdiger Wurzel
Environmental Policy in the European Union

● ● ● ●

Simon Bulmer and William E. Paterson
Germany and the European Union

Phil Daniels and Ella Ritchie
Britain and the European Union

Alain Guyomarch, Howard Machin and Ella Ritchie
France in the European Union

Other titles planned include

European Union: A Brief Introduction

The History of the European Union

The European Union Reader

The Political Economy of the European Union

● ● ● ●

Political Union

The USA and the European Union

● ● ● ●

The European Union and its Member States

Reshaping the States of the Union

Italy and the European Union

Spain and the European Union

The Common
Agricultural Policy

Wyn Grant

First published 1997 by
MACMILLAN PRESS LTD
Houndmills, Basingstoke, Hampshire RG21 6XS
and London
Companies and representatives
throughout the world

ISBN 0–333–60465–2 hardcover
ISBN 0–333–60466–0 paperback

A catalogue record for this book is available
from the British Library.

10   9   8   7   6   5   4   3   2   1
06   05   04   03   02   01   00   99   98   97

Copy-edited and typeset by Povey–Edmondson
Tavistock and Rochdale, England

Printed in Hong Kong

 Published in the United States of America 1997 by
ST.MARTIN'S PRESS, INC.,
Scholarly and Reference Division
175 Fifth Avenue, New York, N.Y. 10010

ISBN 0–312–17393–8

To Alan Curbishley, whose job is more difficult than mine

Contents

List of Tables

Preface

This book seeks to offer a comprehensive review of the Common Agricultural Policy (CAP) taking account of both the perspectives of member states and the development of policies at the EU level. Care is taken to place the CAP within the broader context of the political economy of global agriculture and to take account of agriculture's links with the food processing industry. A central theme of the book is the need for further reform of the CAP and an analysis of the prospects of achieving such reform.

This book draws on a long-standing interest in the politics of agricultural policy which I have pursued for over twenty years. As a native of south-east London who remains an essentially urban person, there is no reason why I should have a particular interest in agriculture. My interest does, however, stem from a more general interest in political economy, broadly understood as the interaction between states and markets. The task of a social scientist is to understand and interpret complexity and there are few more complex policies than the CAP. It is hoped that a student taking a European Integration course who reads this book would then have a good understanding of the principal features of the CAP and its place within the policies of the European Union. I have not sought to use the analysis of the CAP to test competing theories of European integration, although the implicit influence of a liberal intergovernmentalist perspective will be apparent.

I am grateful to Carsten Daugbjerg of Aarhus University, and Michael Winter of Cheltenham and Gloucester College of Higher Education for reading the manuscript and offering the benefit of their expertise. Portions of the manuscript have also been read by Peter Burnell, Graham Cox, Philip Lowe, Charles Jones and Tim Stocker, and I am grateful to them for their comments.

This book makes use of interviews and other materials collected as part of an ESRC-funded study on the politics of agricultural credit policy (R000 23 4553). My collaboration with William Coleman of

McMaster University on that study has been a continuing source of inspiration and intellectual insights.

I would like to thank my wife, Maggie, for her continuing support and tolerance; Sophia, Ros and Milly, who have the good sense not to become academics; and Charlton Athletic football club for providing an absorbing, if sometimes frustrating, distraction from academic work.

Students are invited to update their knowledge of the CAP through my web page:

http://members.tripod.com~WynGrant/WynGrantCAPpage.html.

Please note the WynGrant is one word and case sensitive. In the event of problems, E-mail me at W.P.Grant@Warwick.ac.uk.

WYN GRANT

Introduction

Agricultural policy remains at the centre of the policy making activities of the European Union, yet there is a paradoxical sense in which it is regarded as peripheral to understanding the Union's future development. Keeler observes (1996, p. 128) that 'less than 2.3 percent of the more than 400 articles in . . . *The Journal of Common Market Studies* from September 1966 through September 1992 focused on the CAP. Most of these articles and other publications on the CAP have dealt far more with its economic or technical dimensions than with its political dynamics'. Yet a Common Agricultural Policy (CAP) has been one of the cornerstones of the European Union (EU) since its inception as a common market; it continues to account for around half of the EU's budget; it is the policy which has the greatest impact at the level of individual economic actors; and it presents one of the most significant obstacles to eastern enlargement of the Union.

Analysis of the CAP is a standard element of general university courses on European integration, yet it is often seen as being a rather compartmentalised topic which has little relevance for the more general understanding of the development of the institutions and policies of the European Union. There are three principal reasons why such an approach might be adopted. First, the making of agricultural policy *is* highly compartmentalised. It has its own special set of institutions and actors, and interaction with other policy areas tends to be poorly developed. A high political entry price is imposed by the fact that the various policies associated with the CAP are very complex. Acquiring even a basic understanding of, for example, the agrimonetary system is a long and difficult task likely to dissuade anyone without the keenest interest in the policy area. Whether it is intentional or not, the complexity of the policy process makes it difficult for outsiders to enter the agricultural policy community without absorbing some of the policy assumptions and values of the existing insiders. Complexity also permits policy 'fudges' which

1

convince policy outsiders that there has been real change when in fact very little has occurred.

Second, much of the writing on agricultural policy has been by agricultural economists. Much of this work has been of a very high standard and has made a considerable contribution to the policy debate. In particular, economists have pressed for greater transparency in the policy measures used, and a closer relationship between those measures and the policy objectives they seek to achieve. For example, if one wants to boost rural incomes, then rather than subsidise crops and livestock, one should subsidise farmers. Unavoidably, economists work within their own policy assumptions that lead them to advocate policies which might be optimal in terms of maximising the achievement of stated objectives but which take insufficient account of the political feasibility of their being put into effect. As economists, they conceptualise farming as an economic sector. In doing so, they fail to understand agriculture as a social order that requires sociological understanding, or a set of institutional structures that can be approached through the insights of political science.

Third, the CAP might be seen as a policy of the past rather than the future of the Union. At one time, it might have been seen as the only example of a 'working' Community policy, not in the sense that it achieved its objectives in a cost-effective way, but rather that it influenced decisions taken by individual farmers. However, that claim is no longer a valid one as the EU has expanded its activities in other areas such as cohesion policy, social policy and environmental policy. The CAP's share of the EU budget has dropped from around two-thirds to just over a half. There is an understandable concern with policies which will shape the future development of the Union, such as moves towards economic and monetary union.

The CAP is not, however, going to give up being a significant element of the Union's budget and decision-making activity. Its defenders argue that it will still be there in much the same shape in the year 2010. Others would argue that the external pressures for change will be too great. Whatever happens, the way in which those external pressures are mediated by EU institutions will continue to be a major agenda item for the member states. One should also not assume that the debate about agricultural policy has no lessons for other aspects of the integration process. In the case of agriculture, an attempt has been made to devise a common policy to cope with economies having different levels of involvement in agriculture and food processing, a variety of historical agricultural traditions, and which display divergences in the structure of agriculture in terms of such variables as farm size, ownership patterns and commodities produced. It is not surprising that attempts to devise such a policy have encountered considerable difficulties and it has been necessary to evolve expensive and often incoherent policy compromises. 'As the experience of the agriculture sector demonstrates, it is impossible to have viable common policies without parallel economic development and a convergence of currency values. The EU is clearly far from that stage' (*Agra Europe*, 21 April 1995, p. P/1).

The distinctiveness of this book

There are already many books about the CAP, and no doubt more will appear in the future. This book has a number of distinctive features:

- It is written by a political scientist influenced by an institutional political economy perspective, but is interdisciplinary in the sense that it takes fully into account the research findings of agricultural economists and rural sociologists.
- The political economy of the sector cannot be understood without exploring its linkages with supply and first-stage food processing industries.
- European agriculture has to be understood within the context of the changing global political economy of agriculture.
- The centrality of the relationship between the financial sector and agriculture in understanding the transformation of modern farming into a more input intensive, profit-orientated activity.

What claim is being made when it is stated that this book is written from the disciplinary perspective of a political scientist, working within an institutional political economy perspective? In short, the book is influenced by the 'new institutionalist' perspective, which maintains that analysis of a policy arena has to take account of the institutions that operate within it and the ways in which they shape norms, rules and policy choices. The term 'institution' is defined broadly, to include not just formally defined organisations, but also policy networks, as well as 'standard operating practices that structure the relationship between . . . various units of the polity and economy' (Hall, 1986, p. 19).

An institutional political economy approach thus differs from those based on public choice analysis, or those approaches which, while they might bear postmodernist labels, are rooted in a Marxist tradition such as the regulation school or various forms of post-Fordism. The notion of 'political economy' as used here does not draw on a Marxist tradition, but means that a purely economic or purely political science approach to the understanding of phenomena such as agricultural policy is necessarily inadequate. An economist must temper his or her approach by an awareness of the importance of satisficing behaviour and bounded rationality. A political scientist who seeks to understand economic phenomena must aspire to be economically literate, and in terms of the focus of this book have an understanding of the sector-specific theories and analytical techniques of agricultural economics.

It is also important to be aware of the considerable insights generated by the long-established subdiscipline of rural sociology. Rural sociology was able to establish itself as a viable subdiscipline 'by basing its enquiries upon a recognition that agriculture does *not* develop in advanced capitalist societies in a manner which merely mirrors other industries' (Newby, 1978, p. 25). The architects of the CAP were concerned to bring about a sociological transition: the absorption of the European peasantry into civil society. The CAP was seen as much as a territorial policy – intended to defend and support a rural space and society – as a sectoral policy. The ability of farmers to mobilise politically across Europe in a way that few other social groups could (fishermen were one other such group) helped to perpetuate this definition of the special character of rural needs.

Analysts often emphasise the policy compartmentalisation of agriculture, but it is also important to recognise the linkages that agriculture has with a number of other sectors of the economy, a second key theme of this book. Production and sales levels in these sectors are often directly affected by decisions taken on the CAP. These linkages provide an additional source of political strength for agriculture which has to be taken account when one analyses the political weakening that inevitably results from the declining share of agricultural employment in total employment. Frequently expressed puzzlement about the political displacement of a declining agricultural sector in Europe can be dispelled if one understands the central importance in the European economy of industries, often dominated by large multinationals, which supply agriculture and add value to its products. Agriculture accounts for only 5.4 per cent of employment in the EU, and 1.8 per cent of GDP, but 19.7 per cent of household consumption expenditure. The difference is accounted for by the value added (and appropriated) further down the food chain by food processors and retailers.

A third distinctive theme of this book is that the CAP has to be understood within the context of global agriculture. This does not mean that one has to accept as an uncontentious starting point Le Heron's (1993, p. 2) assertion that agriculture is already 'globalised'. However, the General Agreement on Tariffs and Trade (GATT) Uruguay Round saw the first significant, if still limited, international agreement on liberalising agricultural trade, and this work will be continued by the new World Trade Organisation (WTO). The analytical framework adopted here is not, however, limited to looking at a series of external 'pressures' on the CAP to which EU institutions and policies have to adjust, although that is certainly part of the picture.

Lowe *et al.* (1994, p. 11) identify a number of elements in the globalisation of food systems, taking care to distinguish between genuinely global processes (world-scale socioeconomic processes) from those general socioeconomic processes that happen to be universal. They offer a useful checklist of the findings in the literature. Central to their presentation is the role of multinationals, including their growing prominence in food production, the move towards 'stateless firms' with looser links to national bases and more complex and geographically spread sourcing strategies. Attention is drawn to the way in which technological advances erode the dependence of food production on particular areas of the world and to the internationalisation of consumer preferences. Finally, they emphasise the shift from national to transnational forms of regulation of food production and trade.

It is thus important to understand the extent to which the relative success or failure of the CAP is influenced by events elsewhere in the world, and over which it has little direct influence: for example, the demand for butter from the former Soviet Union or the demand for grain in the People's Republic of China. On the supply side, for all the sophistication of modern agricultural production, it is important to remember that levels and quality of agricultural output are still fundamentally affected by the weather: too much rain or not enough, late frosts, winds that are too strong, a lack of sun at a crucial stage of the ripening process and so on.

Another distinctive theme of this book is the increasing centrality of the relationship between the financial sector and farming in the understanding of agriculture. At the level of the farm, financial and business management skills are becoming as important as the more traditional husbandry and production management skills. The 1994 Report from DGII of the European Commission on *EC Agricultural Policy for the 21st Century* argues that 'The increase in the size of farm units and the value of the output of each unit is prompting larger producers to employ the services of financial and insurance markets . . . The price-fixing mechanism is thus relatively less important as an income stabilizer' (European Commission, 1994a, p. 28). Such an emphasis on financial management skills further disadvantages smaller-scale and more marginal producers.

The main elements of the CAP and the plan of this book

When the nations of Europe got together to form a common market in the late 1950s, agriculture was important to their economies, and even more important to their cultures and societies. They therefore decided that they needed a Common Agricultural Policy (CAP) which was given a set of contradictory objectives, such as increasing earnings for those working in agriculture and ensuring reasonable prices for consumers. The implicit central objective was, however, to make farmers better off so that a reactionary and discontented peasantry would not disrupt progress towards European unity. In so far as this happened, it did not have much to do with the policy, but was the result of increases in productivity made possible by mechanisation and agrochemicals, funded by loans from bankers (who think that farmers underpinned by state guarantees represent a good loan risk). Perhaps the biggest direct impact of the CAP was that it increased land prices, making it difficult for anyone to enter farming except through inheritance.

The basic instruments of the policy were the purchase of surplus produce from farmers and the imposition of import levies to keep out price-competitive produce from elsewhere in the world, together with export subsidies to get rid of the surplus produce. In addition, farmers eventually had their support prices worked out in their own version of

European money, called green money, which meant that their francs and lire were worth more than those of other people. All this had to be paid for by taxpayers and consumers (by higher prices in the shops). The CAP strained relations between European countries and other countries in the world (who wanted to supply the European market with their own cheaper produce), as well as causing environmental damage because of the fertilisers and agrochemicals used to boost production which could be sold into storage.

Why did the EC continue to pursue expensive policies that did not meet their objectives? The policy was so complex that few people understood it, so it was possible to change the policy in a way that benefited its clients, with little criticism. Member states that benefited economically and politically from the CAP defended it. Linked industries were prepared to give it political support when necessary. A number of attempts at reform were made, but they had limited success. However, in the 1990s it at last seemed that real progress towards reform might be possible, in part because of international pressures on the EU, but also because of signs of a changing perspective on the CAP in Germany, a country that had been one of its greatest defenders. Nevertheless, much remained to be done before Europe had an agricultural policy that provided a stable framework for an internationally competitive agricultural sector.

Chapter 1 sets the context for understanding European agriculture. It returns to some of the key themes identified in this chapter, as well as examining technological change in agriculture, and why agriculture is subsidised in most countries of the world. Chapter 2 explores the structure of agriculture and food processing in the member states of the EU, grouping them by shared characteristics. Chapter 3 explains the development of the CAP and why it assumed the shape it did. Chapter 4 unveils one of the greatest mysteries of the CAP, the system of green money, as well as explaining why fraud is a major problem for the CAP. Chapter 5 provides a comprehensible guide to the commodity regimes that lay at the heart of the CAP, paying particular attention to the dairy sector and the bovine spongiform encephalopathy (BSE) crisis, but also providing a lay person's guide to such phenomena as the hot beet syndrome and the dollar banana. Chapter 6 seeks to explain how decisions about the CAP are taken, placing particular emphasis on the role of the Commission, the Council of Ministers and the key member states. Chapter 7 reviews the main pressures for further reform: eastern enlargement; the further liberalisation of agricultural trade; and the difficult relationship between agricultural and environmental policy. Chapter 8 sets out and evaluates more radical reform options and suggests that the objectives of the CAP need to be revised.

My objective in writing this book has been to equip its readers, including those without prior knowledge of the CAP, to:

- understand its main features.
- be able to place that understanding within the context of the changing structure of European and global agriculture.
- understand the pressures for reform and why only limited progress has been made.
- form their own views as to how the reform agenda should develop.

1

The Context of European Agriculture

This chapter sets the context for the analysis of European agriculture in particular countries in Chapter 2. It outlines the main features of European agriculture. It assesses the contribution of technology to the current and future shape of European agriculture. The role of the financial sector in facilitating change in agriculture is discussed. It reviews the main linkages of European agriculture with its supply industries and the food processing sector. European agriculture is placed within its global setting, and it is emphasised that agriculture is subsidised in almost all advanced industrial countries.

The main characteristics of European agriculture

It should not be supposed that European agriculture could not survive without subsidies, or at least subsidies limited to a self-financing safety net that ironed out fluctuations in production caused by variations in the weather:

> For cereals, natural production conditions in large parts of Europe are no less, but probably more, favourable than in any other part of the world . . . once cereals prices in Europe are no longer above those in other parts of the world, there is a very good chance that Europe's pork and poultry farmers can produce for the world market, without subsidies. Indeed, a good part of that grain output which is in excess of domestic use in Europe could probably be

exported in the form of pork and poultry products, thereby enhancing value added in Europe's farming industry. (Marsh and Tangermann, 1996, p. 17)

Agriculture in aggregate in Europe would not necessarily be worse off without subsidies, and the more economically important food processing industry would have its international competitiveness enhanced if it did not have to pay for raw materials at a rate above world market prices. However, many individual farmers would lose out if subsidies were phased out. Those who stand to lose what they already have are a more politically potent force than those who may make uncertain gains in the future. There lies the central dilemma of the CAP: what makes economic sense is often not politically accep-table. Agricultural economists have advanced ingenious ideas for bonds to ease the transition of farmers into other activities, but such elegant solutions do not really provide a means of coping with the raw emotion that a socially cohesive and culturally symbolic industry like farming can generate.

One of the greatest obstacles to the achievement of a common agricultural policy that is more than common in name only is to be found in the considerable structural divergences within European agriculture. These structural divergences lie at the root of the divergent national interests that lead to conficts and tensions in the development, reform and implementation of the CAP and which result in often incoherent and unsatisfactory compromises in the Council of Ministers. These differences have a number of dimensions: size of farm, form of ownership, capital intensity, types of produce and so on. The policy has to try to encompass the different needs and interests of, for example, a wine producer in Italy; a producer of fruit and vegetables using irrigation in Spain; a large-scale cereal grower in Britain or France; a small-scale dairy farmer in Bavaria; or a farmer battling against the climatic disadvantages of Finland.

Particularly within the larger member states, there may be im-portant regional differences in agriculture within a country, and these may affect national agricultural politics and hence the strategies and tactics pursued by a member state at the European level. For example, in Italy, the Po valley represents a more advanced and economically integrated form of agriculture than is found elsewhere in the country. Within France one can distinguish large-scale cereal production in the Paris basin; dairying in Britanny; a variety of forms of viticulture in different parts of the country; areas which specialise in horticulture; and extensive livestock production in areas such as the Massif Central (Charvet, 1994). Neveu has proposed a broad classification of European agriculture into three types of region (Charvet, 1994, pp. 139–42):

1. Competitive regions with good adjustment capabilities. These have good farming conditions which permit the development of commercial strategies and international competitiveness. Examples include cereal production in East Anglia and the Paris basin and a number of areas in Southern Europe such as the Po valley in Italy.
2. Regions in difficulty handicapped by such factors as climate, relief and a domination by small-scale producers. Even with aid from the EU, the maintenance of commercial agriculture in these areas is difficult. The far west of Ireland, much of Finland and many areas in Southern Europe are examples.
3. A rather diverse category of intermediate regions handicapped by such factors as insufficiently modern structures or unfavourable farming conditions. A number of strategies are possible to try and resolve these problems, such as moving towards higher-quality production. This category contains regions that are rather different from one another, such as most of Ireland, the Massif Central and Bavaria.

Overview of the agricultural structure of the EU

Total employment in agriculture in the EU-12 more than halved between 1970 and 1994. The numbers employed in 'agriculture, hunting, forestry and fishing' declined from 16.3 million in 1970 to 7.9 million in 1994 (or from 13.5 per cent to 5.4 per cent of total civilian employment). Most countries were relatively close to the EU-12 mean in terms of the rate of decline in agricultural employment (only The Netherlands showed an increase in absolute numbers). In 1992 two rather different countries maintained 70 per cent of their 1970 levels of employment in agriculture: the UK, which has the smallest agriculture population in the EU, and Greece, which has the largest. Three countries saw a relatively sharp fall in the agricultural population in 1992: Spain with 38 per cent of the 1970 level; Germany (West) with 40 per cent; and France with 43 per cent. Thirty-eight per cent of farmers in Germany had other gainful

employment, the highest level in the EU. This high level of part-time
farming in Germany means that there are more farmers than would
be expected in a highly successful industrial power, a fact that has
significant implications for agricultural politics in the EU.

There is a considerable variation in the agricultural share of the
employed civilian population among the member states, a pattern
also reflected in the share of agriculture in GDP (see Table 1.1). Four
countries (two of them in Southern Europe) have over ten per cent of
their civilian employment in agriculture: Austria, Greece, Ireland
and Portugal. Ireland has one of the EU's economies most dependent
on agriculture and first-stage food processing. The contribution of
Irish agricultural and food exports to net foreign exchange earnings
has been estimated to be of the order of 40 per cent. At the other end
of the spectrum, seven countries in Northern Europe have less than 5

TABLE 1.1

Basic data about European farming, 1994

Country (ranked by value of production)	Value of final production of agriculture (millions ECU)	Share of agriculture, etc.* in civilian employment (%)	Share of agriculture in GDP (%)
France	43 917	4.8	2.0
Italy	32 332	7.9	2.6
Germany	31 396	3.0	0.8
Spain	22 174	9.8	2.7
United Kingdom	17 831	2.2	0.9
Netherlands	16 808	4.0	3.2
Greece	8 722	20.8	7.5
Belgium	6 864	2.5**	1.6
Denmark	6 392	5.7	2.5
Austria	5 412	13.3**	2.2
Republic of Ireland	4 307	12.0	5.4
Finland	3 581	8.3	1.8
Sweden	3 357	3.4	1.0
Portugal	3 217	11.6	2.0
Luxembourg	186	2.8	0.9
EU 15	206 496	5.4	1.8

Notes:
*   Agriculture, forestry, hunting and fishing
**   1993 figures
Source: European Commission, *The Agricultural Situation in the European Union*,
1995 Report.

per cent of their civilian employment in agriculture: Belgium, France, Germany, Luxembourg, The Netherlands, Sweden and the United Kingdom. Four countries are in the intermediate category of between 5 per cent and 10 per cent: Finland, Denmark, Italy and Spain.

Not only does the salience of agriculture in the economy vary significantly from one country to another, but member states also display considerable variations in their agricultural structures in terms of the size and fragmentation of land holdings. Only one state has an average utilised agriculture area per holding of over 50 hectares: the United Kingdom. France, Denmark, Ireland and Luxembourg and Sweden have average holdings of between 25 and 49 hectares, followed by Austria, Belgium, Denmark, Finland The Netherlands and Spain, with average holdings of between 10 and 24 hectares. In three countries, the average size of holding is very small (below 10 hectares): Greece, Italy and Portugal.

The contrast between Greece and the United Kingdom is very strong, with 81 per cent of farms in the UK being reasonably large (over 50 hectares) compared with 88 per cent of farms in Greece being under 10 hectares. Italy and Portugal also have a large proportion of farms under 10 hectares (84 per cent and 89 per cent, respectively). France has more large farms than popular opinion often allows (just under a quarter of them are over 50 hectares).

Technological change in agriculture

It is important to know about technological change in agriculture if one wants to understand the CAP, for two reasons. First, improvements in technology continually boost productivity, offsetting reform efforts which seek to reduce production. Second, there is a growing conflict between the advocates of a high-technology agriculture and those who consider that intensive forms of farming are environmentally damaging, pay insufficient regard to the needs of animals and represent a potential threat to human health. The BSE episode encapsulated and focused consumer concerns about technologically advanced systems of farming. Hence, the application of technology in agriculture is not a politically neutral issue for debate by experts but is increasingly the focus of conflicts which are in part ideological in character.

The emphasis on the maximisation of production in postwar European agriculture encouraged the emergence, particularly in northern Europe, of a modern, technologically-orientated farmer. Although it is well known that farmers vary considerably in their willingness to adopt innovations, the farmer interested in profit maximisation could use his or her increasing, largely subsidised income stream to invest in new buildings and machinery, with banks and specialised agricultural credit institutions increasingly willing to provide loans to meet any shortfall. A considerable amount of advice was available to the farmer who wanted to experiment with new production techniques, from government advisory services or from, for example, the field representatives employed by agrochemical companies. For countries such as the Republic of Ireland, joining the European Community itself initiated a transformation in the direction of a more commercially-orientated form of agriculture.

It is important to appreciate the scale of the change that has occurred in European agriculture:

In the 1950s, the majority of continental European farmers produced and lived much in the same manner as their forebears in the nineteenth century or earlier. They produced cereals and vegetable crops on small, often widely scattered, plots of land, with minimal use of power machinery . . . Horses, oxen and humans provided much of the energy on the farm, so a significant share of farm output was consumed rather than marketed. (Phillips, 1990, p. 23)

The importance of the shift from animal to mechanical power cannot be underestimated. There is a limit to what can be achieved in terms of cultivation with the use of animal draft power, and a considerable proportion of land has to be used to grow crops to feed the animals: 'The shift from animal to mechanical sources of power is an important source of the apparent inherent capacity of agriculture in the industrial countries to expand output for sale or use more rapidly than demand during the transition since the Second World War' (Gale Johnson, 1991, p. 63). Nevertheless, machines largely provide a substitute for human and animal labour. They do not 'change radically the empirical nature of a production process, which remains essentially a complex biological and natural process, technically based on a long-standing accumulation of experience' (Byé and Fonte, 1994, p. 245).

Biotechnology

The future development of agriculture is likely to be substantially influenced by discoveries in biotechnology (in broad terms, understood as the use of genetic engineering to modify plants and animals to carry desired traits such as disease resistance). This is an area in which a number of large multinational companies are active with an emphasis on private-sector research and development. Those critical of the role of multinationals in this area see biotechnology as 'aimed at reinforcing the dependence of farmers on purchased inputs' (Le Heron, 1993, p. 43). Some developments in biotechology such as transgenic plants that are resistant to particular viruses or insects could, however, reduce dependence on purchased inputs such as chemicals. Seeds and plants with a greater resistance to viruses and other diseases as well as weather variations would require fewer agrochemicals to be applied to them. The implications of biotechnology may therefore be somewhat different from that of earlier technologies such as agrochemicals and advanced farm machinery. More sophisticated and diversified demand will tend to produce a more heterogeneous agro-food industry: 'Biotechnologies offer an important opportunity for mastering the transition towards a more diversified production system' (Byé and Fonte, 1994, p. 253).

Historically, biotechnology had its origins in fermentation techniques used in industries such as brewing. After the Second World War 'There were enormous improvements in efficiency, in yields from fermenting cells, in fermenter design and in extraction and purification of the final product' (Marks, 1993, p. 104). In its form as potentially the most important enabling technology of the early twenty-first century, biotechnology is built on the discovery of recombinant DNA and the subsequent use of genetic engineering techniques. It has wide ranging implications for livestock and crop production:

Developments in livestock production include the improvement of animals through genetic selection; enhanced food nutrition; increased reproductive efficiency; greater control of diseases and pests; and the development of growth hormones, bioregulators and diagnostic kits. Plant biotechnologies are being developed to improve resistance to environmental stresses; create new species; regulate plant growth; control diseases; improve plant nutrition; create microbial insecticides; create herbicide-resistant plants;

improve digestibility of forages; and enhance metabolic efficiency. (Marks, 1993, p. 109)

There is often a substantial gap between the development of scientific knowledge and its application in terms of commercial products freely available in the market place, and this is certainly the case for biotechnology. Despite its apparent transformative potential, 'the diffusion of biotechnology in the agro-food system is very slow, its impact is restricted to specific areas and sectors, and commercialized products are still very few' (Byé and Fonte, 1994, p. 242). Some of the most promising developments are in diagnostic veterinary medicine and new vaccines and therapeutics, a number of which have been on the market for some time. In the plant sector, some transgenic plants have been tested in field trials. However, 'Many crops are genetically not well characterised. The number of crops that can be genetically modified is small' (OECD, 1992, p. 19). Genetically modified animals are not in use in commercial agriculture. As in the plant sector, not many useful genes have been identified and many scientific obstacles remain in the way of the production of transgenic animals.

In any case, whether methods of plant and animal breeding and of food production are changed fundamentally in the next few decades in a way that reshapes agriculture 'depends on numerous factors, many of which lie outside the domain of science and technology: economics, legal and safety constraints, public attitudes, industrial and government policies' (OECD, 1992a, p. 11). Even if a technological breakthrough occurs, political obstacles may prevent its commercial use, as the case of BST (bovine Somatotropin) and milk shows.

BST is 'a naturally occurring protein hormone secreted by the pituitary gland of the cow, [which] can now be produced by bacteria through recombinant DNA technology' (Harding, 1989, p. 182). BST can substantially boost milk yield per cow, by as much as 15 per cent per lactation. Produced in a commercial form by multinationals such as Monsanto, BST has been introduced in commercial dairying in the United States, having been certified by the Food and Drug Administration as being completely safe for people and cows. According to OECD estimates, some 43 per cent of US dairy cows are likely to be treated with BST by 1999–2000, compared with just 5 per cent in 1993–4. Milk production per cow is expected to rise by 11.5 per cent (*Agra Europe*, 3 March 1995, p. E/5).

The question of whether BST use should be permitted has pro-voked a prolonged controversy in the EU. In many ways, it has been seen both by the biotechnology sector and by consumer advocates and environmentalists as a test case for the introduction of a new generation of technological advances in agriculture. The Director of the US Pure Food Campaign has 'described BST as "the gateway product". If BST use were allowed . . . a whole stream of biotech products would follow in rapid succession' (*Agra Europe*, 18 November 1994, p. E/9). Fourteen European pressure groups joined together in the 'European Campaign Against rBST' and 257 organisations signed their declaration, which was presented to the serving president of the Council of Agricultural Ministers.

The campaign argued that the use of recombinant BST would go against an expressed consumer preference for natural and wholesome dairy products. It could only be cost effective in intensive dairy farms. Milk production in more marginal areas would fall, and there would be increased concentration in the industry, with more intensive land use practices in the high productivity regions of the EU. In response, the Forum for European Bioindustry Coordination argued that a ban on BST would disregard EU rules and GATT commitments. It claimed that the consequences of deviating from accepted rules would be 'potentially disastrous for a society which must stimulate and rely on innovation for continued economic growth' (*Agra Europe*, 1 December 1994, p. E/10).

The European Commission was concerned about the socioeco-nomic and consumer effects of permitting BST use, but was also aware that under GATT rules decisions about the use of hormones are supposed to be based on the criteria of quality, safety and efficacy, which BST would meet. Member states had three choices: an immediate end to the moratorium; a short extension of one or two years; and the Commission's plan to extend the moratorium until the dairy quota regime expired in 2000, which was accepted. Underlying the ministers' decision must have been a concern about sanctioning a technological innovation that would have increased output of a product already in surplus. Lowe *et al.*, (1994, p. 13) warn against a technological determinism creeping into the analysis of agriculture which detaches technology from social processes. In this case, opposi-tion from consumer, environmental and some farming groups led to a political decision which at least delayed the application of new technology.

It could be argued, of course, that the BST case is less significant than it appears because it really represents the last application of a Fordist model of production to agriculture, an attempt to incorporate a new technology into an existing intensive model of production without upsetting it (Byé and Fonte, 1994, p. 243). What biotechnology is likely to produce is less a biorevolution in agriculture, but rather a political conflict 'between the persistence of a technical model of production still oriented towards quantitative norms and the emergence of new demands and new functions for agriculture and the rural space' (Byé and Fonte, 1994, p. 244). However, while recognising the insights generated by post-Fordist models of agriculture, one must not push them too far. It is very easy to fall into the trap of generalising from particular examples to the whole pattern of food production. Thus the transformation of agricultural products from mass commodities into 'health and medical goods, in the context of a market more strongly regulated by quality, health and environmental norms' (Byé and Fonte, 1994, p. 249) is at most an emergent trend rather than a reality. There are niche markets for high-quality, value-added products such as vegetarian foods, but there is also still a substantial demand for standardised products such as baked beans at the lowest possible price.

The agricultural articles of the Treaty of Rome established as an objective the increase of agricultural productivity 'by promoting technical progress'. Technical progress would have occurred without any stimulation from European institutions, and the concern in the 1990s is that continuing productivity gains will undermine the MacSharry reforms and GATT agreements. It has been noted that 'most advances in agriculture seem to be of the output-increasing and input-using type, and especially of the sort which uses more capital but less labour' (Hill and Ray, 1987, p. 291). This would not seem to be a rational outcome in conditions of structural unemployment and persistent agricultural surpluses:

> Part of the reason is the insulation given to farmers from the market consequences of rising levels of production by various forms of support . . . and the tax and grant environment which, by subsidising capital not labour, creates a favourable climate for labour-saving capital-using innovations. Also, because agricultural scientists have tended to regard more output per acre or more milk per cow as an indicator of their success, the direction of

technological advance has been towards this sort of development. (Hill and Ray, 1987, p. 291)

Productionist assumptions have increasingly been challenged, both because they are no longer seen as solutions to problems but rather as their source, and because of increased public sensitivity to environmental questions. This is reflected, for example, 'in the gradual attainment of a modified insider status in matters of policy-making' (Clunies-Ross and Cox, 1994, p. 73) by the advocates of organic farming. At a European level, increased attention has been paid to agri-environmental policies, even if progress so far has been relatively limited.

Nevertheless, one does not have to be a technological determinist to see that there are underlying forces which continue to promote technological innovation. There is considerable political influence that can be exerted by multinational companies wishing to market products in which they have invested considerable sums of money, even if they did not succeed in their objective in the BST case in Europe. Such firms are, however, continually improving their government relations capabilities in an effort to increase their political influence.

Finance and agriculture

Another set of pressures towards a more high-input, high-output agriculture comes from the financial services sector. The financial services sector understandably only wants to fund commercially viable projects, and in some cases may offer specially favourable terms to the most profit-orientated farmers (Marsden and Whatmore, 1994, p. 123). An Irish bank's agricultural manager commented in an interview, 'I suppose everybody's after the better clients. If we come across a very good client, we'll offer him a good deal and persuade him to come over.' He saw future opportunities for the bank in terms of 'providing more of a specialist service for the larger customers . . . That's the way all banks will go.' 'Banking capital is thus increasingly seeking to police the use of credit, restricting its use to productive enterprises, and as a consequence, pushing the farm family more specifically towards technical methods of production and formal levels of rationality' (Marsden *et al.*, 1990, p. 52).

The rate at which these changes occur will vary from enterprise to enterprise both within and between member states. Some regions of the EU are much more resistant to this process than others. 'Nevertheless, despite this in-built resistance, the increased specialisation of agricultural production among the regions of Europe during the 1970s, and the intensive capitalisation of production in some regions at the expense of others, has been a significant factor affecting the direction of capital penetration into the industry' (Marsden *et al.*, 1986, p. 272).

The need to raise capital and to service loans pushes farmers more in the direction of using profit maxmisation as their principal or sole criterion when making decisions about farming practice. The extreme example of this pressure to secure the best possible return from the available assets of land and capital is seen in Britain, where many farmers have handed over all or part of their farming operations to management companies, one of which (Sentry Farming) is quoted on the Stock Exchange. These companies then put in managers who are trained to secure the best return from the available assets, with the owner of the land securing an agreed portion of the return. The farmer is able to withdraw from active farming, secure in the knowledge that the assets of the farm will be managed in such a way as to provide the best possible return.

Although there are technological and financial pressures which push at least a significant subgroup of farmers in the direction of higher levels of production and more intensive forms of farming, there are also countervailing pressures. Environmental regulations in areas such as dairy farming have become stricter, and a minority of farmers have responded to changing public attitudes by engaging in more environmentally sensitive forms of farming. There remain, however, serious deficiencies in the attention to which education and training for farmers includes an appropriate environmental content (Winter, 1995).

It should also be noted that diversification into the provision of off-farm services or into leisure-orientated enterprises is an alternative to further increases in farm output. Over 40 per cent of agricultural holdings in England undertake some form of non-farm business, with the three most popular types of enterprise being contracting and other agricultural services (21.8 per cent), accommodation (19.7 per cent), and equine (11 per cent) (Country Landowners' Association, 1994, para. 103). Limited tourist activities have long been associated with farming, but these are becoming more sophisticated, while some farmers have diversified into areas such as the provision of golf courses. Throughout the EU, the importance of what is called 'pluriactivity' is underlined by the fact that 'almost a third of all holders of agricultural holdings in the EC-10 have other jobs' (European Commission, 1994, p. 55). The fact that farming remains largely a family activity in most member states gives it a resilience and flexibility in coping with changing economic conditions (Schmitt, 1995).

The linkage industries

As was emphasised in the introduction, the political strength of agriculture is in part because of its links with a number of supply and processing industries whose own well being is influenced by developments in agriculture. The principal industries are:

1. Agricultural machinery and equipment ranging from combine harvesters to milking parlours, with estimated sales of 11 180 million ECU and employment of 97 000 in 1996. In some member states, the supply of irrigation equipment is a significant subsector. The production of tractors and combine harvesters is dominated by a relatively small number of companies, some of which are also car manufacturers. There are also a large number of small and medium-sized companies in the sector producing specialised equipment, often just one product line. Over a third of total value-added in the sector is produced in Germany. Production and sales deteriorated substantially in the early 1990s because the uncertainties associated with CAP reform and the GATT negotiations led farmers to be more cautious about buying new equipment.
2. Forty per cent of world production of agrochemicals (pesticides, herbicides, fungicides) takes place in the EU, reflecting the intensive nature of modern European agriculture. Like most parts of the chemical industry, the need to recoup research costs means that this subsector is dominated by a relatively small number of firms.
3. Fertilisers is another highly concentrated subsector, with the number of independent fertiliser companies in Europe falling from fifty-six in 1980 to twenty-nine in 1990 (Marsden and

Whatmore, 1994, p. 118). 'Set aside' further reduced demand in an industry already suffering from over capacity and weak demand.

4. The EU is the leading world producer of animal feed. The need to keep transport costs low means that independent compounders can be successful, but in Britain three large companies account for over 50 per cent of the compound market (Bojduniak and Sturgess, 1995, p. 77). The multinational companies active in this sector, such as Dalgety, face a situation in which, 'Because of their reliance on the farm sector for a considerable proportion of their raw materials as well as sales, their levels of profitability are particularly sensitive to the fluctuations in farm incomes brought about as a result of changing agricultural policy' (Marsden and Whatmore, 1994, p. 119). CAP reform has led to a slight fall in demand.

5. Seed suppliers. The application of biotechnology to create seeds with disease resistance or other specialised characteristics means that this is an increasingly high-tech sector in which multinational companies are prominent. For example, Ciba-Geigy has developed a maize seed that is genetically engineered to be resistant to weedkillers typically used by farmers, so the maize can be sprayed without any risk of killing the crop. Such products are very politically sensitive as they depend on EU approval which has often not been given readily.

6. Veterinary medicines and other pharmaceutical products, ranging from diagnostic medicines through therapeutics to production stimulants for livestock. The extensive use of, for example, antibiotics, is another indicator of the intensive nature of modern European farming and has implications for human health. This is a rapidly growing subsector, with sales of 1527 million ECU in 1991. A number of large pharmaceutical companies are present in the subsector, although the high research costs relative to turnover have led some to sell off their stakes.

7. The financial services sector providing loans and insurance services to agriculture. In most countries, there are just a few institutions providing such services. Some (Crédit Agricole in France) have been specially set up for the purpose, others have co-operative origins, while others (as in Britain) are specialised agricultural departments of major lending institutions.

8. Specialist institutions and firms providing educational, training and advisory services to agriculture.

9. Specialist agricultural publications in the print media, together with television and radio programmes directed at a farming audience.

On the output side, there is a close link between farming and those 'first stage' food processing industries that prepare agricultural products for human consumption. An example of a 'first stage' food processing industry would be the pasteurisation of milk and its placing in containers for human consumption. 'Second stage' food processing industries typically involve higher value-added transformations to semi-finished products produced by first stage industries, but also often involve the importation of raw materials from outside Europe: for example, chocolate production. First stage processors tend to benefit from the CAP because they produce goods which can be sold into EU intervention stores if necessary, while second stage processors cannot sell into intervention and are adversely affected by levies and duties on essential raw materials imported from outside the EU. A considerable portion of the first stage dairy processing industry in Europe is in the ownership of farmer co-operatives, although these behave increasingly like any other commercial enterprise.

The structure of the food processing industry in a particular country (particularly first stage processing such as dairying) can have a significant feedback effect on farming efficiency. The existence of a vigorous food processing sector in a country, particularly where it has been developed by farmer-owned co-operatives, encourages farmers to grow high-quality produce as cheaply as possible. Conversely, a weak and fragmented food processing sector may hamper the development of more commercial forms of farming. The line of division here is largely one between Northern and Southern Europe, with the food processing industry increasingly dominated by large mutinationals from Northern Europe.

During the 1980s and early 1990s there was a wave of major takeovers in the food processing industry: 'The imperative for growth through acquisition, rather than organic development, has been particularly strong in the food industry because of the key importance of branding as a means of securing markets and erecting entry barriers around them' (Pollert, 1993, p. 6). The US tobacco company, Philip Morris, diversified into food processing, acquiring General Foods, Kraft and the Swiss confectioners Suchard. In the dairy sector, more than 50 per cent of milk processed in Belgium is in the hands of foreign purchasers, along with 25 per cent in Spain, 21 per cent in the United Kingdom and 20 per cent in Italy. The main countries making acquisitions in the dairy sector have been Denmark, France, the Republic of Ireland and The Netherlands (Hall, 1995, p. 12). This surge in take-overs was in large part a response to declining and stagnant markets in the USA and Europe, to the concentration of retailer power, and also to the new opportunities offered by the single market.

There are now few take-over targets left, with many of the remaining firms being either family-owned or co-operatives. As a consequence, there has now been a move towards strategic alliances such as the Danone/Unilever venture, which makes frozen ice-cream and yoghurt snacks. Nevertheless, 'Even successful small companies are vulnerable to takeover, because they cannot finance the capital or the marketing to expand in the face of the cost-barriers to growth established by the larger companies' (Pollert, 1993, p. 9).

European agriculture in its global setting

Even those writers who have advanced a globalisation model of agriculture have emphasised that they are not advancing 'a globalist view' in the sense of 'the equal or comprehensive appearance of phenomena around the globe' (Le Heron, 1993, p. 20). If one examines the three principal dimensions of globalisation – trade, foreign investment and financial integration – it is evident that there has been less impact from global developments in agriculture than in most other economic sectors. Agricultural trade has been constrained by a series of protectionist barriers, not least those erected by the EU. Multinational companies are confined largely to the processing end of the food chain, particularly those second stage companies that have a relatively distant relationship with farming, and to the input side of farming (agrochemical, farm machinery companies and so on.) There has been greater integration of seed producers with agrochemical companies because gene suppliers want to control seed markets or pursue a strategy of 'moving further downstream into crop output markets, in order to capture the industrial value added' (OECD, 1992a, p. 21). In the financial services sector, although country specific agricultural credit institutions have been transformed into more commercial entities in a number of countries, they remain significant agriculturally orientated actors in other countries – for example, Crédit Agricole in France.

It is in trade relationships that there has been seen some of the most economically significant and politically charged transformations. World exports of agricultural products as a percentage of world trade decreased from 13.7 per cent in 1985 to 11.5 per cent in 1992, although their value in real terms increased in line with the general expansion of world trade. A number of developments have, however, reshaped the character of world agricultural trade and produced new political tensions. One of the consequences of the CAP has been 'a marked turnaround in the trading position of the EC from a large net importer of major temperate agricultural products to a substantial net exporter' (Le Heron, 1993, p. 133). This led to the displacement of the United States from traditional markets and recurrent tensions in US–EU agricultural trade relations: 'The Americans were particularly irate because they viewed the United States as the world's most efficient producer and traditionally Europe's major supplier of food imports' (Libby, 1992, p. 4).

Developments on the world market provide the context within which the CAP operates. If, for example, the countries of the former Soviet Union import large quantities of butter, or the People's Republic of China imports large quantities of grain, this will enable intervention stocks in Europe to be run down. World market prices affect the cost of operating the CAP, although the CAP itself also affects world market prices. Another important variable is whether the dollar is appreciating or depreciating. Thus, for example, in 1993, 'The impact of falling world prices on the per tonne market support price in ECU terms was . . . attenuated by the appreciation of the US dollar' (OECD, 1994a, p. 20). In 1995, the depreciation of the US dollar threatened the CAP with a new budgetary crisis.

Cereals and dairy products are the two largest items in the CAP budget. Grains have caused more difficulty in terms of international trading relationships, but the dairy sector contains large numbers of medium-sized 'family farmers', whom domestic politicians have traditionally sought to protect from world market forces. It is therefore worth examining world production and trade trends in these commodities in terms of the impact on the development of the CAP. If one looks at wheat as the single most important cereal product, the United States was projected to account for a little over a third of world exports in 1994–5, with the EU accounting for little under a third. Australia, Argentina and Canada were the other principal exporters. 'The major determining factor in the outlook for cereals remains the future level of demand from developing countries'

(OECD, 1994, p. 79); this is affected by factors such rates of growth, domestic levels of supply and the availability of credit.

For example, China, which has seen a growth in urban populations and bread demand, plans to achieve self-sufficiency in grain by the turn of the century, despite the loss of farmland to industry. Poor procurement prices, the reluctance of farmers to sell to the state, and deficiencies in transport, have all held back domestic supply. In the medium term, China is likely to remain a large importer of wheat and 'the driving force in world wheat demand' (*Agra Europe*, 10 February 1995). The other principal importers of wheat in 1994–5 were the former Soviet Union and North Africa, where local production has been affected by drought. Production in the former Soviet Union has been hampered by a series of problems, including the availability of finance and necessary inputs, land reforms and other changes, while adverse weather conditions can lead to the destruction of up to 15 per cent of the winter wheat crop.

It is anticipated that policy reforms such as those of the CAP will 'produce a lower structural grain surplus in the OECD in the medium term' (OECD, 1994a, p. 78). A reduction in subsidised exports should lead to 'higher world prices, less trade distortion, and improved functioning of international cereal markets over the medium term' (OECD, 1994a, p. 78). Some analysts have suggested that world grain production will not meet rising demand by the early decades of the twenty-first century. Whether this will be the case depends on what assumptions are made about population trends and technological developments, and how far environmental degradation and global warming affect the soil, irrigation systems and air quality. Improvements in agricultural husbandry in the former Soviet Union and Eastern Europe, together with the greater use of biotechnology, could push up production substantially. Much will depend on economic and political stability in such countries, together with the way in which public attitudes towards biotechnology develop in North America and Europe.

In the dairy sector, the EU was expected to account for 29 per cent of world milk production in 1995, a similar proportion of world butter production, but 44 per cent of world cheese production. In terms of exports, the EU accounted in 1994 for some 47 per cent of the world dairy market, with about 2 billion ECU a year being spent on subsidised exports (*Agra Europe*, 3 February 1995, p. P/2). The United States accounts for around 19 per cent of world milk production, with Russia and India also being significant producers.

However, countries such as Australia and New Zealand have a significance out of proportion to their level of production in the trade in world dairy products, with the EU 'losing ground to both Australia and New Zealand for a share of the world market' (*Agra Europe*, 21 April 1995, M/5). Trade in butter is particularly affected by demand from Russia. Surpluses of products such as butter and skimmed milk powder are tending to decline, reflecting policies by OECD countries that have sought to reduce support for the dairy sector, but also an improvement in the world market for cheese and other dairy products. Production growth is forecast to remain low in the medium term, although export levels are also likely to remain below those of the late 1980s.

The CAP has sought to protect the incomes of European farmers by maintaining high prices protected by variable import levies. Surplus production that cannot be absorbed within the EU is dumped on the world market. Countries such as the United States and Japan have also sought vigorously to protect their agricultural populations. As a consequence, world market prices have generally reflected political interventions as least as much as the forces of supply and demand. An increased awareness of the domestic and international costs of such policies has contributed to a process of reform which is at least under way, even if it is inadequate and incomplete. Multilateral trade negotiations have been an important forum in which conflicts over the international consequences of EU and other domestic policies have been fought out and partially resolved. They are likely to be a continuing dynamic for change in the future, but the barriers that have to be removed in terms of various forms of subsidy for agriculture are considerable.

The extensive subsidisation of agriculture

Agriculture has been a heavily subsidised economic activity in most advanced industrial companies. The EU is therefore not unusual in providing high levels of subsidy to agriculture. There are a number of countries which provide higher levels of subsidy, such as Japan, Norway and Switzerland. That does not mean that there should be complacency about the level of subsidy. The EU is such a significant player in the world agricultural economy that its subsidised exports in particular have serious distorting effects.

In order to provide a context for the rest of the book, some of the the distorting effects of high levels of subsidy to farmers will be summarised:

1. A substantial transfer of resources from the population at large to a small segment of the population (farmers) takes place. There may be policy justifications for providing subsidies to rural populations, but there are more transparent and effective ways of doing this than through subsidising agricultural production. There is an increasing recognition of the need for an effective and integrated rural policy rather than simply an agricultural policy. In any case, subsidies principally benefit larger farmers, who are in least in need of them: they could survive in a free market. A substantial proportion of the subsidies provided under the CAP is obtained by agricultural traders, providers of intervention stores and so on, rather than the rural population.

2. Consumers have to pay higher prices for agricultural products than they would have to do in a free market. One must be wary of estimates of the loss to consumers. If the CAP was dismantled, there is a risk that many farmers would go out of business and world prices would rise, so the gains to consumers might not be as great as it would first appear to be the case. Nevertheless, the policy in its present form does impose a significant cost on consumers.

3. Producers elsewhere in the world who have a comparative advantage in agricultural production may be denied access to the EU market by import restrictions, and may face competition in third country markets from EU subsidised exports. Despite the EU's special arrangements with a number of Third World countries under the Lomé conventions, the losers include relatively poor countries.

4. The administration of the policy involves substantial costs. Because of its complexity it offers opportunities for large-scale fraud.

5. It is a source of damaging tensions in relations between the European Union and the United States, and with the medium-sized exporting countries organised in the Cairns Group, such as Australia.

'Agricultural policies in nearly all industrial countries raise prices, redistribute income regressively and towards a small section of

society, and impose economic costs at both home and abroad'
(Winters, 1993, p. 11). How can this outcome be explained? Three
broad categories of explanation can be advanced: economic, food
security, and political.

Achieving a supply and demand equilibrium in agriculture is
particularly difficult. Indeed, this is why there is a distinct discipline
of agricultural economics that has explored phenomena such as
'cobweb cycles'. The underlying reason why surpluses and shortages
occur in agriculture is the influence of variable weather patterns on
production. Consider a commodity such as potatoes. In Year 1, cold
spring weather retards and damages potato growth, hence supply is
short and the price rises. In the following planting season, the high
price encourages a larger acreage to be brought into production.
Weather conditions are optimal, there is a production glut, and the
price falls dramatically.

There is nothing wrong in price variations as they are a means of
conveying information to producers and consumers. However, as
Atkin observes:

It is . . . a well established result in economic theory that very high
levels of volatility create uncertainty that can lead to a lower-than-
optimum level of investment. If the price of a good is very unstable,
it becomes hard to make a sensible judgement about how much of
the good to produce . . . Faced with the inherent uncertainties in
agriculture, there might be under-investment in the sector in the
absence of any government intervention. (Atkin, 1993, pp. 6–7)

4However, as Atkin emphasises, this rather limited argument is
stretched too far. It does not justify the existing scope of government
involvement in agriculture. Atkin places considerable faith in futures
markets as a means of dealing with price volatility, although potato
futures have been a focus of highly speculative activity which has
little to do with the needs of the average farmer. There is probably
more justification for limited, self-funding price stabilisation mechanisms than Atkins allows. Intervention has, however, increased to a
point where it becomes a substitute for the normal functioning of the
market mechanism. For all the talk of reform, 'the major part of
OECD agricultural production has continued to respond predominantly to support policies rather than international market price
signals' (OECD, 1994a, p. 12).

It is possible for the market mechanism to function in agriculture. Potatoes for human consumption have not had a CAP commodity regime (although in the UK they were until recently subject to a marketing board regime which regulated the total amount grown). As a consequence, 'there is a very tight range in prices and the EU's Single Market is clearly working well. Trade is not subject to the agrimonetary distortions which plague the CAP regimes' (*Agra Europe*,7 April 1995, p. M/7). Potatoes grown for starch manufacture do receive production support, and output of them has increased against the background of an overall decline in EU potato production: 'Instead of produce being taken off the market and stored, a surplus of potatoes is largely absorbed by increased consumption because prices are free to fall to very low levels' (*Agra Europe*, 3 February 1995, p. P/7).

Food security was an understandable preoccupation in the years following the Second World War in Europe, when there were real shortages of food in a number of countries: 'In the immediate postwar period of food shortages, the aim was to expand agricultural production by all possible means, both to raise food supplies and to relieve balances of payment' (Tracy, 1989, p. 219). Assuring the availability of supplies was one of the agricultural policy objectives written into the Treaty of Rome. However, 'World economic growth and its associated technological changes have greatly increased international food security during this century' (Gale Johnson, 1991, p. 156). Those who suffer hunger do so 'because they are poor, not because the world does not produce enough food' (Atkin, 1993, p. 5). With the end of the Cold War, arguments for strategic reserves of food-stocks and the need to retain an agricultural production capability of a given size lost whatever credibility they had ever had.

One therefore has to seek a political explanation for the persistence of the CAP in a form that seems to have little economic justification. There would be a strong social justification if support was not so concentrated on the larger-scale farmers. Simplistic popular explanations of the scale of agriculture subsidies would draw attention to the power of the 'farm lobby'. However, farmers are declining as a share of the population in all member states, and the urban population is losing its sentimental view of the countryside and becoming more concerned about environmental issues. As the size of the EU has grown, the scope for disagreement between farm organisations from member states with very different types of farming has grown, while budgetary cutbacks have made it more difficult to forge compromises that give something to everyone. That is not to say that the farm lobby should be written off as a source of influence on policy maintenance and development:

> [If one calculates] the gain of the agricultural sector – from the combined effects of payments from the EAGGF Guarantee Fund and from market protection – at the expense of the consumer/ taxpayer, then the agricultural interest is a substantial gainer in every one of the EU countries . . . By and large, agricultural policy makers do not care about consumers; they do however relate directly to the agricultural lobbies in their individual countries. (*Agra Europe*, 24 February 1995)

However, any explanation that focused, simply on the agricultural lobby at national or European level would be completely inadequate. It is necessary to take account of a whole range of institutions that form a relatively closed agricultural policy community. Among the more important are DG VI, the directorate-general for agriculture; the management committees, which engaged in the detailed operation of commodity regimes; the Special Committee on Agriculture, which is the equivalent of COREPER for other issues; and the Council of Agricultural Ministers, which has relatively frequent and long meetings. These institutions are examined in more depth in Chapter 6. What is clear is that 'The major farm policies survive because of the particular sets of institutions involved in the setting of the policy and the structure of the decision framework in which they operate, as well as the pressures from interest groups' (Moyer and Josling, 1990, p. 203). Member states are crucial actors in the process, and in order to understand their bargaining positions it is necessary to know something about the character of agriculture in each EU country. This understanding is provided in Chapter 2.

2

The Structure of European Agriculture and Food Processing

This chapter will group the countries of the EU into a number of categories in terms of the structure and character of their agriculture and food processing industries. In part, this is done to assist the reader: an isolated description of the agriculture of each country would be difficult to absorb and not particularly useful. It may also help to understand some of the lines of division that emerge within the Council of Ministers. For example, a recurrent line of division is that between Northern and Southern European countries which produce, to a considerable extent, different agricultural products and which have markedly different structures in their farm sectors and food processing industries. However, these are not the only lines of division that have a structural basis.

The following discussion will use a number of broad agricultural and food processing groupings of member states within the EU which will provide a framework for the subsequent discussion, always bearing in mind that each category contains a substantial variation within it. In drawing up this categorisation, two principal variables were taken into account: the centrality of agriculture and first stage food processing in each member state's economy, and its general level of efficiency. A group of five North European countries is set aside because agriculture is not a key activity in their economies. There are then three groups made up of countries in which agriculture is a central activity, but differs in its efficiency from high through medium to low. The last group of countries is distinguished by two other variables: the importance of part-time farming and the priority given to environmental and public health issues:

1. Small north European countries with a high level of agricultural employment, efficient food processing industries and a surplus in trade in food and agricultural products: these are Denmark, the Republic of Ireland and The Netherlands. Ireland has some portions of its agriculture that are highly inefficient, but the success of its first stage food processing industry places it in this category.
2. Northern European countries in which agriculture is not a key economic activity: Belgium, Finland, Luxembourg, Sweden, the United Kingdom.
3. Large countries bordering the Mediterranean, in which agriculture is a significant economic activity and in which progress is being made towards greater efficiency, but current efficiency levels vary significantly within the country: these are France and Spain. Politically, Spain might be said to be closer to the next group but, in the long run, it may develop a different balance of interests.
4. Mediterranean countries with significant but relatively inefficient agricultural sectors: these are Greece, Italy and Portugal.
5. Countries in which agriculture is perceived to be a significant economic activity, although often undertaken by small-scale and/or part-time farmers, and in which environmental pressures on farming are particularly significant: these are Austria and Germany. These two countries voiced the strongest concerns on public health issues during the BSE crisis.

Small countries with successful food sectors

Economic success for a small country can dependent on export-led activities in well defined market niches (Katzenstein, 1985). One such strategy is to develop the value-added export of agricultural products with an emphasis on quality. Denmark and The Netherlands have pursued such a strategy over a long period of time. The Republic of Ireland is a relative latecomer to export-led commercial agriculture, but has displayed increasing success in the period since the country joined the European Community, a success exemplified by the increased presence of Irish food processing enterprises elsewhere in Europe.

A common feature of all three countries is the high proportion of agricultural products sold through farmers' co-operatives: for example the three highest figures in the EU (in 1991) for milk, 98 per cent in Ireland, 92 per cent in Denmark and 84 per cent in The Netherlands, contrasting with a 4.1 per cent figure for the UK. Discussing the nature of the farm co-operative movement, a senior co-operative official in the Republic of Ireland commented in interview, 'we would see co-operatives as something in the middle, but if we were asked what side of the industry we were on we would say effectively this was capitalism but established with a democratic base'. Such businesses had to develop as international enterprises, but if they were converted into conventional companies, there was a risk that institutional investors would begin to dominate and the farmer would be forgotten.

The Danish dairy processing industry is dominated by two large co-operative enterprises: MD Foods and Kloever. MD Foods is an increasingly international player, and has talked of representing all co-operative dairies in Scandinavia. Following a number of acquisitions, it is the third largest supplier of liquid milk in the UK. The Netherlands has three big dairy co-operatives (in order of turnover): Campina Melkunie, Friesland, and Coberco. The Irish dairy co-operative movement has gone through a process of merger and rationalisation and is dominated by the 'big five' (in order of turnover): Avonmore, Kerry, Waterford, Dairygold and Golden Vale.

Denmark

In many ways, Denmark is the exemplar of an economic development strategy based around agriculture. The food industry still accounts for around 25 per cent of the country's merchandise exports. Although its population is only five million, Denmark has a 26 per cent share of world exports of pigmeat, and 10 per cent of world cheese exports. Denmark has also built up companies that are world leaders in supporting industries, such as food processing machinery, food ingredients and instrumentation.

The Danish example had an influence on other countries, such as The Netherlands, particularly in terms of the role of co-operatives. Charvet notes (1994, p. 81) that at the end of the eighteenth century, at the time of the first agricultural revolution, Denmark made a decisive and effective sociopolitical choice to modernise its national agriculture. Instead of imitating the British model, the Danes chose to create an agricultural society based on small and medium-sized owner-proprietors. With an absence of natural resources such as coal and iron ore, Denmark had few alternative options to a strategy based on agriculture, developing high-quality products in areas such as bacon for sale to the large industrial countries of Europe. At one time a major grain exporter, the advent of cheap overseas grain from North America in the 1870s was not responded to by raising protectionist barriers as in other European countries, but by a shift into livestock products. Up to the 1960s, butter and bacon accounted for about 60 per cent of national exports and financed a third of total imports: 'Agricultural products all together made up two-thirds of the total export value' (Just, 1990, p. 137).

Denmark did not enter the EC until 1973, and had difficulty in catching up with the gains made by its rival, The Netherlands, in the common market of six. Tracy notes (1989, p. 295), 'The 1970s were a difficult period for Danish agriculture, hit by rising production costs, high land costs and especially by high interest rates, while in the EEC generally agricultural markets were increasingly oversupplied.' Moreover, Danish farmers are increasingly constrained by a strong environmental movement. In 1995, Denmark introduced an agro-chemicals levy, amounting to 27 per cent of the retail value of insecticides and 13 per cent of the value of fungicides, herbicides and crop-growth-regulating chemicals. This had had the effect of increasing the price of pesticides by 37 per cent and of herbicides by 15 per cent. In overall financial terms, the policy is supposed to have a neutral effect, as the levy is 'channelled' back into agriculture through a reduction in ground rents (Personal communication, Carsten Daugbjerg, 10 September 1995).

The Netherlands

The Netherlands followed a somewhat similar strategy to Denmark in terms of exporting high-quality agricultural products to nearby industrial countries such as Britain and Germany. The product mix was somewhat different, with an emphasis on, for example, cheese, and later a range of horticultural products including flowers, house plants, fruit and vegetables, which accounted for a third of the gross value of Dutch agriculture at the beginning of the 1990s. Dutch agriculture had certain advantages such as 'flat terrain, deep soils, rich pastures, ample water supplies, and a temperate climate' (OECD, 1994b, p. 173). But it also suffered disadvantages such as the need to drain, pump water from and protect the low-lying land; a lack of sunshine; a shortage of land, even allowing for large-scale schemes to reclaim land from the sea; and high labour costs. These disadvantages were turned into advantages – for example, by culti-vating horticultural products under glass to compensate for the lack of sunlight. More generally, capital was substituted for labour, so that 'compared with farmers in many other countries, Dutch farmers have become less and less dependent on the land and the local climate' (OECD, 1994b, p. 173).

Apart from the favourable location of The Netherlands next to so many densely populated countries, a feature that has attracted American investment is its food processing sector; this success was not accidental. The Dutch had to work to overcome a series of natural disadvantages and did so through a distinctive combination of market forces, corporate organisation, corporatist intermediation, and government intervention. Many of the most successful sectors, such as horticulture, have received relatively little government assistance. The country sustains one of the leading European food multinationals (Unilever) alongside a set of highly commercial dairy co-operatives. Corporatist intermediation has played a particularly important role in the maintenance and enhancement of quality standards (de Vroom, 1987, p. 199). Dutch producers have continu-ally upgraded their assets:

> a market-oriented corporate culture, embodied in its numerous co-operatives and in the coordinated network of farmers' organisa-tions; a trained, technologically competent and entrepreneurial labour force; and extensive resources for the creation and dissemination of knowledge. The Government itself has played an important role in fostering the establishment and maintenance of these assets – namely, by facilitating cooperation and integration within the sector and by encouraging the development of human capital. (OECD, 1994b, p. 174)

The horticultural sector, however, faced serious difficulties in the mid-1990s. Fears were expressed that a third of producers might become insolvent. Although perhaps exaggerated, these forecasts did reflect real underlying problems, notably competition from Spain and tighter environmental regulations. It has been claimed that 'Spanish tomato growers were now able to produce all year round with the help of subsidies, whereas Spain had in the past specialised in the production of "winter tomatoes". Spanish horticulture also gained competitive advantages through low wage costs and the strict environmental criteria imposed on Dutch producers' (*Agra Europe*, 16 June 1995, p. N/1).

As in Denmark, environmental pressures are a real concern for Dutch farmers. In many respects, the environmental problems are more serious in The Netherlands. In such a densely populated country, agricultural activities are a significant source of soil, water and air pollution. Dutch livestock farming has become very intensive to offset the disadvantages of small farm structure: 'There are now so many animals on Dutch farms eating so much imported feed that the business of disposing of their wastes on the limited land available has become unbalanced. Indeed, critics have suggested that some areas in the east and south of the country are like a gigantic sewage farm' (*Financial Times*, 26 April 1994).

In the meat sector, the Dutch government has had to intervene to carry out a rationalisation scheme to reduce slaughtering capacity. In 1995 a private company and two co-operatives were merged to become the Holland Meat Group. The flower sector, although recording raised profits, faces increased competition from Africa, India and South America. The forty leading Dutch co-operatives recorded a fall in turnover of 3 per cent in 1994 compared with 1993, the first fall since 1983 (*Agra Europe*, 17 March 1995, p. N/4).

A report commissioned by the Dutch Ministry of Agriculture, published in 1994, warned of an accelerating deterioration of the competitive position of the Dutch farmer. Rather than being an efficient producer of innovative value-added products, it has become a supplier of bulk products with too little variety. The country's agriculture was seen as being less able to react adequately to market changes than are France or Denmark (*Agra Europe*, 21 October 1994, p. N/3). It is little surprise, then, that Dutch farmers are buying up Danish dairy farms where they can get more land and quota for their money and yet feel at home in a very similar country (*Agra Europe*, 21 October 1994, pp. N2–3). Informed observers have concluded that 'Dutch agriculture is in crisis' and that the number of farmers could halve by the end of the twentieth century (*Financial Times*, 26 April 1994). This led leaders of the farm community to initiate a so-called 'Great Debate' (*Ter Zake*, literally 'to work') on the future of Dutch agriculture.

The Republic of Ireland

Irish agriculture and food processing has gone from strength to strength since the country became a member of the EC in 1973. A senior Irish civil servant summarised the changes in an interview:

> The nature of the agricultural business has changed dramatically. The advent of the Common Agricultural Policy and our accession to the EC is probably the most dramatic change in the period. In effect it meant that produce had a market irrespective of whether it was consumed in the market or not, and therefore in very simple terms it meant that the farm product producer was guaranteed a price and therefore guaranteed a profit . . . if you go back a little bit in history, to the relationship between Irish agricultural produce and UK consumer markets, there was a vulnerability there relative to supply and demand that made the business very risk prone. The actual accession to the EC took to a very large extent that risk and that doubt away, and the constancy of income related to the constancy of the intervention system in effect was the key element in that.

It has sometimes been a bumpy ride, as when overborrowing fuelled by a belief in unstoppable expansion led to a farm debt crisis in the early to mid-1980s. The Irish agricultural sector also embraces a wide variety of producers, from highly commercial dairy farms in the east to ageing subsistence farmers in the west who receive a 'farmers' dole'. The overall picture, however, is of an increasingly competitive farm sector, particularly strong in dairying, but also strong in niches such as mushroom production for the British market. The strength of the farm sector is matched by that of the food processing industry which is making its presence known increasingly throughout Europe. From an agricultural sector highly dependent on the British market, the commercial segment of Irish agriculture has been transformed into a modern, forward-looking, European orientated industry. A senior co-operative official commented in interview, 'I couldn't honestly say that Irish farming would survive at any reasonable standard without the European Community's support.'

Using data from the Teagasc National Farm Survey, the Irish Farmers' Association has classified farms into four groups:

1. Economically viable enterprises based on farm income only: 31 per cent of all farms or approximately 50 000 farms.
2. Economically viable based on a combination of farm income and off-farm income; 17 per cent of all farms, or approximately 27 000 farms.
3. Economically non-viable from farming and no off-farm earnings but demographically viable; 31 per cent of all farms or approximately 50 000 farms.
4. Economically non-viable, no off-farm earnings and also demographically non-viable (holder is over fifty-five years old and nobody else in the household is under forty-four: that is, no clear successor); 19 per cent of all farms, or approximately 30 000 farms.

Although very substantial progress has been made since Ireland joined the EU, a number of weaknesses remain. 'Irish farming is splitting into two very distinct parts . . . two-thirds of Irish farm families are existing on very low incomes' (*Irish Farmers' Journal*, 17 July 1993). Over half of the farms have an income level from farming below £Ir5000 and the average income level is £Ir9000 (*Agra Europe*, 3 November 1995, p. N/3). Household income in these farms is often very dependent on off-farm income, typically earned by the wife of the farmer. At the other end of the spectrum, the author read through a set of individual accounts for Irish farms and it is evident that a number of large dairy farmers in particular have good turnovers and are earning substantial returns. There has been criticism in Ireland of the emergence of a new agrarian elite, termed 'ranchers' or the 'hacienda class': 'recently wealthy large farmers and a dependent stratum of provincial business people, whose money derives to a large extent from social changes wrought by the European Union's Common Agricultural Policy over the past 20 years' (*The Independent*, 27 June 1994). The high level of dependence on EU aid in the agricultural economy is a potential weakness with EU subsidies representing an average 41 per cent of farm incomes (*Agra Europe*, 3 November 1995, p. N/3).

Ireland does, however, have some natural advantages, that favour certain types of farming: 'A mild climate . . . combined with well-distributed rainfall . . . provide ideal growing conditions, particularly for grass' (Hussey, 1995, p. 306). Given these conditions, it is no surprise that dairying is the most important sector of Irish agriculture, accounting for over a third of total output. Dairying supplies the great majority of the calves for the beef industry which is second to dairying in terms of employment and exports. Both these types of farming 'are heavily dependent on CAP intervention buying' (Hussey, 1995, p. 308).

Members of the agricultural community in Ireland compare their performance explicitly with Denmark and The Netherlands and are aware of some shortcomings:

> Relative to the continentals – the Denmarks, the Hollands – Irish agriculture would still be under-capitalised. There would be approximately 60 per cent of Irish farmers who do not have bank borrowings. And that reflects two things. There are a lot of Irish farmers who do not have borrowing capacity because of the size . . . Borrowing has been facilitated in Holland and Denmark by longer term loans, therefore making higher borrowings possible from the cash flow point of view relative to here. (Interview with chief agriculture manager of an Irish bank)

From being outside the tax system twenty years ago (apart from local rates), Irish farmers have been brought within a tax system in which many of the special allowances for farmers have been removed and in which a tax rate of 48 per cent starts at a low level by international standards: 'My main worry at this stage is that the tax regime now is encouraging investment to leave farming. Farmers are being facilitated to find a tax shelter out of farming' (Interview with chief agriculture manager of Irish bank).

The Irish co-operative movement has internationalised, investing in, for example, Britain, Belgium, Germany, Hungary and the United States. By 1992, only 41 per cent of turnover of the 'Big Five' was in Ireland, compared with a third in the UK and Europe and 15 per cent in North America, with 11 per cent elsewhere in the world (O'Neill, 1993, p. 16). Even so, Irish companies are still considered to be too small compared to their international competitors. A proposed merger between Avonmore and Waterford was not completed. A senior co-operative official's comment in interview emphasised some of the remaining obstacles to change: 'there was very great pressure from some of the financial institutions and from the Industrial Development Authority to bring about that merger . . . they were looking at a global picture and nobody was looking at the detail on the ground . . . inevitably there were personality problems to be overcome'.

The food processing industry as a whole has been production-rather than market-led. A national strategy for the food and drink industry argued that 'The industry must change its emphasis from being an agricultural processing industry, supplying intervention and other markets with commodity products, to a food industry supplying quality foods for the European market' (IDA, 1991, p. 7). Progress has been made in that direction, but there is still a long way to go. Nevertheless, Ireland's agriculture and food processing industry has been more profoundly influenced by EU membership than most other member states.

Within the context of the peace process, attention has been given to the possibility of an agricultural policy for the whole of the island of Ireland. In both portions of the island, similar climatic conditions have produced a grassland-based agriculture which is economically significant and has to be export-orientated to succeed. Since Britain and the Republic of Ireland joined the EC, agriculture in the north of the island (Ulster) has lagged behind the south. In part this reflects the development of a more effective agricultural and rural policy by the government of the Republic of Ireland (the scandals in the beef industry revealed in the early 1990s notwithstanding). For example:

> As a substantial food exporter the south sought devaluation of the green pound to obtain the maximum possible price increases whereas the United Kingdom, as a food importer, was reluctant to penalize consumers through devaluation. The less rapid devaluation of the green pound in the United Kingdom resulted in southern farmers receiving higher prices for their produce than those in the north and schemes such as the Meat Industry Export Scheme (MIES) had to be introduced to prevent distortions of cross border trade. (Greer, 1996, p. 165)

The Irish Farmers' Association and the Ulster Farmers' Union in 1995 submitted a joint memorandum on agriculture and rural development to the Forum for Peace and Reconciliation. This emphasised structural similarities between the northern and southern parts of Ireland and makes proposals in relation to CAP commodity policy, animal health, and agricultural structures policy. A senior Irish Republic civil servant was more cautious in interview, commenting that he was not in fact sure that there were absolutely common interests north and south. It was hard to say what the interest of the northern farmer was, but it could, for example, be renationalisation of the CAP.

What the example of Ireland shows, in rather dramatic form, is the way in which political boundaries can cut across what otherwise might be geographically coherent regions. Within the EU as a whole, regional variations within countries can be important for agricultural politics.

Northern European countries in which agriculture is not a central economic activity

It is not implied that agriculture is unimportant in these countries, rather that it does not make the central contribution to employment, output and foreign exchange earnings noted in the three countries just discussed. Two of the countries discussed (Finland and Sweden) are at such a northern latitude that their ability to compete effectively in certain products is necessarily limited. In Britain, a high proportion of land is devoted to agriculture but it is a small proportion of the economy or employment as a whole. In Scandinavia the low importance of agriculture is primarily because the proportion of the land area devoted to farming, for climatic and other reasons, is relatively small.

Finland

In Finland, crops such as maize and alfalfa cannot be grown because of the short growing season, which starts in April or May and finishes in August or September: 'The short season also means less pasture and a need for more hay and silage, more insulation and heating in buildings and, by law, manure storage for at least eight months. That all adds up to extra costs' (*Farmers Weekly*, 27 January 1995). Farms are small, with an average size of 13 hectares of farmed land, but there is an average of 50 hectares of adjacent forestry. Although many farmers combine farming and forest management, they do not like to rely too much on forestry because of the long period that elapses before the trees can be felled.

Domestic agricultural policies guaranteed compensation to cover increasing production costs and involved the agreement of producer prices between farmers' organisations and the government. This policy discouraged improvements in farm productivity, led to rising input and land prices, and excessive capital investment: 'The result is an industry ill equipped for EU membership, despite several years of preparation' (*Farmers Weekly*, 27 January 1995). In 1995, Finnish farmers drew direct subsidies equivalent to 85 per cent of the total value of production (*Agra Europe*, 23 August 1996, p. E/5).

Thus, Finnish agriculture in particular is likely to undergo a restructuring as a result of EU membership diametrically opposed to that of the Republic of Ireland, with the emphasis on contraction rather than expansion. A Finnish research institute conducted a study of two regions which estimated that one farm in five would be likely to cease operating by the year 2000 (*Agra Europe*, 12 July 1996, p. N/5). Since Finland joined the EU there has been a surge of exports from Denmark, particularly of meat. The food processing industry is also expected to 'face considerable competitive pressure from EC member countries' (OECD, 1995a, p. 73).

Irrespective of Finland's joining the EU, the Ministry of Agriculture and Forestry stated that 'it is highly likely that hundreds of thousands of hectares of agricultural land will be removed from agricultural use during the next few years – afforestation is one option' (*Agra Europe*, 8 July 1994, p. E/9). Not surprisingly, farmers opposed EU membership when the country held a referendum on the subject. When Finland joined producer prices, which had been 30–60 per cent above the EU average, fell more sharply than had been expected, particularly for eggs (of which there is a national surplus) and pigmeat. Temporary production support was available to offset the fall in prices, but the value of this package was undermined both by the sharper than anticipated fall in prices and the rise of the Finnish mark against the ECU (*Agra Europe*, 13 January 1995, p. N/7).

Research carried out by Tuula Vironen at the University of Helsinki suggests that more than 90 per cent of EU agricultural income support will go to northern farms, although some 40 per cent of active farms are situated in the southernmost regions of the country. Farms in this area have often specialised in crop production, making them most vulnerable to the impact of EU membership. 'According to Vironen, this shift in regional income distribution could damage agricultural production in the best climatic areas of the country' (*Agra Europe*, 21 July 1995, p. N/4).

Agriculture in Finland in 1993 provided 3.3 per cent of GDP and 8.6 per cent of civilian employment, figures which indicate the relative weakness of the agricultural sector. In Sweden, the proportion of GDP accounted for by agriculture was only 0.6 per cent, and the share of civilian employment 3.3 per cent. Sweden had already introduced a reform of its agricultural support programmes in 1990 and further changes were made after the application for EU membership. The ending of dairy quotas in 1989 and the abolition of export subsidies has led to a sharp fall in the number of dairy farmers.

Sweden

Less than 8 per cent of Sweden is farmed. Cropping is restricted to the south of the country, where there has been a shift from oats and spring barley to more profitable sugar beet and winter crops. The Swedish fruit and vegetable processing industry is concentrated in the southern area around Malmö (van Waarden, 1987, p. 86). In the north, where farming has been heavily subsidised, there is a similar pattern of farming to that found in Finland, with an average farm size of fifty hectares, much of that forest land with farmers relying on forestry management to survive.

Levels of concentration are particularly high in the dairy, meat and fruit and vegetable subsectors of the food processing industry in Sweden, with the first two subsectors dominated by farmer-owned co-operatives and multinational companies active in fruit and vegetable processing (van Waarden, 1987, p. 76). Procordia is the only Swedish company listed by Charvet (1994) as being among the top twenty European food processing companies. Originally the food and drink division of Volvo, it was offered for sale, a development which led to some opposition among 'the very vocal section of the Swedish population who resent the idea of [the Procordia companies] falling into foreign hands' *Food File*, 22 March 1995, p. 13). Swedish food exports have increased substantially since the country joined the EU, particularly of salmonella-free poultry and dairy products. This growth in exports has, however, been helped by the weakness of the Swedish Krona.

Belgium and Luxembourg

Belgium has the lowest share of civilian employment in agriculture of any member state apart from Britain. In part, this reflects a common industrial heritage. At the end of the Second World War, 'Belgium was predominantly industrial and imported most agricultural products. No constructive agricultural policy had been developed, peasants had been slow to organise themselves, and many farms were too small and too fragmented to be efficient' (Tracy, 1989, p. 244).

According to a report from the Belgian agriculture ministry, Belgian agriculture has undergone significant structural change since the early 1980s and will continue to do so in the forseeable future. The number of agricultural concerns was forecast to fall by more than a third, to around 36 400 by the year 2005, with the average size of farms rising from 22 hectares in 1992 to 30.1 hectares in 2005. Over a fifth of farms are run by people aged over sixty and over half of the farmers aged fifty or more were not sure about who their successor would be (*Agra Europe*, 10 February 1995, p. N/6).

In 1992, 25 per cent of total agricultural production was accounted for by pigmeat, the second largest share in the EU after Denmark. The share of milk in final agricultural production was the smallest for any of the Northern European countries. Since the introduction of milk quotas, the number of dairy farmers in Belgium has halved, from 49 000 in 1983 to 24 000 in 1993. During the same period, the dairy herd decreased by nearly 30 per cent. One area of considerable expansion in the 1990s has been in apple production, with a 7.8 per cent increase in the area planted with low-stem trees in 1994 alone.

Although Belgium is noted for the production of luxury chocolates, the first stage food processing sector is generally relatively weak. This is not surprising when one considers the relatively small size of the dairy sector, which is an important base for the food processing industry in The Netherlands. The food processing industry in Belgium tends to be dominated by foreign firms, particularly from France, Britain and the United States. The Belgian market is an important one for French agricultural products (Charvet, 1994, p. 98).

Luxembourg is very similar to Belgium in terms of the low share of agriculture in civilian employment and GDP, which is perhaps not surprising given that the two countries first formed an Economic Union in 1922: 'The Union was generally successful, but agriculture was its greatest problem. Farming in Luxembourg suffered from unfavourable natural conditions; the land is broken by steep hills and valleys and much of it is of poor quality' (Tracy, 1989, p. 243). Agricultural production is largely concentrated on three products: milk (42 per cent); beef and veal (25 per cent); and wine (13 per cent). Luxembourg counts for a nominal 0.1 per cent of total EU agricultural output, but is, of course, represented in the Council of

Ministers and has played a role disproportionate to its size in providing presidents of the Commission.

United Kingdom

The inclusion of the United Kingdom in this group of North European countries in which agriculture is not a central economic activity is justified by the fact that agriculture in Britain has the lowest share of civilian employment and GDP of any member state. This is not to say, however, that agriculture is regarded as being unimportant. It should also be noted that the food processing industry is strong, both domestically and, as a result of its expansion and acquisitions, throughout Europe. Of the twenty leading European food processing firms listed by Charvet, eleven are British (Charvet, 1994, p. 89). Those companies that have not had a strong presence in Europe, such as Associated British Foods, are finding it necessary to develop one.

The commercialisation of agriculture in Britain occurred earlier than in any country in the world and helped to provide in the late eighteenth century some of the capital and other background conditions that favoured rapid industrialisation. This industrialisation in turn created the need to feed as cheaply as possible a large urban working class. The repeal of the Corn Laws in 1846 ended the protection of British agriculture for a century. A cheap food policy developed which was based on the importation of food from the 'Dominions', notably Australia, Canada and New Zealand: 'On several occasions in Cabinet action to help British agriculture was ruled out on the grounds that it would harm the Dominions' (Smith, 1988, p. 7). Britain was perceived to be a predominantly industrial country well served by free trade.

After the Second World War there was a determination not to allow a repetition of the depression that had afflicted British agriculture after the First World War, and which had to large extent persisted throughout the interwar period. The 1947 Agriculture Act, although introduced by the postwar Labour Government, reflected a broad political consensus on agricultural policy. In particular, the maximisation of production was seen to be a desirable goal, in pursuit of such objectives as food security and relief for the balance of payments. The wartime experience of the Battle of the Atlantic helped to fix Britain's preoccupation with the security of food supplies. The system of price supports and a variety of grants introduced by the 1947 Act and subsequent legislation introduced a new era of prosperity for British agriculture. Entry into the European Community in 1973 placed support for agriculture on a different basis, but did not undermine its essentially favoured position. Changes in the CAP in the 1980s, such as the introduction of milk quotas, changed the decision-making environment for farmers, but still left the majority of dairy farmers in a position to earn a good living. Perhaps a greater threat to farmers came from growing concern among the urban population (increasing numbers of whom lived in the countryside) about the level of financial support received by farmers; access to the countryside for leisure purposes; anxiety about environmental damage by farmers; and concern about the treatment of farm animals (a stronger preoccupation than in other member states).

One of the characteristics of Britain is the diversity of its topography and climate, even within relatively small areas. Examples of farms in Britain would include a large East Anglian arable farm relying heavily on mechanisation; an urban fringe farm in the Midlands growing fruit and vegetables to sell in its own shops; a small-scale family dairy farm in Devon; a flower and early potatoes farm working small fields on the Isles of Scilly; a sheep farm in Wales covering a large upland area; and a landed estate in Scotland with a strong investment in forestry. Although there is no such thing as a 'typical' British farm, a generalisation that was made in the 1850s but still holds today is 'that between the predominantly arable agriculture of southern and eastern England and the pastoral agriculture of the North and West. In general the boundary between the two areas is that between the highland zone of relatively wet and less fertile uplands and the lowland zone of drier, warmer, flatter and more fertile ground to the east of a line from the Tees to the Exe' (Newby, 1979, p. 77). In terms of the balance of production, approaching 50 per cent of all final agricultural production is accounted for by milk, beef/veal and wheat, in that order.

Viewed comparatively with other member states, what is striking about British farming is the relatively large size of the average farm, nearly twice as large as the country with the next largest average farm, Denmark. Over a third of holdings in Britain are over 50 hectares in size. But whether this represents a more 'efficient' system of farming is a moot point. It certainly represents a form of farming which, at least for most larger farms, can be regarded as a more fully capitalist form of agriculture in which there is a substantial emphasis on profit maximisation. This is reflected in the close involvement of the major banks in lending to farmers; the involvement of the leading accountancy firms in the provision of advisory services to farmers; and the existence of farm management companies (one quoted on the stock exchange) which will take over the running of the farm from the owner so as to maximise returns on the assets held. Britain is predisposed to a more commercial orientation to farming than many other member states.

Large countries in which a relatively efficient agriculture is a major activity

France

France can be regarded as the leading agricultural economic power in the European Union. Nearly 23 per cent of all EU agricultural production in 1994 came from France. France was a major producer in a wide range of products, accounting for over a third of EU production in wheat, barley, maize, oilseeds, fresh fruit and wine. It is also a major milk producer. France is the world's second largest food exporter (after the United States) and has a substantial, although falling, agricultural trade surplus with other EU countries. Because of the shift to direct payments in the CAP, subsidies accounted for an estimated 38 per cent of French farmers' incomes in 1995, compared with 11 per cent in 1991 (*Agra Europe*, 24 November 1995, p. N/1).

Historically, French agriculture suffered from a fragmented structure, low levels of investment and technological change, and the absence of the stimulus of rapid growth in the economy as a whole: 'French agriculture . . . was modernised relatively late. It was only after 1945 that it emerged from the conservative protectionism established during the great agricultural crisis of the late 19th century' (Delorme, 1994, p. 39). Charvet (1994, p. 38) describes the modernisation of agriculture since 1950 as a true revolution. Even if all the objectives set by French decision-makers in the immediate postwar years were not achieved, the emergence of a structural trade surplus on agricultural products in the 1970s is indicative of the extent of change.

Within French agriculture, there are still substantial variations in levels of efficiency and productivity. The cereal producers of the Paris basin are among the most efficient in the world. In 1988 there were 27 000 large cereal-growing enterprises in France, with areas of a hundred hectares or more, a number estimated to rise to 39 000 by the year 2000. At the other end of the spectrum, considerable structural problems persist in Languedoc in Mediterranean France, where there is a concentration of lower-quality wine producers. Charvet (1994, p. 58) argues that this relative inertia in the face of unfavourable economic conditions can in large part be attributed to the role played by numerous small wine co-operatives in the country-side of Languedoc, which assures the relative stability and perma-nence of the existing system of production. The smallest fall in agricultural employment has occurred in wine-growing departments (*Agra Europe*, 2 December 1994, p. N/1). In southern France, it is thought that 'the natural process of structural change is likely to be insufficient to enable farmers starting up in business or wishing to expand existing concerns to obtain enough land to form a viable business' (*Agra Europe*, 18 November 1994, p. N/1).

Nevertheless there has been a considerable restructuring of French agriculture as a whole since the formation of the common market. In 1958, agriculture accounted for nearly a quarter of the total work-force, a figure that had fallen to 6–7 per cent by the mid-1990s (Delorme, 1994, p. 41). This process of restructuring seems likely to continue. The national statistical institute has estimated that the number of farmers (excluding hired workers) in France will fall to around 700 000 in 1998, compared with just under a million in 1990 and 1.45 million in 1982. The expected decline will be concentrated in regions such as Brittany, Île-de-France and Lower Normandy, where the average age of farmers is high, and Midi-Pyrénées, Aquitaine and Pays de Loire (*Agra Europe*, 2 December 1994, p. N/1).

France is the base for a number of major food companies which have a diversified range of interests. Danone (formerly BSN) estab-lished in 1966, is one of the three leading food processing companies in Europe and number four in world rankings. In the dairy sector alone, which accounts for over a third of its sales, it is the largest dairy company in Europe in terms of turnover. Its change of name to Danone in 1994 (after its best-known international brand) is 'be-lieved to precede a large-scale global expansion plan'. Danone is committed to international expansion and is determined 'to closely challenge the likes of Nestlé and Unilever' (*Food File*, 7 October 1994, p. 2). The second-largest French food processing company is Besnier, a privately-owned company concentrating on the dairy sector. Six of the top twenty dairy companies in Europe are French, more than from any other country (Hall, 1995, p. 13). The three leading dairy companies account for around half of all dairy factories, and many smaller plants have been closed. Despite these areas of strength, multinationals such as Nestlé and Unilever are among the leading companies in France, and the general trend of foreign investment in the sector is upwards. Ninety-one agriculture and food projects received foreign investment in 1994, compared with sixty-six in 1993, and eighty-eight in 1992 (the second highest year for such investments). Eighty-two per cent of the investments came from the EU (*Agra Europe*, 7 April 1995, p. N/2).

Spain

It might seem more appropriate to group Spain with the other Mediterranean countries rather than France. However, as noted earlier, Spain is one of three countries (the others are France and Germany) that have seen a particularly rapid fall in agricultural employment. The average size of agricultural holding in Spain is around four times the average of Greece, three times that of Italy, and two-and-a-half times that of Portugal. Although just over half the holdings in Spain in 1989 were below 5 hectares, the proportion in the other Mediterranean countries was higher: just over two-thirds in Italy and Greece, and over three-quarters in Portugal. Spanish farmers have certainly befitted in income terms from membership of the EU, with a rise in incomes significantly higher than the average in the other member states. Subsidies now form, on average, 25 per cent of Spanish farmers' incomes, but in sectors such as cereals, sunflowers and sheep, the figure is as high as 80 per cent (*Agra Europe*, 17 February 1995, p. N/5).

Spanish agriculture faces a number of natural disadvantages: 'The most important physical handicaps to agricultural activity include the climate: low and unevenly distributed precipitation or short, hot summers; the relief: high average altitude and steep slopes; a high risk of soil erosion over most of the country, owing to rainfall intensity, soil type and gradient; and sometimes very poor soil conditions' (Ministerio de Agricultura, 1993, p. 5). The diversity of climatic environments and other factors have combined to create a variety of forms of agriculture. In the livestock sector, measured in terms of numbers of livestock, Spain comes second in the EU after the UK in terms of sheep farming, second after Greece in goat farming, and second after Germany in pig production. Fruit and vegetable production is important, as is wine, although it is estimated that 12 per cent of

Spanish vines have been pulled up since 1988 with another 17 per cent threatened under EU plans (*Financial Times*, 30 June 1993). There is also a significant level of cereal production.

According to Perez-Diaz (1983), Spain underwent a transformation from a largely pre-capitalist, traditional form of agriculture to a modern, capitalist system of farming in the 1960s and 1970s. There was a sharp fall in the labour force, while the use of machinery 'multiplied tenfold between 1960 and 1977' (Perez-Diaz, 1983, p. 4). Of particular importance was a substantial increase in the use of irrigation. Spain is, however, vulnerable to prolonged periods of water shortage, and more than three years of drought in the mid-1990s had a highly adverse impact on rice and cereals and threatened the loss of citrus trees.

The food processing industry in Spain shares many of the weaknesses found throughout Southern Europe. Although it is the fifth-largest food processing industry in the EU in terms of output, 97 per cent of the enterprises have fewer than 50 employees (Ministerio de Agricultura, 1993, p. 31). 'The current problems of the Spanish food industry are reflected not only in the low investment trend, but also in the growing number of bankruptcies' (*Agra Europe*, 30 June 1995, p. N/3). Admittedly, the industry benefits from the abundant supply of raw materials, and family firms can respond very flexibly to changing conditions, also benefiting from paying very low wages: 'On the other hand, the extensive fragmentation of the Spanish food industry, its inadequate levels of research and innovation, and weaknesses in management and infrastructure remain significant handicaps' (*Agra Europe*, 2 June 1995, p. N/2). Foreign multinationals (such as Danone of France) already control 40 per cent of the market. In 1995 the Spanish government launched a strategy programme, expecting it to be funded substantially by the EU, with the objective of consolidating the small-scale, fragmented structure of the industry and protecting it from further bankruptcies and foreign takeovers.

Mediterranean countries with inefficient agricultural sectors

Greece, Italy and Portugal share a predominance of very small producers (at least two-thirds of all holdings are under 5 hectares) and the absence of large scale farmers (no more than 2.2 per cent of holdings in any of the countries is above the 50 hectare level). They are particularly prominent in the production of commodities such as rice, tobacco and olive oil. Given that the accession of Mediterranean countries increased the significance of a number of commodity regimes in the EC, it is worth noting that:

> An undisputable fact is that spending on the southern products has not only declined absolutely in the last ten years, but also significantly in terms of the proportion of the total agricultural support budget . . . As the expenditure on the total agricultural sector has steamed steadily upwards, the amount spent on olive oil, fruit and vegetables, wine and tobacco has increased by very much less in absolute terms . . . As a proportion of total EAGFF expenditure, the Mediterranean group share has never risen above its 1985 level of 20.2% and in 1995 is likely to have fallen back to 13.5%. (*Agra Europe*, 16 June 1995, p. P/2)

Italy

Italy has the smallest proportion of the civilian population working in agriculture (7.9 per cent) of the three countries considered here, although in 1950 the share was 44 per cent. There is considerable evidence to suggest that, leaving aside particular localities and subsectors, Italian agriculture is relatively inefficient and has poor potential for future growth. To some extent, this reflects a historical neglect of agriculture (Neville-Rolfe, 1984).

An exception to the overall picture of inefficient structures and low productivity is to be found in the Po valley. This valley has deep, fertile alluvial soil fed by irrigation canals which draw on lakes filled by melt water from the Alps. Rice is grown here, but also maize and lucerne (alfalfa), which is fed to dairy herds. Average milk production figures exceed those in Britain and The Netherlands. The farmers use a system of production similar to that employed in California, which also records very high milk output per cow. The animals are kept in open concrete yards and have their carefully formulated feed delivered to them. Over 70 per cent of Italy's milk production comes from the Po valley.

Research on the Italian economy has stressed the importance of 'industrial districts', in which small and medium-sized enterprises are able to succeed within a supportive framework developed by public institutions and private collective actors. In certain parts of Northern Italy, parallel 'agricultural districts' are to be found. They are 'characterized by a high level of innovations, intensity and specialization of production' (Merlo and Manente, 1994, p. 138). A network of co-operatives, processing activities and contractors provides a supportive infrastructure backed up by public and private research. In Lombardy, a highly dynamic agriculture is based on intensification and high-quality products, producing a growth rate in value added above the national average in the 1980s (Merlo and Manente, 1994, p. 145).

The cconomic research institute, Nomisma, has suggested that it is not so much Italian agriculture as Italian farmers who need modernisation. The goal of farmers is often to achieve a marginal existence with the aid of subsidies so that some are producing almost exclusively for intervention. Compared with the potential for extensive agriculture of Spain, Italian agriculture has fewer land assets. Italy's potential for agriculture is generally less than in other EU countries, with only Greece comparing less favourably with Italy (*Agra Europe*, 15 July 1994, p. N/1).

Although the Italian food industry has a reputation for high-quality production of particular products, the industry as a whole is greatly fragmented, with an average level of employment within 36 000 concerns of only 10 employees in either. Nevertheless, this average figure conceals a considerable difference between Northern and Southern Italy, with a number of major firms based in the large cities of the North (Charvet, 1994, p. 96). One of the leading Italian-owned firms is Barilla, a family-owned group of over thirty operating companies which controls over a third of the Italian dry pasta market and is a leader in the biscuit and cake sectors. Barilla has a policy of steady international expansion and has been developing its core pasta business in France, Germany and Spain: 'Operating a dual policy of a production presence in Mediterranean markets and an import presence in Northern Europe, the company has found the latter strategy successful in respect of sales growth but not, at least in the short term, so obviously effective in respect of actual sales, whilst the former policy has encountered difficulties, particularly in Spain' (*Food File*, 15 July 1994, p. 2). With the stimulus given to cross-national activity by the internal market, much of the Italian food processing industry is vulnerable to foreign take-overs. Danone already controls a number of Italian firms.

Portugal

Portugal entered the EC with very low levels of land and labour productivity, which were attributed to 'far-reaching structural weaknesses' (European Commission, 1987, p. 14). Portugal had a significant agro-food deficit on its balance of payments, indicating a problem of insufficiently supply:

> Taken overall, the performance of agriculture looks relatively unfavourable when looked at in the context of the country's natural resources and climatic conditions. The level of productivity in agriculture . . . was well below that of the other European countries in 1985: half of the level in Greece and Spain and a quarter of that in the Community. (OECD, 1989, pp. 56–7)

In the South of the country there have been large-scale holdings engaged in grain production, bull breeding, rice growing and market gardening. Insufficient irrigation is a problem in some areas of the South, although productivity has generally been higher there than elsewhere in the country. The 'collective production units set up in the South after the 1974 expropriations proved incapable of modernising the production systems and their efficiency declined.' (OECD, 1989, p. 57). In the North and Centre of the country, dairying, pig-farming and wine production have displayed low levels of productivity because of fragmented production structures (European Commission, 1987, p. 15).

Portugal has received considerable assistance from the EC to improve the structure of its agriculture. The whole of the country is classified as an Objective 1 region, where the GNP is less than 75 per cent of the average in member states. The Portuguese regional development plan for 1994–9 earmarks ECU4.87bn for agriculture and forestry, of which around 40 per cent is funded by the EU (*Agra Europe*, 7 October 1994, p. N/5). A considerable proportion is reserved for the technical and commercial modernisation of agricultural concerns, low levels of education and training among farmers having been one problem in Portugal. The size of the gap between Portugal and other member states is illustrated by the fact that 84 per cent of people employed in farming in Portugal earn what is defined as a very low income (less than ECU4000 per annum). Only one Portuguese family farm worker in a hundred obtains an income in excess of

ECU32 000, compared with one in four in the Netherlands (European Commission, 1994b, p. 44).

The majority of food processing firms in Portugal are very small. One locally owned exception has been Agros, the main association of dairy co-operatives, but its near monopoly in the North has been ended by a deal between the leading Italian dairy group, Parmalat, and a group of farmers *(Agra Europe,* 16 September 1994, p. M/10). French companies, who have only a limited presence there at the moment, see considerable opportunities to take advantage of growing consumer purchasing power, which improved from half of the EU average in 1986 to two-thirds in 1995 *(Agra Europe,* 19 May 1995, p. N/3). As in other Southern European countries, one may expect to see growing penetration of the local market by food multinationals based in Northern Europe.

Greece

Greece has the largest proportion in any member state of its civilian employment in agriculture, and also has the smallest utilised agricultural area per holding. In many respects, agricultural modernisation has not gone very far in Greece, but it would be inappropriate to apply a Northern European model of agricultural development based on an intensification strategy reliant on the use of fertilisers and agrochemicals. In a country such as Greece, this could lead to problems of soil erosion and exhaustion.

Differences of relief and climate within Greece produce considerable diversity in agriculture. In mountain areas, agriculture has declined and there has been significant rural depopulation: 'The Greek mountains, along with certain semi-mountainous zones which lack up-to-date production structures, are cut off, maintaining very lower labour productivity' (Goussios, 1995, p. 324). In contrast, there is mechanised cereal production dependent on irrigation on the large plains of the mainland, together with fruit and market garden crops, often under glass, on small coastal plains and in some inland areas (Goussios, 1995, p. 324).

There is a well-developed agricultural co-operative movement in Greece, which sells a considerable proportion of the two main crops produced in the country, cereals and fruit. However, they have lacked both the material infrastructure and entrepreneurial mentality found in most of their counterparts elsewhere. These deficiencies are in large part because of the traditional government relationship with the co-operatives. These have either been used as a means to promote national economic goals (unsuccessfully), or as a tool to consolidate party political support (more successfully). The state has used the co-operatives to implement social welfare policies in rural areas, policies from which the ruling parties have benefited politically: 'Every policy by the Greek State is aimed at fulfilling the needs of an agricultural society made up of small landowners. This practice is politically and socially essential for anyone whose goal is to achieve and secure political power' (Goussios and Zacopoulou, 1990, p. 28).

A marked increase in real wages in Greece has led to a demand for better-quality food. Although the Greek food processing industry compares favourably with other sectors in the domestic economy, its performance is less good when compared with other countries. There is a relatively small number of large private companies that dominate their particular subsectors such as '3E' in fruit juices, with the balance of production accounted for by the co-operatives. The few large food processing enterprises in Greece are able to cope with increased demand in the domestic market but seem less well equipped to deal with changing consumer demands for higher-quality products in the wider European market. There seems to be less interest in inward investment by multinational food companies than there is in Portugal, which is perceived as having made good use of EU aid to improve transport infrastructure. However, Danone has a stake in the dairy, ice-cream and fruit juice group, Delta Dairy and Barilla has a pasta subsidiary, Misko AE. Despite increased outside interest in Portugal, 'Greece and Portugal remain relatively unscathed by the international appetites of others, because of their location, size and lower economic wealth' (Hall, 1995, p. 12).

Germany and Austria: the significance of small-scale farming and the importance of environmental pressures

Germany

The share of agriculture in GDP in Germany is the lowest of any member state (0.8 per cent). This figure, however, gives a misleading impression of the political displacement of agriculture in Germany. In part, this is because German agriculture has a very skewed structure. Before the division of the country in 1945, Germany had historically been dependent on agricultural supplies from the east of the country.

There is a considerable number of large farms, particularly in the former East Germany, but also in the north of the former West Germany. For example, in the new länder, 212 hectares is the average, while the figure for Schleswig-Holstein is 40 hectares, with nearly 30 per cent of arable farms over a hundred hectares. In contrast, in Southern Germany, there is a considerable number of very small farms. For example, in Bavaria, the average farm is 16 hectares. Nearly 30 per cent of farms in Germany are under 5 hectares, and these very small farms are generally worked on a part-time basis by farmers who also have a job in industry or some other sector of the economy. Thirty-seven per cent of German farmers have some other main employment, the highest figure for any member state.

Germany thus has one of the most diverse farming structures of any member state, even more so since unification. This diversity has deep historical roots: 'The diversity of farm structures reflected different paths of evolution from the feudal society of the Middle Ages in the German territory of the Holy Roman Empire' (Tracy, 1989, p. 83). By the end of the nineteenth century, 'in the provinces of the Kingdom of Prussia lying east of the Elbe, estates of more than 100 hectares accounted for 43% of the agricultural area . . . In the rest of Germany a more varied farm structure was found' (Tracy, 1989, pp. 86–7). Given this historical background, it is not surprising that:

> Trying to portray what is typical in German agriculture is not simple. There are huge differences in size of holdings and herds, as well as a remarkable diversity of farm produce. Crops vary from tobacco, kiwifruit, soybeans and wine, as well as all the usual temperate crops and enterprises. (*Farmers Weekly*, 3 December 1993)

Unification greatly increased the diversity of German farming. Small farms in the west were brought together with large farms in the east. These large differences in farm size have persisted since unification, with an average farm size in the east of 195 hectares compared with 21.5 hectares in western Germany (*Agra Europe*, 5 January 1996, p. N/1). The inefficiencies of eastern agriculture have, however, been substantially reduced. Although the livestock sector remains problematic, with pig numbers at a third of their 1990 level, dairy productivity has improved, with 40 per cent of the pre-unification dairy herd producing milk at 60 per cent of the pre-unification level

(*Agra Europe*, 26 January 1996, p. N/2). Overall average grain yields at 6.01t/ha in 1995 were very close to the levels in the western länder, whereas yields of 5 tonnes per hectare had been thought to be unattainable before unification.

All this progress has, however, been achieved with the aid of subsidised interest loans that pay some three-quarters of fixed interest charges on long-term bank borrowing, and DM950 million of investment aid from the federal and Land governments. There have also been substantial subsidies from the EU. An east German arable farm of 4000 hectares can expect to be drawing 535 000 ECU in arable aid payments and 104 000 ECU in set aside in 1996. Often, land is rented by western farmers from families who occupied it in the pre-Communist era. A West German farmer who took over an eastern holding shortly after unification commented, 'We repaid our capital investment in two years solely out of the subsidies we were paid from Brussels' (*Agra Europe*, 23 December 1994, p. P/2). Some farms in the east have had up to 90 per cent of their land in five-year set aside (*Agra Europe*, 9 February 1996, p. N/4).

In an economy that has the most successful manufacturing industrial sector of any member state, it is not surprising that there has been a substantial movement of labour out of agriculture, much greater than in most member states: 'During the past 40 years, one million farmers have left the industry and another 300,000 farmers – about one half of the present total – will probably leave within 15 years' (*Farmers Weekly*, 3 December 1993). Between 1987 and 1995, an average of almost seventy farms a day went out of production, of which around three-quarters were part-time farms. There has been a particularly marked structural change in the dairy sector where, according to the German Farmers' Union (DBV), virtually every second milk producer gave up farming in the ten years up to 1995 (*Agra Europe*, 9 June 1995, p. N/5). In part, this reflects a sharp fall in milk prices which fell almost 20 per cent between 1989 and 1995. In the east, the number of people employed in agriculture fell from 850 000 before unification to 175 000 in 1996 (*Agra Europe*, 26 January 1996, p. N/2).

The Green movement has become an entrenched feature of the political landscape in Germany at both federal and land level in a way that has not happened in most other member states. Environmentalists are opposed to productionist models of agriculture and concerned about the pollution that results from intensive methods of farming. Farming practices are affected by these political pressures.

For example, in the high pig population centres of Northern Germany, stocking rates have been reduced on pig farms to prevent potential pollution from slurry spreading.

Only one German food processing firm (Südzucker, a specialist firm) is among the top twenty European food processing firms by turnover (Charvet, 1994, p. 89). The dairy sector, which is the largest in terms of turnover, is dominated by co-operatives, but even the largest (Milchwerke Köln/Wuppertal) is smaller in terms of ECU turnover than the three largest producers in The Netherlands or the two largest in the Republic of Ireland (figures from Residuary Milk Marketing Board, 1994, pp. 90–1). No German company figures in the list of Europe's top twenty dairy companies, reflecting the fact for dairy products that 'Germany is . . . quite a regional market in character' (Hall, 1995, p. 12). Südmilch, the leading producer of yoghurts, filed for bankruptcy in 1993 and was eventually purchased by the Dutch co-operative, Campina-Melkunie.

The three largest food processing firms in Germany are foreign owned: Unilever, Nestlé and Coca-Cola. Most food processing firms in Germany constitute a dense network of relatively small firms (Charvet, 1994, p. 93). The prosperity of German consumers means that it is possible for small firms to develop niche markets in high-value-added products. Nevertheless, most growth in 1994 came from exports, which grew by 7.1 per cent to reach DM20.51 billion, although that is less than 10 per cent of total sales (*Agra Europe*, 26 May 1995). The attractions of the domestic market, and the ease of export to nearby large concentrations of population, helps to explain why German food processing firms are less strongly represented as producers elsewhere in the EU than firms from some other member states.

Austria

Agriculture accounts for around 2 per cent of GDP and 13 per cent of civilian employment in Austria, suggesting a relatively inefficient agricultural sector. Nevertheless, there has been a sharp fall in agricultural employment since 1960, when nearly a quarter of the labour force was employed in agriculture. Structurally, it shares a number of features with Germany: 'The size distribution is very skewed, with nearly 40 per cent of holdings being under 5 hectares and over 50 per cent under ten' (OECD, 1992b, p. 43). Another similarity with Germany is the presence of large numbers of part-time farmers, with 80 per cent of farms under 10 hectares being run on a part-time basis (OECD, 1992b, p. 69). Where Austria differs from Germany is that large parts of the country are mountainous, with a quarter of the land used by agriculture and forestry being mountain pasture. Farming in mountainous areas is only possible with substantial subsidies. Indeed, 'In some ways the CAP is less interventionist' (OECD, 1992b, p. 73) than the national policies followed by Austria before it joined the EU. However, payments to farmers in mountainous areas seem likely to increase under the EU regime (OECD, 1995a, p. 60).

Austria is noted as a country which has had highly developed corporatist arrangements and these have been particularly apparent in the dairy sector, the most important sector of the agricultural economy. The first objective of the law relating to the dairy sector is to protect the domestic industry and high milk prices have been one means of supporting mountain farming. An Austrian analyst of the domestic dairy regime had to admit that it was 'somewhat ponderous' and noted 'the still unsolved problem of chronic overproduction in the sector' (Traxler, 1985, p. 164).

Austria has given increasing emphasis to environmental protection as a policy objective of agricultural policy and has developed an extensive agri-environmental programme. There has been a 'steep upward trend in government support for organic farming' (OECD, 1995a, p. 59). While he was still Austrian agriculture minister, before he became the commissioner for agriculture, Franz Fischler argued that agri-environmental measures should become a policy objective of the CAP in their own right (*Agra Europe*, 29 June 1994, p. E/6). Such a policy emphasis would, of course, be beneficial to smaller farmers in Austria.

The food processing sector has been the industry hardest hit by Austria's membership of the EU. This is a serious development, given that the food and drinks sector remains Austria's largest industry, but not a surprising one when one considers that Austria has one of the most fragmented industries in Europe, with only one concern in the top hundred companies (Food Industry Bulletin, 1995, pp. 6–7). For decades, the sector existed comfortably within the context of 'the country's generous farm support system and a closed market' (*Financial Times*, 6 July 1995). The chief economist at the Federal Chamber of Commerce has estimated that a fifth of the 50 000 jobs in the sector could disappear (*Financial Times*, 6 July 1995). Many domestically owned plants in sectors such as dairying have been small and uncompetitive, while multinationals such as Unilever have had to consider the future of plants making small batches of a range of products for the Austrian market which could be made at plants elsewhere in the EU.

Conclusions

The relationship between the structure and economic displacement of agriculture in a member state, and the stance it takes on agricultural issues at the EU level, is necessarily a complex one. In most member states, the political displacement of agriculture far exceeds its economic significance. For example, 'The Austrian landscape has been strongly influenced by agricultural activity and, since the decline in agricultural employment has been relatively recent and rapid in historical perspective, agricultural interests are still very strongly represented in political decision-making' (OECD, 1992b, p. 47). In the case of Germany, the limited importance of agricultural in the German national economy bears no relationship to the vigour with which Germany defends the national interests of its farmers at the EU level, sometimes, it would seem, at the expense of more pressing national concerns.

Nevertheless, before attempting to understand the political strategies and tactics of member states at the EU level, it is necessary to have some understanding of the form and character of their own agricultural economies. This is what this chapter has sought to do. The Mediterranean countries have in general relatively uncompetitive agricultures, although Spain may have more potential for making progress than the other countries. The contrast between Northern and Southern Europe is even stronger in the case of the food processing industry where, with a few exceptions, firms from Southern Europe are often small, fragmented, family-run and unable to compete outside their own domestic or local markets. They face increasing competition from Northern European multinationals who are moving into their markets to meet the demand for higher quality products from consumers with larger disposable incomes.

At the other end of the spectrum from the Mediterranean countries are Denmark and The Netherlands, with well-run agricultural sectors sustaining highly competitive food processing industries. The Republic of Ireland is at least a candidate member of this group. Britain and Sweden take a highly commercial approach to agriculture and are advocates of reduced subsidies. It is no accident that they are some-times aligned in the Council of Ministers, occasionally with Denmark and The Netherlands. Agriculture is far from being the most im-portant economic interest of Belgium and Luxembourg, and Lux-embourg can sometimes play a disproportionate role in the EU decision-making process, as a mediator and provider of compromises. Austria and Finland are countries whose long-protected agricultural sectors face enhanced competition from other EU countries. How far-reaching the structural changes that follow will be depends on how the transition process is handled.

The most important economic actor in European agriculture is undoubtedly France. It accounts for nearly a quarter of EU agricul-tural production, it is the second largest agricultural exporter in the world, and it is the base for a number of the leading food processing firms in Europe. Agriculture has had a high national priority for France since the Second World War and it has a particularly vociferous farmers' lobby. France cannot, however, act unilaterally on agricultural matters, and at the very least it requires the support of the other most important actor in the EU, Germany. In order to understand the relationship between France and Germany on agri-cultural questions it is necessary to consider the events surrounding the formation and early development of the CAP, which is the subject of the next chapter.

3

The Development of the Common Agricultural Policy

The Common Agricultural Policy is essentially the product of a compromise between France and Germany. There was a significant Dutch input to the discussions about the formation of the CAP and the impact of their more commercially-orientated approach to agriculture might have been greater if Britain had also been involved as a member state. However, Britain was committed to unrealistic proposals for a European free trade area that excluded agriculture, and by the time Britain entered the EC in 1972 the CAP was established in a form that could not be modified significantly to accommodate new entrants. As far as Italy was concerned, 'Preoccupation with domestic political issues has had a marked and on the whole harmful effect on Italian attitudes to the development of the CAP, especially during the important formative period between 1958 and 1967' (Neville-Rolfe, 1984, pp. 160–1).

France's interest in the negotiations leading to the establishment of the common market was to ensure that its farmers secured outlets for their produce in Germany. Only if this objective was secured was France prepared to allow German manufacturing exports access to the French market. Given the physical fragmentation and economic weakness of German agriculture, and the strength of the German manufacturing sector, the underlying interests of Germany would appear to lie in as few barriers to trade as possible. In other words, one might think that Germany would be prepared to sacrifice the interests of its farmers to advance the interests of its manufacturers.

However, Germany had a very strong agricultural lobby, with close links to the governing parties. Indeed, 'the objectives of the CAP, are an almost faithful reflection of the aims as contained in Germany's "Agricultural Act", passed in September 1955, which institutionalised the generally-held view that agriculture deserves special treatment' (Hendriks, 1995, p. 59).

In 1955 the foreign ministers of the European Coal and Steel Community met in Messina to discuss the basis for further steps towards a united Europe. They established a committee chaired by the foreign minister of Belgium, Paul-Henri Spaak, to suggest how their agreement at Messina might be put into effect. The Spaak report 'did not contain concrete suggestions regarding the way agricultural policies should be treated in the Community. But it left no doubt concerning the fundamental importance of including agriculture in the process of European economic integration' (Tangermann, 1992, p. 409). The Spaak report was accepted by the foreign ministers of the six in 1956 and it was used as the basis for negotiations at val Duchesse in Brussels: 'Although *ad hoc* working parties were formed to deal with particular issues, there was no formal group concerned with agriculture. Much of the day to day work was left in the hands of relatively junior civil servants, many of whom subsequently transferred to the service of the Commission' (Neville-Rolfe, 1984, p. 193).

The Common Agricultural Policy is covered by Articles 38 to 45 of the Treaty of Rome. The crucial article is Article 39, which sets out the objectives of the CAP. However, it is worth noting that Article 38 defines agricultural products as including first stage food processing. The products subject to the provisions of Articles 39 to 45 are set out in Annex II of the treaty: 'Annex II excludes manufactured foods, yet it is these which contribute most to European GNP and to the value of our exports' (Land Use and Food Policy Inter-Group 1995, p. 8).

The objectives of the CAP set out in Article 39 are criticised frequently in the mid-1990s by reformers because of their emphasis on a productionist policy that neglects environmental considerations. Article 39(1) sets out five objectives. The first is to increase agricultural productivity through the promotion of technical progress and the optimum utilisation of factors of production, especially labour. Technical progress has, of course, occurred in European agriculture, stimulated by the multinational companies that produce powered machinery, agrochemicals, fertilisers, veterinary drugs and, more recently, products based on biotechnology. Intensive forms of agriculture have increased output in a way that has made it difficult to avoid the accumulation of surpluses. Labour was shed particularly in conditions of fuller employment, when younger workers found it attractive to take advantage of the higher wages available in manufacturing industry. Farmers are generally an ageing group in the European population.

The second objective was stated to be 'to ensure a fair standard of living for the agricultural community, in particular by increasing the individual earnings of persons engaged in agriculture'. The founders of the EC were concerned that the disparity between urban and rural incomes in Europe might become a source of social unrest. However, 'In the formulation of the CAP the relationship between price policy and standards of living in the farm sector was never finally established' (Le Heron, 1993, p. 128). The gap between industrial and agricultural incomes was not eliminated. Indeed, in many respects, the impact of the CAP on income distribution has been negative, as the principal beneficiary of its policies has been the larger-scale farmer, along with those trading and storing agricultural products.

A third objective was to stabilise markets. This objective could be said to have been achieved to a large extent, but at a substantial budgetary cost, and at the price of the distortion of world markets by the export of subsidised surpluses from Community countries. A fourth objective was to assure the availability of supplies. This reflected the recent experience at the time of a shortage of supply, or in Germany after the Second World War, of insufficient food to sustain an adequate diet. It is very difficult for those who did not experience rationing in the immediate postwar years to appreciate the priority given to this objective by those engaged in the early discussions about the formation of the CAP. Food security continued to be a concern through the years of the Cold War, but seems of less importance in the highly integrated global economy of the last years of the twentieth century, even given sometimes exaggerated concerns in the mid-1990s about world grain supplies. A final objective was to 'ensure that supplies reach consumers at reasonable prices'. Much depends on how one interprets the word 'reasonable', but the CAP has generally operated by maintaining prices within the EU at above world levels.

Article 43(1) of the Treaty of Rome stated that 'In order to evolve the broad lines of a common agricultural policy, the Commission shall, immediately this Treaty enters into force, convene a conference of the Member States, with a view to making a comparison of their agricultural policies, in particular by producing a statement of their resources and needs.' This conference was held at Stresa on Lake Maggiore in Italy in July 1958: 'Although the agreement reached at Stresa was not legally binding, the final resolution offered a more coherent view of the CAP than was presented in the Treaty of Rome' (Fearne, 1991, p. 27). However, many of the aspirations expressed at Stresa were not achieved in the subsequent evolution of the CAP: the development of trade without threatening established relationships with third countries; an equilibrium between production and market outlets; and an effective structural policy. It is significant that there was discussion of a price policy, although it was hoped that policy objectives could be achieved without surpluses. In contrast, the objective of supplying consumers at reasonable prices 'did not attract a great deal of attention either in the working party reports or, with two exceptions, in the ministers' speeches' (Neville-Rolfe, 1984, p. 198). Part of the general context for the discussions was the view that world markets were 'dominated by the United States against whose hegemony the Community was at least in part a political expression' (European Commission, 1994a, p. 63).

That agreement was possible at Stresa at all was largely a result of the efforts of Commission officials and, in particular, the former Dutch agriculture minister who was to serve as commissioner for agriculture until 1972, Sicco Mansholt. Careful management of the conference ensured 'that from conflict came compromise, and from ambiguity came cohesion' (Fearne, 1991, p. 27). Stresa helped to establish the CAP routine of complex intergovernmental bargaining brokered by the Commission. There have been many occasions when the Commission has been able to bridge seemingly irreconcilable differences within the Council of Ministers. However, the objective of enabling the CAP, and hence the Community, to continue to function has often been achieved at a high price. Additional budgetary costs have been incurred in order to placate particular member states or interests; surplus product has distorted the world market; or problems have been transferred from one sector to another: for example, surplus skimmed milk has been fed to pigs, affecting the feed trade; or wine has been turned into industrial alcohol, to the annoyance of the chemical industry. Above all, there has been a preference for fudged compromises rather than tackling the underlying structural problems that are the source of the CAP's difficulties. In a complex system of intergovernmental bargaining, first seen in operation at Stresa, arriving at an acceptable decision has understandably often been preferable to attempting to reach the right decision; that is, one that is optimal for the long-run development of the CAP rather than politically palatable in the short run.

The final resolution agreed at Stresa set out the objectives of the CAP, but did not specify the mechanisms to be used for their achievement. A complex set of negotiations followed, centred on the cereal sector. The cereals regime established in 1962 (although not put into effect in terms of common prices until the 1967/8 crop year) represented the effective birth of the CAP, and its principles and mechanisms were adopted for subsequent commodity regimes: 'Cereals held a key position for agriculture: while being a basic food directly affecting the price of bread, they are also the input into further production of livestock and therefore indirectly affect meat, eggs and milk' (Hendriks, 1991, p. 51).

Three institutional prices form the basis of the EU's pricing mechanisms. The target price is the basic reference point from which the other prices are derived. It is designed to represent a satisfactory level of return to the farmer. Threshold prices represent minimum entry prices for imports and are designed to ensure that target prices cannot be undercut. They are calculated by deducting the cost of transport from the target price. This is done by setting the target price where the particular commodity is in shortest supply. In the case of grain this is Duisburg in the Ruhr: 'The threshold price for grain is defined as the Rotterdam price for imported grain that, adjusting for transportation costs, is consistent with the Duisburg target price' (Atkin, 1993, p. 64). The intervention price provides a floor to the market by providing a price at which national agencies have to buy products offered to them into intervention stores if they meet quality standards. The other elements of the commodity regime for cereals which were widely adopted were variable import levies to bring imports up to the threshold price (these were adopted from the Dutch method of protection), and export refunds to make up the difference between the price within the common market and the average world price.

Import levies offered a means of contributing to the cost of the CAP. Alternative methods of support, such as the British system of deficiency payments, were seen as being likely to place too great a strain on the Community budget. Under a deficiency payments system, farmers sell their produce on the market at the best price they can get, but they receive compensation for the difference between the average market price and a guaranteed price. The cost of deficiency payments can rise sharply if world market prices fall, and this feature of this type of price support caused increasing concern in Britain in the years leading up to Community entry (and had led to the introduction of some import controls in 1963). However, deficiency payments do not cause surpluses, with produce being sold off at market clearing prices to the benefit of poorer consumers while the burden falls on better-off taxpayers.

During the course of the discussions about the shape of the CAP in the early 1960s, three basic principles emerged: market unity, Community preference, and financial solidarity. Although these principles are 'often quoted and held to be sacrosanct, [they] have somewhat vague origins' (Fennell, 1979, p. 14). The market unity principle requires a single market for any commodity under the CAP, with a common system of marketing and pricing throughout the EU. In practice, this principle has been eroded by the operation of the agrimonetary system, discussed in Chapter 4. The second principle, Community preference, 'means in effect that producers inside the Community should always be more favourably placed than competing overseas suppliers' (Fennell, 1979, p. 14). The third principle, financial solidarity, requires joint financial responsibility for the funding of the CAP. Atkin argues (1993, p. 54) that the second and third principles were 'major victories for France, since they, in effect, committed other European countries to provide markets for French produce and to contribute jointly to the cost of doing so'.

The system of prices

Having decided a system of pricing within the common market, the actual prices had to be fixed: 'The price of wheat was the crux, determining the price of bread and, through its influence on grains for feeding animals, of meat and other livestock products' (Pinder, 1991, p. 80). The highest prices were in Germany and, if these had been adopted across the common market, they would have pushed production up to unacceptable levels, as well as protecting German farmers from French competition. The underlying politics of grain prices in Germany differed from what might be deduced from the country's agricultural structure:

In the Federal Republic grain production represented some 10 per cent of total farm produce only, but the political influence of grain farmers is great. Cereals producers predominate among the farm deputies who represent Germany in various professional groups and consultative bodies at Community level. (Hendriks, 1991, p. 51)

By 1964 the French had become so exasperated over the lack of progress on the harmonisation of cereal prices that they threatened to withdraw from the Community unless agreement on grain prices was reached by the end of the year. Germany did then agree to lower prices, which it presented as a substantial concession in the interests of European solidarity, a claim greeted with some scepticism by the other member states (Neville-Rolfe, 1984, p. 227). In any case, the wheat price was well above world prices and the average in the member states and certainly 'was considerably higher than the Commission or the French wanted' (Pinder, 1991, p. 81) and promoted over-production. For example, given the relatively high level of cereal prices established, Dutch farmers responded by rapidly and substantially increasing wheat production' (Fearne, 1991, p. 39). Although other member states might benefit from the decisions taken, 'the outcomes can most easily be understood as compromises between French and German interests' (Atkin, 1993, p. 56). Yet 'Germany saw itself as the loser' (Hendriks, 1991, p. 55). Germany became more determined to protect its national interests in the future, with the agrimonetary system eventually serving as a convenient device to sustain the incomes of German farmers within the common market (see Chapter 4).

The question of financing the CAP provoked the dispute with France that led to the Luxembourg Compromise. The Commission, not unreasonably, took the view that common financing implied a greater role for Community institutions in scrutinising the use of the funds and suggested that the European Parliament should be involved in the approval of the budget. The French saw this as a threat to their national sovereignty and withdrew from participation in Community institutions in the second half of 1965, the so-called 'empty chair'. This dispute was resolved by the 'Luxembourg Compromise' of 1966, which overrode the proposed introduction of qualified majority voting for agricultural issues by an understanding that where very important interests were at stake, the Council would endeavour to reach a unanimous agreement. This agreement 'which might more accurately have been called the Luxembourg veto, led to the general use of the unanimity procedure in the Council for about

two decades, thus consolidating the dominance of the intergovernmental method of operating the Community and diminishing its
capacity for action' (Pinder, 1991, p. 82). Germany used the veto to
oppose cuts in cereal prices in the agriculture Council in 1985,
although, as events developed, this had little practical effect.

The Mansholt Plan: the first attempt at reform

The Mansholt Plan of 1968, officially a Commission memorandum to
the Council on the reform of agriculture, was the first attempt to
tackle the underlying structural problems of Community agriculture.
Its fate was indicative of the problems encountered by subsequent
attempts to reform the Community. Mansholt and other members of
DG VI were aware that the prices agreed by the Council would push
up production, leading to an increasing burden on the budget.
Mansholt recognised the implications of technologically-driven agricultural productivity in a relatively risk-free environment protected
from external competition. Recognising that only those producers
with a high rates of technical innovation are going to create sustainable productivity gains, the plan sought to reduce real prices by
basing them on the cost levels of the more efficient farmers (Le Heron,
1993, pp. 128–9). Structural adjustment might make good sense, but
it was not good politics.

The memorandum started with a succinct review of the economic
situation of European agriculture. Consumption of agricultural products was not increasing as fast as production. There were already
increasing surpluses of common wheat, milk and sugar and the report
correctly forecast that surpluses could be expected to develop in fruit
and vegetables. The products most commonly in surplus could not all
be disposed of on the world market. Agriculture in the Community
suffered from serious structural imperfections, with too many small
farms and too many elderly farmers with inadequate training for
modern conditions. The gap between incomes in agriculture and
other sectors of the economy had generally not diminished, and
income disparities had grown considerably within agriculture. Market and support policies alone could not solve the problems of farming
and there was a risk of intolerable costs to the Community without
any effective improvement for farmers (Secretariat-General of the

Commission, 1968, pp. 9–12). For clarity and perspicacity, it would be difficult to improve on this analysis.

The report saw the problems of agriculture as being essentially a social problem. Although the farming population was falling, the rate of decline must be greatly accelerated: 'The only way to provide farmers with an equitable income and better living conditions, and at the same time ensure the indispensable balance between output and sales outlets, is to reshape the structure of production' (Secretariat-General of the Commission, 1968, p. 21). The price policy then in place was seen as encouraging marginal farms to stay in business. The proposed 'Agriculture 1980' programme envisaged the steady reduction of guarantee expenditure. Measures should be introduced to enable farmers to withdraw from agricultural production, particularly older producers, permitting consolidation of land into larger enterprises, although the total area of cultivated land should be reduced considerably.

The Commission acknowledged that this call for radical structural reform 'may even call forth negative reactions' (Secretariat-General of the Commission, 1968, p. 23). Even if one allows for the understatement of bureaucratic language, this was a serious underestimation of the furore that ensued. The plan 'proved too radical to be politically acceptable. It was seen as destructive of too many family farms and too great a departure from the policy of market price support' (European Commission, 1994a, p. 13). 'In France, in particular, there [was] bitter reaction, as the debate took place against a background of concern about the prospects for the farm community, faced by acute problems of transition from a peasant-type, small-scale farming pattern, depending almost exclusively on family labour and making little use of purchased inputs, to larger-scale, mechanised and capital-intensive units' (Tracy, 1989, p. 287).

Although three directives on structural policy were agreed in 1972, they fell far short of the radical plan that the Commission memorandum had envisaged. Whereas it had originally been intended that a third of the agricultural budget would be spent on structural measures rather than price support, the guidance section of the Guarantee and Guidance Fund generally remained below 5 per cent of total expenditure. There has been some increase in expenditure on rural development since the late 1980s as part of the effort to promote cohesion, but guidance expenditure still accounts for only 7 per cent of all agricultural expenditure in the 1995 budget.

The first enlargement

'For a CAP reform proposal to be adopted, it is . . . important that
the distribution of costs and benefits between Member States does not
change dramatically as a result of its implementation and also that it
is perceived in each Member State not to do so' (European Commission, 1994a, p. 33). A reform as radical as the Mansholt Plan clearly
failed this basic test, as did all subsequent fundamental attempts at
reform until the MacSharry reforms in 1992. Paradoxically, the first
enlargement in 1973 may have made it easier for the CAP to survive
unreformed: 'Had it not been for British entry in 1973, and the
diversion of imports into its large market from its traditional overseas
suppliers to the Community farmers, together with the large British
contribution to the Community budget, the burden of surplus
production would have become intolerable for the Community sooner' (Pinder, 1991, p. 86).

The CAP had been one of the main stumbling blocks to acceptance
of membership of the Community in Britain. Britain had relied on
imports from Commonwealth countries to keep food prices as low as
possible. The productionist alliance between the Ministry of Agriculture, Fisheries and Food and the National Farmers' Union since
the 1947 Agriculture Act had boosted domestic production. With its
larger farms, Britain was seen to be a more efficient agricultural
producer than its continental counterparts, although much of this
efficiency had been obtained with the highly subsidised substitution of
capital inputs for labour. However, with the deficiency payments
system under pressure from the Treasury, British farmers came to see
that most of them would benefit from high prices in the CAP: 'The
issue of Britain's relations with the Commonwealth, which had
seemed intractable in 1961–3, now broke down into a limited number
of relatively technical problems' (Tracy, 1989, p. 287). There had to
be lengthy negotiations about New Zealand, which was then highly
dependent on the British market for the sale of its dairy products and
lamb. Indeed, 'The problem of New Zealand butter became another
recurrent issue in Britain's relations with the Community' (Tracy,
1989, p. 288).

One of the issues of particular concern to Britain was the maintenance of assistance to hill and upland agriculture. Such assistance
was viewed by the original member states as a distortion of competition and potentially incompatible with the Treaty of Rome. This
problem was dealt with through the Less Favoured Areas Directive

adopted in 1975. It was originally thought of as the Mountain Areas Directive, with France pressing for a definition that would have excluded British hills and uplands. However, the British emphasis on latitude as well as altitude won the day, and the Directive represents the one clear example of a British policy being incorporated into the CAP. Other member states came to see less favoured area status as a way of securing additional funds for their farmers and the areas designated as less favoured gradually expanded. By 1995, 56 per cent of the utilised agricultural area of the EU was designated as being less favoured.

Britain, Denmark and the Republic of Ireland joined the EC in 1973: 'Ireland, with its agriculture becoming increasingly competitive, was able to sit back and reap the rewards from the decisions influenced most heavily by the more powerful member states' (Fearne, 1991, p. 53). In Britain, producer prices did not rise as much as farmers had hoped because the government used the 'green pound' to restrain the rate of price increases. The development of green currencies from the late 1960s undermined the operation of the CAP as a common market and presented a recurrent set of policy problems for the Community, which had still not been resolved by the 1990s. The agrimonetary system is one of the most complex and important aspects of history of the CAP and it will be treated separately in Chapter 4.

The Lomé Convention

One other consequence of British membership was the first Lomé Convention negotiated in 1975, which provided a framework for the EU's relations with developing countries. Former British colonies wanted to enjoy the same privileges as had been granted to former French possessions under the earlier Yaoundé conventions, so that they could continue to sell to their traditional markets. For its part, the EU had an interest in securing stable supplies of such commodities as palm nuts, cloves, cocoa and groundnut oil. What the original convention provided to the Third-World countries in the Lomé convention was 'a privileged position in terms of preferential access for their exports, stabilization measures for their earnings from the export of primary products (STABEX), and access to financial resources from the Community, mainly in the form of grants' (Pedersen, 1993, p. 140).

The Lomé convention has been renegotiated on a number of occasions, with the ten-year Lomé IV agreement being reached in 1990. This was focused originally on the former colonies of the European states: namely the African, Caribbean and Pacific (ACP) countries: 'Enlargement of the Community in 1986 broadened the geographic field of north–south relations by allowing the EC to reinforce its relations with . . . countries of Central and Latin America' (Lowe, 1996, p. 15). The forty-six countries covered in Lomé I had increased to sixty-nine in Lomé IV.

Opinions about the efficacy of the Lomé arrangements for the Third-World countries vary. Certainly, it is more comprehensive and far-reaching than other arrangements between developed and developing countries. Thus it can be claimed that 'even if it had by no means resolved development problems' it had at least 'gone further than any other instrument in trying to address them' (Lowe, 1996, p. 16). However, a basic asymmetry of power exists between developing countries dependent on one or a limited range of products, and wealthy, developed countries which add value in their own factories to the primary products they import. It is possible to argue that developing countries would be worse off without Lomé, but also that it is not an adequate offset for the distortions of world agricultural trade brought about by the CAP.

The reform imperative

As surpluses increased and more money was spent on dumping subsidised exports on world markets, 'CAP spending doubled in real terms between the mid-1970s and the mid-1980s' (European Commission, 1994a, p. 14). After a temporary respite in the late 1970s because of poor harvests and a recovery on the world market, 'The 1980s were years of almost unrelieved crisis for the CAP, with rapid growth in budgetary costs . . . growing surpluses in all main crop and livestock sectors [and] a variety of uncoordinated attempts to discourage overproduction' (European Commission, 1994a, p. 15). There was a parallel crisis in the Community's agrimonetary system which was of such importance and complexity that it deserves separate treatment in the next chapter. At this point it should be noted that the complexity of the 'green money' system allowed decision-makers in the agricultural policy community to claim that they were 'freezing' support prices when they were in fact being increased in terms of the payments made to farmers in national currencies.

The development and implementation of the important reforms in the cereals and dairy sectors, and the attempt to introduce reforms in other sectors, is discussed more fully in Chapter 5. Here the focus is on the broad outline of the reforms, and in particular, the imperative behind them: what was it that permitted the logjam of resistance to reform to be broken? In broad terms, the imperative in the 1980s was a budgetary one. In the 1990s, budgetary pressures fell into the background, and the international trade negotiations conducted in the Uruguay Round moved into the forefront. In the first decade of the twenty-first century it may well be that eastern enlargement of the EU will provide the main imperative for further reform (see Chapter 7).

In the 1980s, reform became necessary because the CAP threatened to break the Community's budget, leading to the introduction of dairy quotas in 1984 and budgetary stabilisers in 1988. Dairy quotas brought spending on the dairy sector under control. Although differing from sector to sector, the general objective of budgetary stabilisers was to reduce the attractiveness of production for intervention by lowering prices when the quantity produce exceeded a threshold, and reducing intervention guarantees. The hope was to stop intervention purchasing acting 'as a risk-free market outlet in its own right, so that its original function is restored, namely to cushion farmers against short-term production fluctuations which are not structural in nature' (European Commission, 1989, p. 16). Agriculture expenditure was not to be allowed to grow by more than just under three-quarters of the increase in Community GDP, restricting market support expenditure to no more than 2 per cent a year in real terms. Although a substantial reduction from the 6 per cent growth rate in prices (in constant price terms) between 1980 and 1987, the Commission's claim 'that the new rule is a draconian one' (European Commission, 1989, p. 16) seems exaggerated. As the Commission itself subsequently recognised:

the stabilisers policy has not involved – and indeed did not have as an objective – a fundamental reform of the CAP. As its description suggests, it was a policy to stabilise production and spending, through a largely automatic mechanism whereby the price and the guarantee reduced beyond a certain production threshold. This policy did not attack the underlying problems [of the CAP] viz.

that support through the EAGGF remains proportionate to the quantity produced: this factor preserves a permanent incentive to greater production and further intensification. (European Commission, 1991, p. 8)

Aided by a relatively favourable market situation in 1988 and 1989, the Community did manage to reduce stocks and budgetary costs. Having risen from 12.4 billion ECU in 1982 to 27.5 billion ECU in 1987, farm spending levelled at about 27 billion ECU at the end of the 1980s (*Financial Times*, 14 December 1989). As a share of the total budget, the CAP accounted for 75 per cent of the total in 1985, a figure that fell to 65 per cent at the end of the 1980s. In 1994 European Agricultural Guidance and Guarantee Fund (EAGGF) expenditure amounted to 55 per cent of the EU's total budget (compared with 53.8 per cent in 1993) (*Agra Europe*, 8 December 1995, p. E/3). In part, this fall in the CAP share of the budget reflected the growth of spending on other policies, such as cohesion. Total projected EAGGF expenditure for 1996 was 54 per cent above the 1990 level, at 38.5 billion ECU (*Agra Europe*, 15 December 1995, p. E/4). More generally, budgetary crises do not provide a sustained imperative for effective reform:

There is a limit . . . to the efficiency impetus created by a budget crisis. As soon as enough resources have been saved to deal with the crisis, the pressure is removed to take any further action. That . . . was evidenced in the EC milk quotas and stabilizers debates. (Moyer and Josling, 1990, p. 201)

The Commission's 1988 'Rural World' green paper stimulated further debate about the role of the CAP, and added urgency was given to this debate when budget projections for 1990 and 1991 showed further rises in CAP spending which were likely to continue. The breakdown of the Uruguay Round negotiations in Brussels in 1990 brought home the international price that might have to be paid for a failure to reform the CAP. The 'Reflections' paper published by the Commission in 1991 clearly recognised that more fundamental reform of the CAP was required. The paper stated 'that the mechanisms of the CAP as currently applied are no longer in a position to attain certain objectives prescribed for the agricultural policy under Article 39 of the Treaty of Rome' (European Commission, 1991, p. 3). The paper warned that 'the Community's agricultural policy cannot avoid a succession of increasingly serious crises unless its mechanisms are fundamentally reviewed so far as to adapt them to a situation different from that of the sixties' (European Commission, 1991, p. 9).

As the Commission admitted in the Reflections paper, there was nothing new in this analysis. There had been a whole series of Commission papers since the early days of the CAP providing trenchant analyses of its fundamental weaknesses, such as the 1975 'Stocktaking' paper. What was different in 1991, however, was the political context in which the analysis was presented – the Uruguay Round trade negotiations that had begun in 1986 and had broken down at their supposed concluding meeting in Brussels to a large extent because of disputes between the USA and the EU over agricultural trade. The Reflections paper, and the ensuing MacSharry reforms, provided a means of restarting the negotiations. This was always denied by DG VI for political reasons. 'De-linkage' of evidently inter-linked issues is politically necessary 'as agriculture ministers traditionally show resistance to the notion of forced external changes to the CAP' (*Agra Europe*, 10 November 1995, p. P/1). In practice, 'the GATT negotiations and the process of preparing for CAP reform went in parallel' (Tangermann, 1996, p. 12).

In July 1991, agriculture commissioner Ray MacSharry issued a package of reform proposals based on the principles outlined in the Reflections paper. These were mainly directed at the cereals sector, but their novel feature was that, in return for compulsorily setting aside land, farmers would receive arable aid compensation payments. These thus introduced a partial decoupling of support from production – at least from yields, if not from land – something that agricultural economists had long advocated. The most controversial aspect of the proposals were what is known as 'modulation' in Commission jargon: the targeting of assistance away from larger farmers towards smaller farmers. The Commission had argued in its Reflections paper that 80 per cent of assistance went to 20 per cent of farmers, although no figures have ever been produced to justify this conclusion (which is not to say that it is not an acceptable 'stylised fact'). The proposal to place a 7.5 hectare upper limit on compensation for set aside land was opposed by Britain and Germany, and had to be dropped. The cut in cereal prices had to be reduced from 35 to 29 per cent, and various other detailed concessions had to be offered to member states, such as extra subsidies for the East German länder (for further discussion of the reform package, see Swinbank, 1993a).

In broad terms, however, the package remained in place. Moreover, agreement was reached in ten months, by May 1992, allowing further progress to be made in the Uruguay Round negotiations.

There are two views of the MacSharry reforms: the sceptics' and the optimists'. The sceptics point out that, in the medium term, the reforms have forced up the budgetary cost of the CAP because of the compensatory payments to farmers. The CAP budget for 1996 exceeded 40 billion ECU for the first time. Moreover, because of a rise in world market prices, cereal farmers have received compensation for price cuts that have not in fact occurred. The critics also pointed out that the policy would be more expensive to run (requiring satellite surveillance systems to check on set aside) and more burdensome and intrusive for the individual farmers (who had to fill in complicated forms covering every parcel in the holding). The reforms failed to 'tackle the underlying problems of European farming's dependence on support and the policy's excessive cost' (CAP Review Group, 1995, p. 4). Johnson argues (1995, p. 7): 'While the CAP reform was of major importance, it cannot be said to have been revolutionary in nature; perhaps it may be described as evolutionary.'

For defenders of the MacSharry reforms, they represented a real break with the past: 'The May 1992 reform package was the first truly important recognition by EC governments that the price support system could no longer square the circle of maintaining farmers' incomes and at the same time bring markets into better balance' (European Commission, 1994b, p. 19). Agricultural economists saw the reform as pointing the CAP in a new policy direction, arguing that 'the 1992 Reform established the precedent for significant policy change in the CAP to meet changing circumstances' (Josling and Tangermann, 1995, p. 5). Tangermann argues (1996, p. 1) that in political terms, 'the MacSharry reform was an absolutely remarkable achievement, and a major departure from earlier attempts at reforming the CAP', though he also admits that in economic terms the reform was not large enough, was bought at too high a cost, and left much unfinished business. As is evident from the discussion of commodity regimes in Chapter 5, it has proved difficult to deal with unreformed sectors such as wine, and fruit and vegetables.

It is not intended to provide here a detailed account of the negotiations on agriculture in the Uruguay Round and their many complications (such as the red, amber, green and later blue 'boxes'). A number of excellent accounts are available elsewhere (Ingersent *et al.*, 1994; Josling *et al.*, forthcoming; Stewart, 1993; Swinbank and Tanner, 1996). A chronology of the principal events in the agricultural negotiations is provided in Table 3.1. Three general observations do, however, need to be made. First, the EU was more successful in defending its position than were the USA (and the Cairns Group) in advancing theirs. Second, the presence of the Round affected the decision-making process on the CAP by bringing in a wider and more senior range of actors from outside the agricultural policy community. Third, the immediate impact of the conclusion of the Round on agricultural trade was not that substantial, but its longer-run implications are more significant.

The United States entered the negotiations with the so-called 'zero option'. The term was borrowed from strategic arms limitations talks, but in agriculture it meant eliminating trade-distorting barriers over a ten-year period while removing all barriers to market access over the same period. This was clearly an unrealistic 'wish list', and by starting from an unrealistic position, albeit one on which they were prepared (and had to) make substantial concessions, the USA got the negotiations off to a bad start. In taking such a position, the US government was urged on by its agribusiness and trading lobbies. The USA also seems to have believed that the EC was internally weak, 'that European unity was a chimera, and that strong pressure could succeed in having the Europeans change course' (Dupont and Sciarini, 1994, p. 12).

This was an unrealistic perception. The EC made it clear in an opening statement from the Council of Ministers issued in October

TABLE 3.1

Key dates in the Uruguay Round agriculture negotiations

September 1986	Round mandated at Punta del Este, Uruguay
December 1988	Mid-term review in Montreal
July 1990	Houston G–7 summit. Agreement on how farm subsidies talks could proceed interpreted differently by EC and USA
December 1990	Brussels talks, intended to complete round, fail
November 1991	US–EC summit at The Hague (Bush–Delors)
December 1991	'Dunkel draft' tabled in Geneva: includes possible solution on agriculture
November 1992	USA and EU reach Blair House agreement
December 1993	USA and EU reach 'Blair House II' agreement leading to conclusion of Uruguay Round

1987 that it was determined to preserve the fundamental mechanisms of the CAP. It was resolved that no single commodity would suffer a severe cutback in support, and that the existing subsidy regime should be supported by firming up prices: 'The EC was primarily interested in the management of world trade, whereas the US was willing to let the prices be freely determined by market forces' (Dupont and Sciarini, 1994, pp. 14–15). The Australian-led group of medium-sized agricultural exporting countries, the Cairns Group, could have acted as a mediator between the USA and the EU, but moved rather quickly in a position close to that of the US, leaving countries such as Sweden and the GATT secretariat to perform a mediating role.

In terms of the handling of the talks, despite considerable difficulties with France's position and tensions between the commissioners, the EC displayed a remarkable degree of cohesion and effectiveness. In part, this was because the EU was following a defensive strategy based on 'the continuation of . . . very high levels of effective protection and isolation from world market forces' (Hathaway and Ingco, 1995, p. 30). Moreover, US negotiators were constrained by a requirement to consult Congress and the private sector. Thus, during the Brussels talks in 1990, the US command centre at the President Hotel was full of business executives, members of Congress and their staff milling around, creating an atmosphere that one observer described as akin to a high school reunion.

Reducing the impact of EU export subsidies on the world market was always a key US goal. From starting off by demanding a 90 per cent cut in such subsidies, the figure was reduced to 35 per cent at the US–EU summit in November 1991; and was eventually agreed as a 36 per cent cut in export subsidy expenditure and a 21 per cent cut in the volume of subsidised exports. The Blair House II agreement modified this further by allowing a choice of starting point for cuts in exports subsidies, and exempted EU grain stocks from the calculations. The overall effect was to allow the EU and USA to engage in more subsidised exporting than had been envisaged in the original agreement. Moreover, the progress that the USA was able to make on export subsidies was offset by excluding EU compensation payments from the scope of the agreement, a key goal for the EU. The implementation of the agreement has led to renewed tensions between the EU and the USA, and has proved to be something of a bureaucratic nightmare (Doran-Schiratti, 1996).

The negotiations did, however, widen the circle of decision-makers in the EU involved in agricultural issues. In particular, it led to the involvement of heads of government, who were concerned about the wider effects on the world economy of trade war started by a failure to reach a settlement with the USA on agricultural trade. France was particularly resistant to any settlement that might erode its position as a major agricultural exporter. French resistance ensured that they extracted the maximum concessions possible from the negotiating process. In reopening the Blair House agreement, they renegotiated an agreement which the USA and France's European partners had regarded as final.

Within Germany, the manufacturing sector, which is highly export dependent, became increasingly concerned about the consequences of a failure to reach an international trade agreement because of agricultural problems: 'With GATT negotiations at stake, German industry began to exert pressure on the federal government. The Federation of German Industry wrote several times to the Federal Chancellor, urging him to use his power and authority on his EC partners who might still hesitate to meet US demands' (Hendriks, 1994, pp. 158–9). Chancellor Kohl used his rights under the German constitution to set policy guidelines on the negotiations, instructing his cabinet that 'The GATT round must not end in failure' (Hendriks, 1994, p. 159).

Although Germany emphasised that it stood by the original Blair House agreement, 'The August monetary crisis in the European monetary system helped France, insofar as it induced Chancellor Kohl to give closer attention to French complaints' (Dupont and Sciarini, 1994, p. 38). Germany became engaged in September 1993 in detailed discussions about a French proposal setting out how the Blair House agreement could be changed without a full renegotiation (the EU eventually agreed in November to seek 'clarification' of the Blair House accord). Germany listened carefully to France's concerns, with top officials from the chancellor's office and the ministries of agriculture and foreign affairs meeting with their counterparts in Paris. While being careful not to criticise France in public, Chancellor Kohl conveyed to the French in private 'the vital German interest in a successful outcome to the round' (Preeg, 1995, p. 166). Germany did not want to sacrifice its manufacturing industry, nor did it want to jeopardise its relationship with its principal European ally. In the end, it succeeded in achieving both objectives.

The eventual impact of the agreement on agricultural trade was less than the tortuous and often heated nature of the negotiations might have led one to expect. In part, this was because the 1986–8 period, when world prices were exceptionally low, was chosen as the basis for the tariffication of trade barriers. This base period gave a high level of protection, leading to 'markedly little liberalization for most products in most countries' (Hathaway and Ingco, 1995, p. 15). Market access was not greatly improved, with barriers to low-cost exporters remaining largely in place. Despite the sometimes exaggerated claims made for the agreement on agriculture, 'it does not represent a significant reduction in border protection or a major increase in access to protected markets' (Hathaway and Ingco, 1995, p. 31).

This does not mean that the agreement was without significance. The trend towards greater agricultural protection in developed countries was put into reverse, and agriculture was placed firmly on the agenda of international trade negotiations, from which it had been largely excluded for so long. The Uruguay Round agreement places a set of constraints on EU agricultural policy. Even more significant, there have to be discussions on further reform of agricultural trade starting in 1999. Hence, the pressures on the CAP from the liberalisation of international trade are not a one-off effect, but are likely to persist. Future prospects in this area are discussed in Chapter 7.

The CAP is still recognisable as the set of policies created in the 1960s, and there are those who would like it to continue in this form well into the twenty-first century. A start has been made on the process of reform, but there is still a policy that absorbs a disproportionate share of the EU budget; is expensive to administer and prone to fraud; disadvantages consumers; encourages intensive farming that often harms the environment; is unhelpful to the food processing industry; imposes costs on Third-World countries; introduces tensions into relations between the EU and the USA and Cairns Group countries; has forced up land prices; and has done little to improve farm incomes. Why such a situation has been allowed to persist requires an awareness of the political entry price imposed by its complexity, illustrated by the following chapter on the agrimonetary system; and an understanding of the bargaining processes that lie at the heart of its politics, provided in Chapter 6. In Chapter 7, the analysis will return to the agenda and imperative for reform.

4

System Failures: The Agrimonetary System and the Fraud Problem

In the previous chapter the establishment of the EC's price support system for farmers was reviewed, and the difficulties it ran into were discussed. The green money, or agrimonetary, system of the EU was an alternative mechanism for protecting the interests of farmers. Its retention long after it had outlived any technical usefulness was a political act intended 'to obfuscate and protect. The green money system is manipulated to provide an additional element of protection for farmers against exchange rate protection; and the sheer complexity of the system renders the whole apparatus of the CAP less vulnerable to critical review by outsiders who are not steeped in the arcane world of farm policy' (Swinbank, 1996b, p. 1). This chapter also considers another area of failure in the CAP, the perennial problem of fraud. Indeed, by increasing the complexity of the CAP, the agrimontary system was one of the factors that has made fraud more likely to occur.

The emergence of green money

As has already been noted, one of the fundamental principles of the CAP is common pricing. This objective was implemented initially through the establishment of an artificial unit of currency, the unit of account. Under the Bretton Woods system of fixed exchange rates, this was set at par with the US dollar, which was at that time convertible into gold. CAP prices set in terms of the unit of account were then translated into national currencies to provide target prices, intervention prices and so on: 'Thus the CAP would achieve common prices within a common market despite the existence of different national currencies, but Community-led decisions would be in terms of its own supranational currency' (Hill, 1984, p. 60).

The disturbances in France in 1968 placed the French franc under increasing pressure in foreign exchange markets, particularly in forward markets. This opened up opportunities for speculative trading and French farm products were bought for the German market at cheap prices, driving down prices in Germany and building up intervention surpluses there. In August 1969 the French franc was devalued by 11 per cent, followed by the revaluation of the Deutschmark in October. If the green franc had been devalued at the same time, no problems would have arisen. However, 'France was unwilling to accept a further price increase because of the impact that would have on consumers and might have on the rate of inflation' (Swinbank, 1978, p. 19). There was therefore a phased devaluation of the green franc and a phased revaluation of the green mark. This led in turn to the introduction of what were supposed to be a temporary system of border taxes and subsidies known as monetary compensation amounts (MCAs) to 'permit agricultural commodities to be traded between the countries as though common prices existed' (Hill, 1984, p. 63). These MCAs, however, created new opportunities for fraud, as in the 'carousel' which involved smuggling pigs and cattle across the border between the Republic of Ireland and the six counties of Northern Ireland whenever significant MCA disparities developed (the direction in which the animals moved depended on the nature of the disparity). Intensive efforts by the authorities to stop this trade met with some success, but were complicated by the security situation and the alleged involvement of paramilitary organisations.

As the dollar weakened in the early 1970s, and as the world moved from a system of fixed to floating exchange rates, what had been intended to be a temporary adjustment to allow France and Germany to cope with the impact of the currency changes in 1969 became more entrenched. Rates were fixed separately for each currency, so there was a green lira and a green guilder, and were often different for each commodity, adding a new layer of complexity to the CAP. Adjustments to the green rates 'tended to become part of the annual price proposals package' (Mackel, 1977, p. 6). However, this did not happen in a way that could be understood easily by non-specialists, making agricultural policy even more inaccessible to informed outside criticism. Reviewing the agrimonetary system in 1989, the Court of Auditors commented (1989, p. C128/4) 'without detailed knowledge of the impact of the agrimonetary system, it is not possible either to understand fully the real meaning of the annual agricultural price fixing decisions, or to interpret the accounting information presented by the Commission'. In other words, another formidable political entry barrier had been erected around the CAP.

The green money system also undermined the integrative force of the CAP. For member states, the green currency mechanism became a means of pursuing national agricultural and food policies while remaining within the common market. By devaluing their green rates, countries with falling currencies could increase the amounts received by farmers in their national currencies. For a country whose currency was appreciating, a green currency revaluation led to a fall in national farm prices. Thus, if their farmers were to receive a price increase it had come from upward movement in the prices agreed by the Council of Agricultural Ministers: 'Consequently it was in their interest to argue for a larger common price increase than that proposed by the Commission' (National Consumer Council, 1988, p. 16). In practice, it also meant that devaluations were achieved more readily than revaluations, leading to an inflationary effect.

In Britain between 1974 and 1979 the Labour government maintained an overvalued green pound. This had the effect of holding down the price the consumer paid for his or her food, as intervention prices were lower than they would otherwise have been, and imports were subsidised through MCAs. Farmers' organisations pressed for a phased series of green pound devaluations, but faced opposition from the trade union movement, while the food manufacturers were divided. (Grant, 1981, pp. 317–21). The matter was not, however, simply a question of domestic politics. The UK government had to negotiate with the Commission and other member states over green pound rates. In 1977, Britain had to concede a 2.9 per cent green pound devaluation, less than half of the devaluation the Commission had originally wanted. In 1978, the government lost a House of Commons vote and was required to press for an immediate 7.5 per cent devaluation. The two-stage devaluation agreed by the Community was rather closer to what the Labour government had been prepared to concede than the amount the House of Commons had voted for (Grant, 1981).

By 1978, individual governments had been 'so successful in maintaining their own national food and farm price preferences that [there were] now seven price zones in place of the theoretical common price' (Swinbank, 1978, p. 20). The CAP price level in Germany was about 35 per cent higher than in Britain, with a UK MCA in February 1978 of −23.7 per cent, and with a positive MCA in Germany of 7.5 per cent. (Negative MCAs were applied in weak currency countries as a subsidy on imports and a levy on exports, and positive MCAs were applied in strong currency countries as a levy on imports and a subsidy on exports.) 'The Commission was dismayed by these huge price differences and tried to encourage members to phase out MCAs, that is to re-align green currency rates with market rates and thus return to common prices' (Hill, 1984, p. 66). At this stage, the future of the agrimonetary system became entangled with the development of the European Monetary System (EMS), a relationship between two discrete policy arenas that was to become significant again in the 1990s. France advanced proposals that would have fixed the ECU against the agricultural unit of account at parity. Given that this would have 'implied a 21 per cent reduction in agricultural prices in real terms' (Hill, 1984, p. 66) this proposal was blocked by Germany, which would have faced more intense competition for its high cost products. France then blocked the introduction of the EMS at the beginning of 1979, an impasse that led to the signing of the so-called 'Gentleman's Agreement' (the UK refused to sign, so it was not a formal document). This agreement made the provision that any reduction in MCAs should not lead to a reduction in prices in national currencies; in effect, a codification of the existing reality.

The green ECU

This undertaking would not have caused difficulties if common prices had continued to rise: 'But when the Commission started trying to freeze or cut common prices, German mca's could not be phased out without contradicting the Gentleman's Agreement, yet for the French, in particular, getting rid of German mca's was a political priority' (Tracy, 1989, p. 312). In 1984, a way out of these problems was found, through a major change in the green money system, which had the long-term effect of substantially increasing CAP support prices. A new green ECU was introduced, based on the strongest currency in the European monetary system – normally the Deutschmark (but sometimes the Dutch guilder) – rather than a basket of currencies. This was accompanied by a 'switchover mechanism' which 'was designed to protect farmers from 75% of the pricing consequences of currency appreciation of those countries participating within the narrow band of the exchange rate mechanism' (Swinbank, 1996b, p. 3). Positive MCAs posed a greater political problem than negative ones, because dismantling them entailed a reduction in prices in a national currency. The solution adopted in 1984 was to 'switch' positive MCAs into negative ones through the use of a corrective factor applied to the ECU.

The ingenious design of the correcting factor means that one can revalue one's national currency for reasons of general economic policy management without affecting the agricultural conversion rate and disadvantaging farmers. Initially 1.033651, the correcting factor was changed each time there was a realignment within or affecting the EMS. For example, when the Deutschmark and other currencies were revalued in January 1987, the correcting factor was increased to 1.137282. By May 1993 it was 1.207509 (the correcting factor was never reduced).

Adapting in a more fanciful manner a hypothetical example presented by Swinbank (1993b), let us imagine that there is an independent principality on the southern borders of Germany which is an EU member state. The principality is in the EMS and its currency (the ducet) closely shadows the D-mark. The country produces one CAP commodity, for which the support price is 120 ecu/tonne, with 1 ECU = 2 ducets. This means that the level of price support for farmers is 240 ducets per tonne. Following a revaluation of the D-mark, the ducet is also revalued, so that one ECU now equals 1.6 ducets. If this was applied to agricultural prices, farmers would find they were receiving 192 ducets per tonne when they sold into intervention. This would leave the farmers 48 ducets per tonne worse off, which might make them less willing to contribute to a present for the forthcoming wedding of the prince's daughter, or even lead them to surround the prince's castle in an angry mood. To overcome this problem, EU rules allow the application of a correcting factor of 1.25 to maintain an agricultural conversion rate of 1 ECU = 2 ducets, so that the support price in real or 'commercial' ecu is 150 ducets per tonne. Multiplying 150 ducets by the new exchange rate of 1.6 ECU = 1 ducet means that farmers continue to receive 240 ducets per tonne. The farmers are able to live happily ever after (or at least until the MacSharry reforms), the wedding is a great success, and consumers and taxpayers remain in blessed ignorance.

The official rationale is that this change was introduced as a move towards market unity by providing 'a means of overcoming the difficulty of dismantling positive MCA's during a period when price increases in ECU were severely restrained' (Court of Auditors, 1989, p. C128/12). As the Deutschmark had appreciated, Germany had developed a high positive real monetary gap (RMG), the gap between the real and 'green' ECUs. As Swinbank (1992, p. 4) succinctly explains the underlying political realities:

A number of Member States, France in particular, were determined that this large positive RMG should be reduced to curb the price advantage German farmers enjoyed over their competitors elsewhere in the EC. Germany, however, was insistent that the price received by German farmers, expressed in deutsch-marks, should not be reduced. Finally, with the EC facing a severe budget crisis, Ministers were adamant that CAP prices expressed in ECU should not be increased. These entrenched positions were incompatible, until the goal-posts were moved.

The introduction of the switchover mechanism meant a shift to a more complex green money game with new goalposts. As has been noted, the green ECU necessitated the introduction of a switchover mechanism with a correcting coefficient. As a consequence, 'very few people other than the specialists in the Commission, the Member States' administrations and in commerce understand what the system now involves' (Court of Auditors, 1989, p. C128/18). The old joke that only six people in Europe fully understand the operation of the CAP had to be changed, to revise downwards the figure used.

The important points about the 1984 changes is that they increased complexity, reduced transparency and raised prices. Complexity was present at three levels: conceptual; rules for calculation; and the day-to-day application of the system. The switchover mechanism made the jargon of the agrimonetary system even more complex: 'the part of a Member State's negative MCA which results from the operation of the switchover is called the "artificial" negative MCA, that part which results from changes in the exchange rate of the Member State's currency is described as a "natural" MCA' (Court of Auditors, 1989, p. C128/33). Government departments, trade associations and firms developed their own computer models to understand what was happening as variable MCA rates changed week by week. In an attempt at reassurance, the Court of Auditors noted (1989, p. C128/

18) that 'The problem of complexity . . . should not be overemphasized: few people need to know the fine details of how calculations are carried out, for most people affected by the system it is sufficient to know how to apply the results.'

Such a complex system does, however, have an inbuilt bias in favour of larger traders who know how to manipulate it. It is also liable to error and fraud, as well as imposing significant administrative costs. It should also be noted that after 1984 there was an increase in the number of different green rates for particular commodities within member states. Thus, for example, in 1988, France had six green rates and the United Kingdom had five (Court of Auditors, 1989, p. C128/8).

Transparency is a key criterion in relation to important public policy decisions and significant budgetary allocations. It is not a criterion that was met in the case of green money. The Commission has itself been obliged to admit that the growing complexity of the green money system has 'increasingly robbed it of all transparency' (COM(87)64, final of 27 February 1987, p. 25). Increases in common prices occurred in a way that was hidden from citizens of the European Union.

Even if relatively few people really understand what is going on, the pricing and budgetary consequences of the 1984 changes are all too apparent. Because of the creation of an effective Deutschmark zone for agriculture, common prices were over 20 per cent higher than what they would otherwise have been by 1994. The switchover mechanism was supposed to allow positive MCAs to be dismantled while keeping the CAP budget under control, but in practice agricultural incomes were protected by increases in common prices or, in some cases, by other forms of compensation.

The attempt to reconcile Germany's insistence on looking after the interests of its farmers with the EU's policy preference of avoiding new positive MCAs through the switchover mechanism, led to a situation at the end of the 1980s that was well summarised by the Court of Auditors:

the annual decisions of the Council fixing the level of agricultural prices in ECU do not reflect real developments in institutional prices: following each EMS realignment the application of the switchover mechanism to avoid the creation of positive MCAs in effect raises the common price level in line with the strongest currency in the EMS, the DM. These increases in the common price level, however, are essentially hidden. The impact of these hidden price increases feeds through as increased budgetary expenditure in a manner that is obscure. The switchover, therefore, has not improved the management of expenditure in the agricultural markets. It has, also, resulted in the exchange rates used for agricultural purposes becoming further removed from real exchange rates. (Court of Auditors, 1989, p. C128/4)

The exchange rate mechanism and green money

The agrimonetary system was, however, influenced by changes in the broader policy context, notably the single market programme and the evolution of the exchange rate mechanism (ERM) into a quasi-fixed rate system between 1987 and 1992, and moves towards economic and monetary union (EMU). With a single currency, there would be no need for green currencies – perhaps one of the most convincing reasons for introducing a single currency. As part of the price package agreed in 1987, the Council of Agricultural Ministers agreed on a system for dismantling automatically any new MCAs created at future currency realignments with different timetables for 'natural' and 'artificial' MCAs. In 1988 it was decided to phase out the remaining MCAs in the narrow band EMS (affecting five countries) by 1992, to seek to dismantle the monetary gaps for Italy, and to tackle the other four member states with variable MCAs (the UK and the three Southern countries). At the 1991/2 farm price review, narrow band ERM countries 'eliminated all residual gaps then remaining between their green conversion rates and the central rates, within ERM, of the *green* European Currency Unit' (Swinbank, 1992, p. 1). In early 1992, however, variable MCAs remained in place for the UK and the three Southern countries. Writing early in 1992, Swinbank saw a window of opportunity to make all support payments in ECU. By the end of the year, Italy and the UK had left the ERM, which was effectively abandoned through the introduction of wide fluctuation margins in 1993. A new set of green currency problems emerged. British farmers came to regard the exit from the ERM as 'Golden Wednesday', because it was the first devaluation in twenty years that had not been eroded by a rapid increase in input prices, ushering in a period of prosperity for most British farmers.

With the creation of the single market in January 1993, MCAs were abolished because they were incompatible with the supposed absence of border checks. Adjustments of the green rates were supposed to occur only if currencies moved outside the narrow ERM margins. Otherwise, the green rates floated within the narrow bands rather than being adjusted by decisions taken in the annual price review process: 'If currencies in the wide band fluctuated, green rates were to be adjusted according to a new automatic formula – supposedly immune from political lobbying – that should have forced farmers with an appreciating currency to take a price cut' (*The Economist*, 25 September 1993). The single market should have seen the end of the green money system. 'But the Commission, and the Member States, largely on German insistence, botched the job' (Swinbank, 1996b, p. 1).

The consequences of ERM collapse

When the ERM virtually collapsed in August 1993, a new green money crisis ensued, not least because German farmers were faced with the unthinkable, a price cut. As the head of currency affairs at the German agriculture ministry put it, 'It is a principle of the Common Agricultural Policy to protect the income of farmers against abrupt changes in institutional prices and amounts caused by revaluation' (Schwinne, 1993, p. 1). It was certainly not a principle discussed when the CAP was established, and it is difficult to see why farmers should be protected against currency changes when manufacturing industry is not. But from a German perspective, the impact of the ERM collapse on the agrimonetary system was 'merely accidental' and could not alter decisions taken about the future of the agrimonetary system as 'part of a very comprehensive compromise which contained other elements extremely difficult for Germany' (Schwinne, 1993, p. 2). (The latter remark is believed to refer to bananas; see Swinbank 1996b, p. 4n).

With the drop in the value of the franc and the Danish krone, more French and Danish products appeared on the German market, pushing prices down. As the switchover was triggered by a political decision formally to realign within the narrow ERM bands, it became defunct under a system of wide fluctuations, which made a realignment highly unlikely. Germany attempted to argue that switchover should apply to green rate adjustments even when there had been no ERM realignment, a policy that would have greatly increased the cost of the CAP. Faced with having to make some response to German demands, and having no coherent policy position, the Commission decided to freeze green currency rates. This decision incensed the food processing industry, which had been trying to hedge its currency risk, showing that German farmers carry more political weight than food manufacturers. For its part, Germany argued that what happened in practice after 1993 was that the core currencies continued to trade in narrow bands, putting farmers in those countries at a disadvantage compared to farmers in Britain, Spain or Italy. In particular, Bavarian dairy farmers were seen to be disadvantaged in relation to exports to Italy.

At the end of December 1993, the green rates were unfrozen, and the 'floating franchise' system restored. A succession of green rate devaluations followed. The agrimonetary system continued to be costly for EU citizens, increasing the cost of operating the CAP:

> This is because the 'floating franchise' approach tends to allow positive monetary gaps to be maintained or widened, while negative monetary gaps are much more likely to be reduced by means of green rate devaluations. When a country has a positive monetary gap, its farmers are being paid more than would have been the case if the green rate had been aligned exactly on the prevalent market rate . . . By contrast, a negative monetary gap implies lower spending on the EU's part, because the green rate is being maintained at below the 'common price' level. (*Agra Europe*, 26 August 1995, p. P/5)

The budgetary consequences of the 'floating franchise' concerned the Commission. Since 1984 what one DG VI official called the 'last dinosaur' had cost the EU an extra 6.5 billion ECU in agricultural support (*Agra Europe*, 18 November 1994). The problem was how to get rid of the green ECU and the switchover while avoiding the political costs of reducing the income of German farmers. Currency turmoil since 1992 had left the Germans virtually isolated in their support of switchover. In any case, their concern was the substantive one of protecting the income security of their politically influential farmers rather than the mechanism by which this objective was achieved. The solution arrived at was to remove the difference between the green ECU and the market ECU by dividing all green rates by the switchover coefficient which, by the end of 1993, had risen to 1.207509. Germany was able to insist successfully on the preservation of the 'mini-switchover', which provided for an increase across the EU in arable and livestock aids whenever there was a green rate revaluation. Any such increase would apply in all countries, even those with devaluing currencies.

Under the agreement, the basic spread of monetary gaps was allowed to move to up to 5 per cent on the positive side before triggering a revaluation. Any 'appreciable' revaluation, as defined by a table in the Regulation, would have to be decided by qualified majority vote of the Council of Ministers. Before a revaluation was put into effect, there was to be a 'period of reflection' of fifty to sixty days to confirm the currency trend that had triggered the revaluation. There were also provisions for emergency green rate changes in the case of sharp currency fluctuations. In all, there were four different 'periods of reflection', two for appreciable revaluations, and two for non-appreciable revaluations. There was thus still plenty of scope for specialist conferences seeking to explain the complexities of the agrimonetary system.

A half-hearted reform that didn't work

The new arrangements were implemented at the beginning of February 1995, but quickly ran into trouble when faced with turbulence on the currency markets, which saw a 'flight to quality' and the appreciation of currencies such as the Deutschmark. A Commission official commented, 'Back in December when the markets were quiet nobody thought this would happen' (*Financial Times*, 3 May 1995). It quickly became apparent that the periods of reflection were unworkable. Speculative trade began to develop to take advantage of monetary distortions. 'The failure to adjust the strong currency reference rates means that potential exports to third countries are now being re-routed from weak currency country ports to those of the strong money group in order to claim the largest possible export restitutions' (*Agra Europe*, 21 April 1995, p. P/2). Purchasers and commodity dealers were able to obtain inflated profits in a way that was entirely legal. Apart from this unwanted redistributive effect, the emergence of speculative trade showed that the agrimonetary system in place was fatally flawed: 'The basic aim in operating an agrimonetary policy has always been to ensure that CAP intervention mechanisms are not undermined by speculative trade' (*Agra Europe*, 14 July 1995, p. P/2).

At the end of March, the specialist newsletter *Agra Europe* launched a scathing attack on what it called the 'half hearted' December reforms. *Agra Europe* is often critical of the progress towards reform of the CAP and often seems to be quite close to the perspectives of agricultural economists. Nevertheless, the concerns it was raising were more widely shared:

> It is now clearer than ever that a common price system based on the Deutschmark cannot be sustained without considerable cost to the taxpayer, market distorting windfall gains to some agricultural producers in some countries, and the continuous adjustment of average prices in an increasingly internationally non-competitive direction. The claims which were made at the time, to the effect that the notorious 'switchover mechanism' had finally been abolished, obscured yet another confidence trick by the agricultural clique: the introduction of a mechanism to jack up the MacSharry compensatory subsidies in all EU countries in line with the largest rate of revaluation by the DM group of countries. (*Agra Europe*, 24 March 1995, p. P/1)

The Commission became increasingly worried about the implications of this new green money crisis for the budget and the Mac-Sharry reform programme. It was calculated that triggering the 'mini switchover' would add an additional one billion ECU to the budget, undermining the MacSharry programme by pushing up its costs to unacceptable levels. Direct arable aids are converted into national currency using the green conversion rates on a single day, July 1, a date that concentrated minds on the need to find a new policy solution. An underlying issue was Germany's *de facto* role as paymaster of the EU, and the way in which any policy changes might increase the gap between Germany's EU contributions and receipts.

Faced with a renewed threat to the well being of their farmers, the Germans started coalition building among their hard currency allies. In March, the 'Aachen Five' group was formed when the agriculture ministers of Germany, Austria, Belgium and The Netherlands, plus a senior official from Luxembourg, met at the instigation of the Germans at a hotel in Aachen to discuss agrimonetary questions. Denmark subsequently joined the group after becoming a candidate for a green currency revaluation. This coalition building was paralleled at the level of farming organisations with a grouping formed by the German farming organisation with their counterparts in the other five hard currency countries. This grouping advocated adjustments to value added tax (VAT) rates as a form of compensation to farmers, a device that had already been used in Germany. At a European level, before Denmark aligned itself with the hard currency countries, Finnish support was important to the hard currency countries as it enabled them to form a blocking minority under qualified majority voting. Finland supported the 'Aachen Five' in placing the question of green pound revaluations on the agenda of the Special Committee on Agriculture in March (*Agra Europe*, 10 March 1995, p. P/2).

At the beginning of May, the Commission proposed that the mini-switchover should be abolished and that national financial ceilings should be introduced for compensatory payments to farmers in revaluing countries. The Commission's proposals were immediately opposed by Germany, Belgium and Luxembourg, but won support from three of the Northern reform-orientated countries – Denmark, Sweden and the UK. The Netherlands, Austria and Finland appeared to be prepared to give support, while the Southern countries were concerned that, if the Commission's offer of 100 per cent compensation to German farmers for five years was taken up, it would be difficult to fund reforms in the wine and fruit and vegetable sectors. Germany came up with a counter proposal to fix aids in national currencies, which the Commission viewed as tantamount to dismantling the CAP.

The temperature between the Commission and Germany rose quickly. German agriculture minister Jochen Borchert insisted that guaranteed protection against revaluations was 'an essential German concern' (*Agra Europe*, 19 May 1995, p. E/1). Franz Fischler retorted that 'The Commission is dismayed by the unwanted aggressiveness and lack of objectivity shown by the German agriculture minister in his discussion of the proposal to compensate farmers for possible adjustments of the DM green rate' (*Agra Europe*, 26 May 1995, p. E/4).

Such a rift between the Commission and the EU's leading member state had to be healed, and a compromise was arrived at with the assistance of the French presidency of the Council. Strong currency countries implementing an appreciable revaluation between the end of June 1995 and January 1996 would be able to convert aid into national prices using the pre-revaluation rates, that is, their farmers would receive higher payments. It is more than likely that such an arrangement will be extended to future revaluations. These countries would also be entitled to specified amounts of compensation for income losses, partly funded by the EU. This point was of particular concern to France, whose farmers had suffered income losses because of cheaper imports in 1994 and 1995. Strong currency countries were given the option of revaluing their green currencies once the positive gap exceeded 4 per cent (rather than 5 per cent). Countries able to show that farmers have suffered considerable income losses as a result of monetary movements occurring in other countries can grant national compensatory aid on a reducing basis over three years, subject to the approval of the Council of Ministers.

The last of these changes represented a significant move towards renationalising the CAP. *Agra Europe* commented (14 July, 1995, p. P/1) that, in allowing this change, DG VI, which enthusiastically supported it, had taken 'a fateful step towards the eventual disintegration of the European Union's Common Agricultural Policy'. In its view, the scheme was 'little more than a method to allow Paris to make political payments to France's fruit, vegetable and wine sectors – the less efficient part of French agriculture – which are being hammered by Spanish and to a lesser extent Italian competition' (*Agra Europe*, 14 July 1995, p. P/1). A scheme was subsequently introduced for Belgium, but a German proposal to use the VAT system to compensate farmers was rejected in October by both the agricultural and financial affairs councils.

Even with the new arrangements, 'the freezing of green rates for aid conversion in strong currency countries is likely to lead to increasing distortions not only between countries but also between sectors, because the CAP Reform aids apply only for cereals, oilseeds, protein crops, beef and sheep' (*Agra Europe*, 27 October 1995, p. P/4). This gives these sectors an advantage over the dairy and sugar sectors, where there are no CAP reform aids. The conversion rates used for structural aid also attracted comment, with a different date being used for Sweden than for other countries. Not that Swedish farmers had cause for complaint, as they were receiving 11–14 per cent more in Swedish kroner per hectare than they might have expected (*Agra Europe*, 22 March 1996, pp. E/6–7).

As is so often the case with policy compromises in the EU, the June 1995 'mini-switchover' deal seems likely to increase the budgetary cost of the CAP, despite being presented at the time as a money-saving deal. Increased costs of, for example, cereals aid payments and special beef premium payments will place additional demands on EU finances until 1999, alongside the financial strain produced by the

BSE crisis. It has been estimated that the budgetary cost in Germany, The Netherlands and Belgium alone will amount to at least 68 million ECU each year (*Agra Europe*, 20 September 1996, p. E/4).

EMU and the future of green money

Hopes for finally eliminating the distortions and costs of the green money system have centred increasingly on the establishment of EMU in a form which would remove the need for an agrimonetary system. However, while the abolition of green money is an argument in favour of EMU, it is not of itself a decisive argument. Moreover, an agrimonetary system would still be need to cope with trade between those countries in EMU and those countries outside it. The meeting of finance ministers at Verona in April 1996 effectively recognised that a two-track system would be unavoidable, which means that the green currency system would not be abolished if partial EMU was achieved in 1999: 'So long as there is any variation between currency values there has to be an adjustment system for agriculture where centrally set subsidies and support prices are maintained' (*Agra Europe*, 12 April 1996, p. P/5).

Even Commission officials have called the agrimonetary system a 'dinosaur', and it has effectively undermined the principle of common pricing and led to moves towards the renationalisation of the CAP. Its defenders use three kinds of argument: one from integration, one from structural diversity, and one based on the political process. The integration argument, advanced by officials at the German ministry of agriculture, is that green money is indispensable because 'Farming, more than any other industry, is integrated into Europe and as we have common prices and no common currency, we will have to take care of currency divergences' (*Financial Times*, 1 March 1995). The structural diversity argument maintains that such co-operation as has been possible has been achieved because the green money system has provided a mechanism for taking account of economic divergence:

On the one hand it can be argued that with the limited economic and monetary co-operation between the Member States that has existed since 1969 the flexibility in the common price system that results from the use of green rate has been essential to the continuing functioning of the common market organisation: if this flexibility had not been provided by the agrimonetary system, it would have to have been provided in some other way, as otherwise the strains on the common market organizations would have been too great. (Court of Auditors, 1989, p. C128/9)

The Commission places some emphasis on political considerations, taking the view that 'on the political level, the switchover mechanism has made the fixing of agricultural prices easier' (Court of Auditors, 1989, p. C128/40). In particular, it believes that the switchover mechanism 'helped on the political level to facilitate the annual agricultural price fixing operation'. (Court of Auditors, 1989, p. C128/43). The development of green money has undoubtedly represented a series of political compromises, but at what price? As the Court of Auditors note (1989, p. C128/9), 'it is an unsatisfactory situation where Member States are able to use the green rate system to pursue national pricing policy objectives which conflict with the Community common price interest'. The underlying political dynamic has been to satisfy the interests of German farmers. Their interests are allowed to be placed at the centre of the CAP as a whole because of the determination and skill of Germany in relation to agricultural questions and its role as a major net budget contributor.

The green money system has thus operated as a means of supporting a high-cost German agriculture that would not be price competitive without some form of support: 'The crux of the 25-year old agrimonetary problem is the reluctance of strong currency countries to face the implications of a common pricing policy' (*Agra Europe*, 20 May 1994, p. E/5). The problem is, however, not just one for Germany and other strong currencies. Farmers throughout the EU have come to expect to be protected against currency fluctuations. Industrialists can, of course, hedge against currency risk, something that only a very few large and financially sophisticated farmers are able to do.

Nevertheless, the green money system has led to higher CAP support prices than would otherwise have been the case. Price signals from the EU to producers have thus been blunted, while member states have been allowed to follow their own national support policies. This outcome has been achieved through a system which, even if its complexity is not intentional, has the consequence of reducing the transparency of the CAP and its exposure to effective external criticism.

The problem of fraud

It is not possible to measure the full extent of fraud in the CAP because only those frauds that are detected are recorded. Both the House of Lords (1994) and independent experts such as Professor Klaus Tiedemann of Frieburg University (*Financial Times*, 19 May 1994) have estimated that as much as 10 per cent of the EU's budget is wasted through fraud and improper use of funds. The Commission's response is that there is no evidence that the figure is so high, although they also accept that the detection rate (1.2 per cent of the budget in 1994) underestimates the extent of the problem. Although the Commission has its own anti-fraud unit (UCLAF) it is dependent to a substantial extent on the discovery of fraud by the member states. A National Audit Office noted that member states faced a conflict of interest: 'They want to demonstrate that they are diligently guarding against error and fraud, but at the same time they do not want unfavourable publicity or invidious comparisons with other member states if error or fraud are discovered' (*Financial Times*, 20 December 1995). At the EU level, the Commission is eager to demonstrate that it is seeking to tackle the fraud problem, but also has to be aware of the fact that Euro-sceptics use evidence of fraud as ammunition against the EU. Members of the European Parliament are concerned that the Commission puts 'on a "big show" of talking tough about fraud but has not been resolute enough in tackling it' (*Financial Times*, 19 May 1994).

The level of fraud in the agricultural sector is in line with its share of the overall budget. There are many types of fraud, but most of the CAP frauds are 'either claims for subsidy payments on products which do not exist, or the misrepresentation of a less valuable form of a commodity as a more valuable one' (*Agra Europe*, 29 July 1994, p. P/2). Export subsidies are a major target of organised frauds, and the meat carousel is a favourite scam. For example, live animals are imported to Italy from eastern Europe and sold there. Low-quality meat is exported to Malta and then sent to Italy before being exported outside the EU to obtain a refund (House of Lords, 1994a, p. 29). Another alternative is to use forged customs documents to pretend that meat is being sold outside the EU, thus gaining export subsidies and higher meat prices within Europe. Frozen meat offers even more possibilities: 'One shipment of east European beef recently went from Italy to Malta, back to Italy and then to Austria with the refunds paid twice' (*Financial Times*, 19 May 1994). Another variant is to export a product to an African, Caribbean and Pacific (ACP) country with a subsidy, make slight changes to it and re-import it taking advantage of preferential import duties. For example, cheese or milk powder might be sent out in bulk form and packaged into smaller units.

Another favourite scam is to label something as a higher-value product to gain the maximum refund, while placing a lower-value commodity in the container: for example, claiming that a commodity is a high-value-added product: 'The boxes of bones presented as prime beef, the cheese or milk powder whose true fat content is at odds with that which is presented, and the "processed" products which turn out to be nothing of the sort; these are examples of this basic scam' (*Agra Europe*, 29 July 1994, p. P/4). Other ploys are claiming for invisible goods in intervention stores through false invoices, or, as rural development programmes have grown, claiming for infrastructure projects that have never been finished.

Farmers have their own variants of these scams, largely based on claiming for livestock that do not exist or crops that have never been grown. Problems have been encountered in the past with Greek cotton. With the development of set-aside payments, satellite surveillance is being used increasingly. However, to check livestock scams it is necessary to count the animals, and farmers have attempted to evade such checks through impersonation.

The incidence of fraud varies considerably from one member state to another, reflecting the effectiveness of the local administration and the involvement of criminal organisations in fraud. Almost 60 per cent of EAGGF frauds in 1991–4 occurred in Italy. It has been claimed that 60–70 per cent of Italy's meat imports 'avoid VAT through fictitious companies that import the product from Europe and go bankrupt or disappear just before any VAT is paid' (*Agra Europe*, 9 February 1996, p. N/7). Greece ranks second in terms of discovered fraud, followed by Spain. It is therefore not surprising that exporters in Northern Europe were concerned about proposals to deal with carousel frauds, which might have penalised them for events outside their control involving slight reprocessing of products in third countries, but would not greatly affect Southern states which do not export large quantities of such goods.

It should not be imagined, however, that Northern member states are immune to fraud. The Intervention Board in Britain has a fraud squad of nearly fifty and investigated 200 cases between 1991 and 1993. A more recent case that led to prosecutions involved the delivery of 'black' milk to unregistered purchasers. Milk was produced outside the quota system and taken direct from farms, sometimes unpasteurised. It was then sold through a chain that was often unsupervised in terms of hygiene and quality controls to retailers and caterers in other areas. Of course, if there was no quota, farmers would be able to sell as much milk as they liked, subject to the operation of the price mechanism.

The sheer complexity of the CAP is one of the main sources of opportunities for fraud which is difficult to detect. Much of the blame for this complexity rests with the agriculture ministers who elaborate 'basic Commission proposals with endless derogations and legal nuances in the interests of cobbling together an acceptable political fudge' (*Agra Europe*, 29 July 1994, p. P/1). The agrimonetary system represented a gigantic political fudge whose incomprehensibility masked a set of deals to protect farmers' incomes, and the incomes of German farmers in particular. It is the commodity regimes, however, which lie at the heart of the CAP and which often embody some of the most cherished interests of particular member states. The next chapter explores how the main commodity regimes have developed.

5

Butter Mountains, Wine Lakes and Beef Wars: The Commodity Regimes

In January 1995, what was described in the press as an 'angry swarm' of around two thousand beekeepers, some dressed as bees, picketed the meeting of the Council of Agricultural Ministers to demand subsidies to help combat cheap imports of honey from Mexico and China. In October 1995, a spotter plane flew low over the rooftops of Brussels as a long cavalcade of trucks organised by tomato growers blocked the streets of the Belgian capital, their cacophony of horns disturbing the peace of the Brussels parks on a mild autumn day. Such demonstrations are part of the Brussels routine, at least suggesting that those demonstrating recognise the city as a locus of political power.

These demonstrations about specific products also reflect the existence of a series of commodity regimes or 'market organisations' in the CAP, each with its own distinctive problems and patterns of politics. However, taken as a whole, 'This system has shown remarkable resilience over the years and the number of major changes to the commodity regimes has been limited' (Josling, 1993, p. 41). Since the MacSharry reforms, there has perhaps been less of a commodity-specific emphasis within the CAP. In the arable sector, the emphasis has been on arable systems rather than particular crops, while the encouragement of extensification could promote mixed systems of farming. Nevertheless, the commodity regimes remain deeply embedded in the CAP's decision-making structures, in particular through the management committees.

It will not be possible to discuss each of these commodity regimes in depth in this chapter and an emphasis will be placed on drawing general lessons about the nature of the CAP, the limits of its reform, and its decision-making processes. Nevertheless, particular attention will be devoted to the two most important regimes in terms of the proportion of EAGGF expenditure they absorb, cereals and dairy products, which were estimated to account for fractionally under 50 per cent of all expenditure in 1996. Following the BSE controversy, it will also be necessary to examine the beef regime in some depth. The crisis in the beef sector threatened to destablise the whole CAP, with Franz Fischler declaring that the chaos unleashed had been so precipitous and of such magnitude that it was unparalleled in the history of the CAP (*Agra Europe*, 12 July 1996, p. E/3).

The two principal livestock regimes: beef and veal; and sheepmeat and goatmeat, accounted for almost 17 per cent of all expenditure in 1996. Fruit and vegetables and wine together account for less than 7 per cent of all expenditure, but require some attention because of the intractable problems they present. The sugar regime, which also poses considerable problems and accounts for 5 per cent of expenditure, will also be considered at this point. Part of the difficulty of the politics of the commodity regimes arises from the fact that some products are produced in a relatively small number of countries. This particularly applies to a group of products produced in Southern member states: cotton, olive oil, rice and tobacco. A summary of the various commodity regimes is presented in Table 5.1.

Life without a commodity regime

It is possible to farm successfully and profitably while operating outside a commodity regime, but producers without one often feel that they are disadvantaged and lobby to be brought within the CAP's embrace. In 1993, guided by an Italian rapporteur, the European Parliament's Committee on Agriculture, Fisheries and Rural Development produced a report on the plight of bergamot growers, of whom there are some five thousand families found along a coastal strip in Calabria. The bergamot is a citrus fruit tree which spread by spontaneous hybridisation in the middle of the eighteenth century. Three products are extracted from the fruit. The most valuable is bergamot essential oil, which is used to help provide the aromatic fruity notes of perfumes. However, for cheaper perfumes, this is being displaced by synthetic essence. The pulp of the fruit is

TABLE 5.1

Commodity regimes ranked by share of EAGFF expenditure, 1996 budget

Commodity regime	Percentage share
Arable products	42.1
Beef/veal	13.4
Dairy products	10.3
Sugar	4.8
Olive oil	4.4
Fruit and vegetables	4.2
Sheepmeat and goatmeat	3.3
Wine	2.7
Tobacco	2.7
Textile plants and silkworms (mainly cotton)	2.2
Dried fodder and dried vegetables	0.8
Rice, seeds, hops and other miscellaneous products	0.8
Pigmeat	0.4
Eggs and poultrymeat	0.4
Other measures for livestock products	0.4
Other items (accompanying measures, Annex II products etc.)	6.5

Source: European Commission, 1996.

used in the food industry in 'bitter' drinks and citrus juice mixtures. The squeezed rind or 'mash' is used principally as an animal feed.

Bergamot is the only citrus fruit not to receive any EU assistance, although bergamot juice is classified as an agri-food product. For a number of reasons, future bergamot production is threatened because of the competition from synthetics to which we have already referred; the nature of the fruit itself, which is delicate and susceptible to sudden climate changes; and the excessive fragmentation of holdings. The price of the product went up at a time when the demand for luxury perfumes was hit by the world recession. As a consequence, bergamot-producing land is being sold for urban development.

A reasonable person used to the operations of a market system might ask at this point, why should the forces of supply and demand not be allowed to operate? Those farmers who can obtain a good price for their land should be allowed to sell, and the social problems faced by those who cannot realise their assets should be dealt with by transitional aid to allow them to shift to other forms of production or employment. Perhaps one farmer could be assisted to operate a rural museum devoted to bergamot growing.

Nevertheless, with only one abstention, the Committee on Agriculture, Fisheries and Regional Development voted to ask the EU to introduce a scheme to support industrial processing of the bergamot. This decision can, of course, be excused as a gesture of support for a fellow MEP, with no practical consequences. What is of broader significance about this otherwise minor example is the spurious arguments used to support the resolution. The resolution adopted first states that bergamot growing is a 'vital source of income for some 5000 families in a Community region facing severe social and economic difficulties'. This, however, is a case for assisting the person rather than the product, and for tackling the broader structural problems of the area. Secondly, the resolution states that 'the bergamot is a typical regional product with very important applications in the perfume and pharmaceutical industries and whereas the necessary production and support must be provided for it'. The reference to a typical regional product is an appeal to Southern solidarity, and indeed the proposals had been supported by CLAM (Comité de liaison de l'agrimiculture méditerranéenne). If the product was as important as is stated it would be able to survive without support, but the third line of the resolution reveals the real problem, by stating that the crop's survival is being threatened by high production costs and competition. The resolution then refers to 'the importance of bergamot growing in ecological terms and for the countryside', but it is never stated in the report what the ecological contribution is, other than to prevent urban development, which might be a better use for the land. The final line of the resolution is supposedly the clinching argument, 'whereas no specific Community assistance is being granted for the product at the present time' (European Parliament, 1993, p. 4).

Demands for support for beekeepers, including an annual pollination bonus, reveal a similar line of reasoning. Climatic conditions means that it costs more to produce honey in Northern Europe than elsewhere; imported honey undercuts European producers, who then receive 'unacceptable' prices; beekeeping is claimed to be important in maintaining the rural economy in less favoured areas; and 'bees are the most important pollinating insects and are thus of exceptionally great economic and environmental importance' (European Parliament, 1992a, p. 4). It is not the defective logic of these arguments that have undermined the beekeepers' case, or the ludicrous nature of demands for a compulsory register of productive bee colonies or a uniform definition of honey, but the fact that most of the apiculturists are part-time hobbyists. Commission officials have so far been able to brush aside their demands with bureaucratic jokes such as 'We'll have to keep them sweet' (*Financial Times*, 25 January 1994).

Rather more serious are the attempts to introduce a potato regime (referred to in Chapter 1), on the grounds that this is necessary to complete the single market. France, among other countries, has argued that 'all other crops are now strictly regulated, and the potato sector risks becoming the "poubelle" (dustbin) into which problems from other sectors can spill over' (*Agra Europe*, 19 August 1994, p. P/4). It is a sector in which there are a number of national subsidies, but these 'nationally-funded withdrawal operations for potatoes are confined to surplus years and production levels are determined by the operation of supply and demand' (*Agra Europe*, 23 June 1995, p. E/10). Germany and Britain have opposed many aspects of the proposals brought forward, both countries being concerned about the budgetary cost. With the abolition of the Potato Marketing Board and its quota system, British producers are, however, anxious to ensure that they are not disadvantaged by more favourable national aid schemes in other member states. Southern member states would like some form of intervention buying and help to modernise their potato sectors, but the eventual outcome may be controls on the quality of imports. By the summer of 1966 it appeared likely that a 'lightweight' regime, which would make national aids illegal but would not introduce quotas and market intervention, might be in place by the end of 1996 (*Agra Europe*, 28 June 1996, p. P/8).

The dairy sector

The regime for milk products has been of central importance to the development of the CAP, not least because there are significant numbers of dairy farmers present in every member state. Milk has the largest share of final agricultural production of any product in the EU (17.3 per cent in 1994). It is of particular importance to the agricultural economy in smaller countries such as Denmark, the Republic of Ireland and The Netherlands. Processing factories are an important source of employment in rural areas, although firms such as Avonmore from Ireland now have over three-quarters of their production located outside the Republic of Ireland. The formation of the European Dairy Association in 1994 to provide one voice for the sector was seen as a reflection of internationalisation, restructuring and concentration, not just in the dairy sector itself, but also in customer industries and the retail trade.

The dairy sector has been in many respects the greatest reform success of the CAP. Between 1973 and 1980, 'milk accounted, on average, for 39 per cent of the total annual expenditure of the Guarantee Section' (Neville-Rolfe, 1984, p. 363). The butter mountains, and those of skimmed milk powder, became symbols of the inefficiency of the CAP. The introduction of quotas in 1984 brought production in the sector under control and introduced a better balance between supply and demand. Assisted by world market developments, the intervention surpluses had virtually disappeared by the mid-1990s, and the sector's share of EAGFF expenditure had fallen from 43 per cent in 1980 to 10.3 per cent in 1995 (see Table 5.2). Looking at the situation from an industry viewpoint, Jachnik comments (1996, p. 2) that 'out of 100 litres of milk deliveries in the European Union, 75 are sold without any subsidy on the domestic market and 25 are sold with subsidies, 12 on the home market and 13 for export to third countries'. Taking a less sanguine view, a quota broker, Ian Potter, has commented:

> every UK producer is subsidised by about 4p a litre, or £200 a cow for an average yielder through export subsidies, import tariffs and intervention. And EU milk production is still about 15% higher than demand. GATT means we cannot go on dumping subsidised product on the world market, and our prices have to fall. (*Farmers Weekly*, 2 February 1996)

Production quotas were introduced in 1984 'rather abruptly', at the time representing 'a step into the unknown' (European Parliament, 1994b, p. 6). For once, the Community was prepared to act relatively quickly and decisively (after extensive discussions at two summits of heads of government). The impetus for action was the threat that the dairy sector could bankrupt the CAP and the Community as a whole if some remedial action was not taken. Given the complexity of the situation, and the unfamiliarity of producers with quotas, their introduction required some courage on the part of the Council of Ministers, but the decisions were taken 'in the context of a budgetary crisis without precedent' (Élégoët and Frouws, 1990, p. 11). This meant that actors outside the agricultural policy community, such as finance ministers, became involved.

TABLE 5.2

The reducing burden in the dairy sector

	1985	1990	1994
Quantity and value of dairy products in storage (millions/tonnes)			
Skimmed milk powder	513.8	333.2	58.1
Butter	1098.1	251.8	51.3
Value of dairy products in storage as percentage of value of all products stored	40.1%	24.0%	9.6%
	1980	**1990**	**1996**
Dairy product expenditure as percentage of EAGFF expenditure	43%	19%	10%

Source: Derived from various annual reports from the European Commission on *The Agricultural Situation in the Community/European Union.*

The way in which the dairy regime had operated had encouraged dairy production: 'Dairy farmers had particularly strong incentives to produce a surplus in that they could use low-cost cereal substitutes and soybeans for feed while the EC guaranteed them a high price for whatever amount of milk they marketed' (Moyer and Josling, 1990, p. 67). The adoption of quotas raised difficult questions of internal politics within the Commission and among member states. (For a full account, see Petit *et al.*, 1987.) However, 'The trade-off was a stark one – either the dairy programme was changed or the CAP would collapse' (Moyer and Josling, 1990, p. 70).

Compared with some other sectors, it was relatively easy to administer quotas in the dairy sector, because all but relatively small amounts of milk were delivered to central plants for processing. There was thus an administrative structure, at least in most countries, that could be used to allocate quotas and impose heavy financial penalties ('super levies') for over-production. However, it is evident that the quota scheme was administered with varying degrees of effectiveness, and in different ways, in each member state. An unintended consequence of the introduction of quotas was that they increased the freedom of action of member states in the dairy sector. For example, in relation to the allocation of additional quotas to groups such as smaller producers or new entrants, 'the criteria proposed by Member States differ so widely that it would not be going too far to say that producers are treated differently depending on where they live'

(European Parliament, 1994, p. 7). This represents a specific example of the general problem that the EU is dependent on member states for the implementation of its policies.

Policy adjustments to suit particular national circumstances are one matter, but wholesale evasion of the policy is another. It became apparent that the quota regime had not been properly applied in Italy. It was not until 1995 that Italy brought its production in line with EU rules. Other member states were not slow to draw attention to 'the injustice of a situation where one member state has been allowed to get away with blatantly disregarding the curbs imposed on it' (*Agra Europe*, 13 April 1995, p. P/4). Indeed, Italy benefited from its misbehaviour, as it was granted, along with Greece, a permanent increase in its quota in 1995.

Quotas provide existing farmers with a capital asset: advertisements for farms for sale in Britain invariably include reference to any quota that would be transferred with the sale. They therefore erect entry barriers for new producers wanting to enter dairy farming, a problem accentuated by the general absence of any special entry arrangements, such as the sharemilking scheme common in New Zealand (Grant, 1991, pp. 47, 75). 'Quotas once introduced become difficult to dislodge. Those that have quotas view them as entitlements to be guarded' (Josling and Tangermann, 1995, p. 12). It is, of course, not impossible to get rid of quotas, as the example of dismantling potato quotas in Britain shows, but fewer farmers were affected in that case, and they did not generally rely on potatoes as their main product, as do many dairy farmers.

How large the entry barriers are depend on the arrangements for quota transfer between farmers, with only Britain and The Netherlands initially permitting the trading of milk quotas. In Britain, there is a well established market for the sale and lease of quotas operated by quota agents. In the 1994–5 quota year, leased quota prices increased from 6p a litre to 20p a litre, while quota sale prices rose from about 45p a litre to 70p a litre. Following allegations of manipulation of the market by speculators, an investigation was carried out by the House of Commons Select Committee on Agriculture, which found no evidence of significant speculation. In the UK, quotas can be bought and sold without land, but in The Netherlands they are supposed to be attached to land deals, leading to artificial rented grazing transactions. The Irish system of quota transfer is so complex that the IFA has had to issue a thirty-page guide. Germany permits quota leasing, but this has produced resentment about 'sofa milkers' (often from the new länder) who do not own a single cow. Considerable difficulties have been encountered in devising a workable quota transfer scheme in France, and the young farmers, the group most interested in the issue, have called for a higher levy to 'siphon' off a greater proportion of transferred quota into the reserves for young farmers. The more general point is that the creation of quotas is a welfare transfer to farmers which then leads to a pseudo-market in which quotas are traded to the benefit of existing producers and those who make a living out of operating the market. None of this can be said to be a means of reducing the price paid for milk and dairy products by consumers.

Quotas cannot be traded between member states, a restriction that in principle is incompatible with the idea of a single market. A number of reformers have called for cross-border trading in quotas: 'To make quotas fully saleable, across farms and across borders, would at a stroke end one of the major economic drawbacks to quotas. The market in quotas would allow those with lower costs to bid more and end up with the most production' (Josling and Tangermann, 1995, p. 13). Such proposals have received particular support from Britain, which has a much lower quota per head of population than other countries such as the Republic of Ireland and The Netherlands. Hence the UK can meet only eighty-five per cent of its domestic dairy product needs, while the Republic of Ireland has a large surplus for export. This outcome does not reflect, as has sometimes been suggested, the incompetence of British ministers in the 1984 discussions on quotas, but rather the historical structure of the British dairy industry, which was orientated towards producing milk for liquid consumption, with dairy products such as butter being imported from Commonwealth countries, principally New Zealand (Barnes, 1995). British calls for cross-border trading of quotas (which is permitted for fishing quotas) have therefore won little support from other member states, France and Germany in particular regarding the social costs as being too high. The National Farmers' Union has suggested a more modest scheme for the transfer of unused quotas.

The introduction of dairy quotas prevented the burden of the dairy regime from increasing any further, and stabilised its budgetary cost by fixing production at around the 1983 level. However, 'Even in 1995, with highly favourable world market conditions, the dairy sector budget still amounts to around 4.3bn ECU' (*Agra Europe*, 15 September 1995, p. P/1). This is a reduction on the 1984 budget of

5.5 billion ECU, particularly when one takes account of inflation, but it does not represent a sharp fall in the total cost of the dairy regime. Any success was therefore of a partial character. This is not because of the nature of the policy instrument itself, but rather the way in which it was used. It is the pricing policy and the level of quota available that is crucial. Quotas have broadly achieved the levels of production they set out to achieve, but policy-makers have often failed to grasp the nettle of reducing quotas so that surpluses are fully dealt with, and reducing prices so that long-term quotas might be removed without risk of unleashing surpluses once more.

A structural surplus remained in the dairy sector and increased in size as the result of the entry of three new member states in 1995: 'The reason for this is simple: the Community produces some 15–18 million tonnes more milk than its domestic market can absorb and this excess has to be exported with substantial subsidies which currently represent some 60% of the total dairy sector budget' (*Agra Europe*, 15 September 1995, p. P/1). The limits to the success of the quota regime are not altogether surprising: 'Quotas do not solve any underlying problem. They mask the symptoms and allow a partial solution to obscure the market imbalance' (Josling and Tangermann, 1995, p. 12). Given market access commitments and restrictions on subsidised exports under the Uruguay Round agreements, quotas might need to be reduced by 3 per cent by the year 2000 if the EU's milk market is to be kept in balance (*Agra Europe*, 2 February 1996, p. E/1). After the year 2000, the United States and the Cairns Group will be pressing for further liberalisation of trade in dairy products.

The fundamental problem in the dairy sector is that demand is in general stagnant, while supply is liable to increase. This is in a context where Europe is a less efficient producer of milk than either the United States or New Zealand. On the demand side, there is little population growth in Europe that might fuel increased consumption, while the demographics of an ageing population tend to depress demand. Particularly in Britain, milk has become a commodity product used as a loss leader in retail stores. The consumption of butter and skimmed milk powder has shown a long-term decline, with production of both commodities in the EU falling by nearly a third between 1984 and 1994. (*Agra Europe*, 29 September 1995, p. M/8). Consumption of butter in principal European countries fell in the late 1980s and early 1990s, while consumption of margarine increased (Residuary Body, 1995, p. 179), reflecting a longer-term trend. Consumption of cheese, particularly speciality cheeses, increased over the same period, while yoghurts, speciality ice-creams and frozen desserts were other value-added products of increasing importance in the dairy sector. As dairy companies seek to move the balance of their production towards more value-added products, cuts in manufacturing capacity have concentrated on butter, skimmed milk powder and hard-pressed cheese, although such plants are often located in areas where there is little alternative employment.

The more innovative dairy companies can thus rearrange their product balance, but improvements in animal breeding, record keeping, veterinary care, milking plant and general management tend to produce more milk per cow. The dairy herd in Europe declined by 29 per cent between 1984 and 1994, but the decrease in production was only 12 per cent because of higher yields (*Agra Europe*, 29 September 1995, p. M/8). Despite these improvements, because of herd sizes, levels of investment and climatic factors, Europe remains a high-cost producer. Prices and production costs have been estimated by an official of the *Deutscher Bauernverband* as being at one-third of the EU level in New Zealand and Australia, and two-thirds of the EU level in North America (*Agra Europe*, 21 October 1994, p. E/2). In the UK, according to estimates produced by Norman Coward, agriculture director of Midland Bank, the cost of quota, land and the cow is about £1.40 per litre of milk produced, compared with 35p a litre in California, which has the highest yields in the world; and 25p a litre in New Zealand, which has very favourable conditions for dairying (*Farmers Weekly*, 17 November 1995). Thus 'The essence of the problem is that while the EU remains a high-cost producer in world terms, the authorities continue to maintain high support prices and thus encourage a level of production well above domestic consumption' (*Agra Europe*, 3 February 1995, p. P/1).

As countries such as New Zealand and the United States benefit from the liberalisation of agricultural trade resulting from the Uruguay Round, the EU may see its share of the world dairy products market declining, especially in areas such as the Middle East. The EU's exports are largely made up of staple products such as butter and milk powders. This indifferent export performance reflects the underlying problems of the industry:

> The basic problem remains that support prices are too high in relation to both the level of production and the levels of productivity. Paradoxically, the dairy processing industry is short

of raw material and in many parts of the EU is having to operate at less than full capacity with a consequent loss of efficiency and international competitiveness. (*Agra Europe*, 23 February 1996, p. P/1)

Quotas are supposed to expire in the year 2000, but are likely to be renewed beyond then, although perhaps in a form which eventually links them to cows rather than milk, and transforms them into a form of support for more marginal farmers. Although initially greeted with alarm by farmers, quotas are now well entrenched, and their abolition would produce significant problems:

> It is estimated that without milk quotas, Europe has the capacity to increase milk production by 30%. This would have a significant downward effect on milk prices and force smaller, less competitive producers out of business. In most member states, it would be a politically unacceptable move. (*Farmers Weekly Dairy Event Supplement*, 16 September 1994)

In 1996 there appeared to be some support within the Commission for the introduction of a system of two- or three-tier quotas after the year 2000, based on the arrangements existing in the sugar regime. Franz Fischler engaged in some kite flying on this idea during a visit to Britain in January, in order to open up the debate. Quotas would remain in place for 'A' quota milk sold for use or production within the EU. Support prices would be reduced to take account of the growth in productivity since 1974, with farmers being compensated by a premium payment per dairy cow. Learning from the mistakes made in the cereals regime, these payments would be variable in response to world and EU market conditions. The more efficient farmers would be able to produce 'C' quota milk, which could be sold on the world market at a competitive price without export subsidies. This would allow the more efficient farmers and sectors of the dairy processing industry to expand without breaching GATT limits on subsidised exports.

This might appear to be a neat way of reconciling apparently irreconcilable objectives: finding a means of 'encouraging the most efficient sectors of the industry while gradually eliminating the use of the dairy policy as a barely concealed rural area welfare system – particularly in the southern regions of the Union' (*Agra Europe*, 23

February 1996, p. P/2). However, the proposal faced a number of internal and external political obstacles. One of the main drawbacks of such a scheme would be the likely budgetary cost of the dairy premiums, a new subsidy to farmers. In order to keep costs under control, they would probably have to be 'modulated'; for example, not paid to the herds of more than fifty cows who make up a third of all EU cows, but account for more than half of production. Such a policy would not be popular in countries such as Britain, which have a concentration of larger herds. Farmers are likely to resist any threat to what they regard as the valuable asset of quotas. In Denmark, the Dairy Board suggested the introduction of a two-tier system to protect Danish dairy exports, but encountered opposition from farmers who feared that the quota system would be undermined (Personal communication, Carsten Daugbjerg, 17 April 1996). It quickly became apparent that the majority of member states were opposed to two-tier quotas.

Internationally, the EU's dominant position in the world dairy market, where it accounts for more than half of all exports, means that cross subsidisation of the B quota milk which would be produced as a marginal addition to supported A quota would tend to undermine the world price: 'If the EU goes ahead with this type of system for the dairy sector, it can be sure of strong opposition from other dairy exporting countries in the new WTO negotiations on agricultural trade' *Agra Europe*, 28 June 1996, p. P/6).

Given the political obstacles, and the administrative difficulties of operating any such scheme, Fischler made it clear in July 1996 that A and B quotas were not the only options for change in the sector. An alternative would be a grassland area aid scheme to compensate farmers for falls in the market price for milk, similar to that in the arable sector, which would give the Commission a new lever to control stocking densities. One difficulty would be whether to pay compensation per hectare, or per cow, or on the basis of milk yields, which differ considerably: 'High yielding countries such as Denmark and the Netherlands could be expected to favour a per kg option' (*Agra Europe*, 12 July 1996, p. E/3). As with the arable aid scheme, much would depend on the world price that was used as the basis for calculation. Fluctuations in the world price could lead to farmers being over- or under-compensated.

Quotas seem set to continue in some form well into the twenty-first century. Informed commentators do not believe that there is going to be 'a sort of big bang in milk: such a scenario is not realistic politically, budgetarily, socially' (Jachnik, 1996, p. 3). As Atkin comments (1993, p. 79):

> They in no way reduce the protection of European farmers from more efficient producers overseas. What is more, they institutionalize inefficiency, and reduce incentives for individual farmers to innovate. Since they cannot be traded from one country to another, they prevent an efficient allocation of resources within the Community.

It is worth noting that the debate about the dairy sector has been driven by concerns about the impact of any policy changes on dairy farmers. The 1994 European Parliament report, for example, emphasises the importance of attending to the problems of smaller producers and introducing structural improvements which benefit family farms. There is no mention of the dairy processing industry, which employs some 250 000 people with an annual turnover of 80 billion ECU. Such a narrowness of focus was apparent when quotas were introduced in 1984 (Cox *et al.*, 1989). The continuation of this neglect is no great surprise, given the 'great imbalance of involvement in policy making between agricultural producers . . . on the one hand, and secondary processors and consumer interests on the other . . . decisions affecting the food industry have often been taken in an ad hoc way by a number of different departments within the Commission' (European Parliament, 1989, p. 18).

Cross-border trading of quotas would be beneficial to an industry that has sometimes been slow to internationalise, take advantage of market opportunities, and to engage in product innovation. Quotas 'imposed a strait-jacket on company development. Growth often came to depend on buying other businesses to source extra milk supplies' (Hall, 1995, p. 12). However, cross-border trading of quotas would produce winners and losers. As a 1992 Economist Intelligence Unit report noted, French and Danish dairy companies are most likely to become multinational players in the single market, followed by the large Dutch and Irish companies which have more limited product range and added value. UK companies are large, but have not been active in continental markets and have 'a limited range of products, disappointing growth in [domestic] markets, and a lack of innovation'. The Italian, West German and Spanish industries were 'poorly developed structurally, still look predominantly at regional rather than national markets and are psychologically less prepared for competition on a European scale' (Economist Intelligence Unit, 1990). In terms of both the CAP itself and its impact on the food processing industry, the emphasis is always on protecting existing national interests rather than on maximising competitiveness across Europe as a whole.

Cereals

In order of their share of final agricultural production in the EU in 1994, the principal cereal crops forming part of the commodity regime are: wheat (5.0 per cent); maize (1.8 per cent); and barley (1.6 per cent). Over 50 per cent of all EU wheat production was in two countries in 1994: France (34 per cent) and the United Kingdom (17 per cent), followed by Germany with 16 per cent and Italy with 13 per cent. Germany, France and Britain (in that order) dominate barley production, accounting for two-thirds of EU output in 1994. France is the leading maize producer, with a 50 per cent share of EU production in 1994.

It is important to emphasise that Britain and France would have the potential to be important cereal producers in a free market agricultural economy. Climatic and soil conditions are favourable on the best cereal growing land and yields consequently are high. However, an analysis by the *Farmers' Weekly* shows that fixed and variable costs are much higher on a cereal farm in the UK compared with similar farms in the main competitor countries outside the EU (Argentina, Australia, Canada, the USA). The UK farm was spending much more per hectare on seed, fertiliser and sprays, and also had much higher bills for labour, equipment repairs and rent, not to mention miscellaneous items such as fuel, insurance and telephone (*Farmers' Weekly*, 6 November 1992, pp. 60–2). The major differential in rental costs, which is one of the factors producing a higher break-even point in the UK, is significant, as it has been suggested that one of the main consequences of the CAP has been to force up land prices. It has been estimated that the main consequence of eliminating agricultural protection would be that land rental would fall by 40 per cent (Johnson, 1995, p. 32).

In a tight supply and demand situation which forced up world prices (such as the situation in the mid-1990s), British and French producers should be able to compete in a world market without protection. However, the margins for survival are very tight, and depend on trends in input costs and green money. Reporting on the east of England, where the most viable cereal farms are located, the University of Cambridge (1994) noted that, at the prices then prevailing, even if variable costs were reduced by 10 per cent, there would be a loss of £10 per hectare: 'In the absence of some form of compensation payment the average wheat producer in the Eastern counties could not continue for very long' (University of Cambridge, 1994, p. 66).

Wheat farmers from eastern and central England are a powerful force within the National Farmers' Union, and recent ministers of agriculture in Britain have been drawn preponderantly from areas of eastern England where cereal farming predominates. Cereal farmers are also a significant force in French rural politics where, in part because of the dues structure, they have been the dominant force in the Fédération Nationale des Syndicats d'Exploitants Agricoles (FNSEA). France has, of course, been the main beneficiary of the export subsidy programmes of the European Union. Finally, Germany has been anxious to protect the high prices received by its often less-efficient grain producers, even using the veto in the Council of Agricultural Ministers in an attempt to prevent a cereal price cut in 1985.

Faced with this triumvirate of key countries with an interest in maintaining support for the cereals sector, achieving a measure of reform was not easy. Essentially, progress was stimulated by budgetary pressures and achieved through the design of new policy instruments: 'High support prices have been a feature of the cereals regime since its inception. Production of cereals has grown dramatically during the last twenty-five years while consumption has remained stagnant' (National Consumer Council, 1995, p. 59). Phillips (1990) has traced with great care the evolution of price policy in the 1980s, and the shift from a system dominated by the farm lobby with farm incomes as the main preoccupation to a more market based system.

Once the problems in the dairy sector had been 'solved' in 1984, the cereals regime became the main agenda item for the EC. A co-responsibility level was introduced to fund part of the cost of subsidised exports. Budgetary stabilisers were introduced in 1988, based on the idea that whenever production broke through a ceiling set in advance, support for the product would be reduced automatically. The Commission would have preferred straightforward price cuts and the resulting arrangements were complicated and depended to a considerable extent on whether the Maximum Guaranteed Quantity (MGQ) was set at a level that was likely to trigger reduction in support. As Tracy notes (1989, p. 318) it was questionable how farmers would react to such complicated mechanisms, which did not provide 'such clear signals as an explicit programme of price reductions'. 'In practice, the Council of Ministers tended to be generous in setting maximum production levels and there was often controversy over actual production levels' (European Commission, 1994, p. 16). In 1989/90, when output in both the United States and the European Union was affected by drought, the additional co-responsibility levy was reimbursed in full. In 1990/91, the overrun of the MGQ led to a 3 per cent cut in intervention prices. However, this did not represent a major change in production incentives, and cereal intervention stocks continued to increase.

In its 1991 reflections paper, the Commission noted 'the trend on the cereals market is especially worrying' (European Commission, 1991, p. 6). The EC had already introduced a scheme of voluntary set aside and under the MacSharry reform proposals it introduced a system of compulsory set aside for cereal producers, complemented by compensatory arable aid payments made direct to farmers. These reforms also facilitated a satisfactory conclusion to the Uruguay Round negotiations, despite EU protestations that there was no direct link between the two processes. As a political arrangement, set-aside payments had a number of advantages, particularly once British objections had been met by not capping payments to their large-scale arable farmers, seven of whom received payments in excess of half a million pounds in 1994 (*Agra Europe*, 5 May 1995, p. P/2). 'Because Germany had more non-competitive farms, it was also more willing than France to consider quantitative controls on production that would tie support to individuals' (Phillips, 1990, pp. 110–11). Given that farmers received compensation for price cuts which did not happen because of world market conditions, French cereal farmers had no cause for complaint. Indeed, in the main arable farming areas of northern France land prices rose by nearly thirty per cent between 1992 and the middle of 1994 (*Agra Europe*, 5 May 1995, p. P/2).

The budgetary costs of this solution to the problems of the cereals sector are high, with support expenditure projected to double from six billion ECU in 1992 to twelve billion ECU in 1996 (*Agra Europe*, 5 May 1995, p. P/2). By 1994 arable sector compensation accounted for just under 40 per cent of all EAGGF spending. The Commission has had to invite tenders for interpreting satellite surveillance photographs to check fraudulent claims for set aside. Pressure from countries such as France has led to reductions in the total area of set aside, so the EU may have some difficulty in meeting its commitments under the GATT agreements. The EU has tended to underestimate the effect of continuing productivity gains and overestimate increased disposals for animal feed. The main internal players in cereals policy – Britain, France and Germany – have, however, been provided with a reform package that meets their particular concerns.

One of the ironies of the solution arrived at was that shortly after it was brought into effect, world cereal prices started to rise, in large part because of bad weather in major producing countries in 1994 and 1995 (although they started to ease in 1996). Farmers were thus compensated for a fall in prices which did not in fact occur. By the end of 1995, the EU had replaced its export subisidies for cereals with a punitive export tax. Set aside was reduced to 5 per cent for the 1996/7 crop year and could have been reduced to zero for crops other than oilseeds. Instead of dumping subsidised products on the world market, the EU was forcing up its price by withholding it, introducing a novel source of tension in US–EU agricultural relations. Following the BSE crisis, the Commission proposed a 7 per cent cut in arable area aids and a 27 per cent cut in set-aside compensation, to fund assistance to the beef sector.

The rise in cereal prices reflected a tight world supply and demand situation which had both long-term and proximate causes. The world grain market changed significantly between the mid-1970s and mid-1990s, with developing countries accounting for an increasing share of production and consumption: 'The share of the [developing countries] in world wheat production has increased from around 38% in the 1970s to a current 47%, and their share of coarse grains output has increased from around 30% to over 40%' (*Agra Europe*, 10 November 1995, p. P/3). Asia outside the Indian subcontinent, with a growing disposable income, is the leading world import market for wheat and maize. More than 50 per cent of the growth in global grain imports between the years 1995 and 2000 will be in Asia (Coyle, 1996). By 2005, Asian countries could account for 45 per cent of global grain imports, depending largely on the rate of growth in GDP. There has been a shift away from the traditional rice diet towards more convenient wheat-based products (for example, the rapidly growing pot noodle industry in Indonesia), while increasing consumption of dairy products has led to increased use of feed grains (*Agra Europe*, 10 November 1995, p. M/8).

From the early 1970s, the Soviet Union was a somewhat unpredictable large-scale purchaser of grains, often producing panic price reactions. Since the dissolution of the Soviet Union, Russia has been largely absent from the international markets, but its place as a major purchaser been taken by the Peoples' Republic of China, which has moved from being a net exporter to a net importer of grain. China is dependent on irrigated land for two-thirds of its production, and some of the land has been used for industrialisation or diverted by farmers to crops which produce a better return in a cash economy (*Agra Europe*, 10 March 1995, p. E/6). In 1994–5, consumption of grains was at a high level, while stocks were depleted because of low production resulting from drought and a variety of other factors in Australia, China, the former Soviet Union and the United States (*Agra Europe*, 11 August 1995, p. P/1). It is difficult to forecast future production levels in China because there is reason to believe that China has been understating its land base for some time, and therefore the data may be unreliable. There may also be scope for increasing production, given that levels of fertiliser use in the interior provinces remain low.

Grains experts disagree about whether the tight supply and demand in grain is a short-term phenomenon, or a harbinger of new world food shortages early in the twenty-first century. Although the recent supply/demand pattern has been volatile, industry sources consider that 'production potential should match or exceed rising consumption' (De Maria, 1996, p. 1). On the supply side, yields have increased for the past thirty years, with plenty of scope for further increases as a result of technological advances in seeds, and improved management. In the past twenty years, cereal yields have increased by around 50 per cent (*Agra Europe*, 5 January 1996, p. P/2). Policy measures taken in the EU and the United States have reduced the area planted to cereals in the world by almost 9 per cent (*Agra Europe*, 5 January 1996, p. P/1). However, by 1996, set-aside provision in the EU had been reduced to a minimal level. In the former Soviet Union, the acreage planted could increase in Russia, while yields could improve in the Ukraine. In Russia, Ukraine and Eastern Europe, 'Domestic production will increasingly cover the growing demand, since domestic production is cheap, favoured by low costs of land and labour, logistical advantage and advantageous import levies' (Bielders, 1996, p. 1). Scare stories in the press about a global food shortage are, therefore, just that.

Some observers were concerned that there could be a repetition of the situation in the mid-1970s, when a slight fall in production combined with a surge in demand from the Soviet Union 'stoked up world prices, stimulated production to the point where it moderately exceeded consumption . . . and led to the building of massive stocks in the 1983–86 period' (*Agra Europe*, 10 November 1995, p. P/3). This, in turn, led to serious tensions in US–EU economic relations, which threatened to spill over into other areas of trade. Whether the lessons of past policy errors have been learnt is open to question.

By the autumn of 1996 the wheat market was shifting to become a buyers' market, signalled by trends on the futures exchanges in Chicago and Kansas City. The International Grains Council predicted a 4.5 per cent rise in wheat output in 1996/7. One wheat trading specialist commented, 'The world has more wheat than anybody originally thought and the buyers' appetites aren't that big' (*Agra Europe*, 13 September 1996, p. M/12).

In the cereals sector, EU farmers have received the benefits of compensation payments without suffering from a fall in prices. This was not the intended policy outcome, and illustrates both how the CAP operates in a context of uncertainty set by world market conditions, and how difficult it is to remove privileges that have been given to farmers, whether they are in the form of payments or quotas. A major difference between the dairy and cereals sectors is in terms of their exposure to international trade. Subsidised exports have been a mechanism for disposing of surpluses in the dairy sector. However, although individuals have specialised in that trade, there have been no equivalents of the major grain trading firms such as Cargill and Continental Grain, who have been the main beneficiaries of American export subsidy programmes (Libby, 1992). In that sense, cereals are a more globalised sector than the dairy industry and one in which the US is more likely to make decisive interventions to protect the interests of its agribusiness sector.

Livestock regimes

'The European Union produces some 15% of total world production of beef and veal (second only to the USA) and through its exports in particular accounts for about 25% of the world trade in beef and veal' (European Commission, 1995, p. 87). Cattle farming is predominantly concentrated in the Northern countries of the EU; 55 per cent of beef and veal production in the EU takes place in Britain, France and Germany, while beef production is of central importance to the Irish agricultural economy. Around two-thirds of the cattle slaughtered for meat production still come from dairy herds, but the share of specially-bred beef cattle is increasing (Court of Auditors, 1994, p. C356/7). Beef as a meat has faced intensifying competition from other meats, particularly white meats: 'The continuing reduction in feed grain prices will stimulate the pig and poultry sectors and continue to diminish the share of the EU meat market held by beef' (*Agra Europe*, 28 April 1995, p. P/5).

In a liberalised trading environment, countries with low production costs and appropriate technology for providing processed products to meet specific consumer demands are likely to benefit from the growing world market for meat, which is driven by population increases and rising living standards. The USA is likely to gain at the expense of the EU, whose meat industry has high fixed and variable costs and faces growing animal welfare and environmental costs (*Agra Europe*, 8 December 1995, p. M/3). These animal welfare problems are particularly apparent in relation to veal, where the confinement of livestock in crates for production purposes has attracted increasing criticism.

The Community market in beef and veal suffered from gradually increasing surpluses from the early 1980s. Special factors between 1990 and 1992 such as the Gulf War, developments in Eastern Europe, and the BSE controversy meant that 'the Community market underwent an unprecedented crisis which, as from the financial year 1991, led to soaring Community budgetary expenditure in the sector' (Court of Auditors, 1994, p. C356/3). The MacSharry reforms attempted to tackle the problems in the beef sector by reducing intervention prices and quantities purchased, and increasing premiums (subsidies) to producers. It became possible to claim a subsidy twice in an animal's life rather than at slaughter, also making it possible to double the number of claims per business: 'The extension of potential claims sits strangely against the need to control expenditure, and looks particularly inept when it is considered that the second claim is a virtual inducement to keep the animal longer and to a higher slaughter weight, therefore increasing the supply of beef' (Neville and Mordaunt, 1993, p. 68). It should be noted, however, that the number of second premiums claimed in 1994 amounted to only 10 per cent of the claims for first payments (Personal communication, Michael Winter, 18 September 1996).

It was no surprise that these contradictory 'reforms' attracted a highly critical report from the Court of Auditors. They drew attention to several irregularities in policing the control and management of intervention stocks. The report concluded:

> the 1992 reform has ultimately done nothing to correct the imbalance [in beef production and consumption], which has expensive implications for the Community's finances . . . the Commission will inevitably have to put forward proposals for measures to eliminate the persistent structural surpluses in the beef sector, otherwise the intervention costs of buying and storing the surplus will continue to be substantial. (Court of Auditors, 1994, p. C356/31)

Very high levels of exports to the former Soviet Union, combined with a fall in production of 16 per cent between 1992 and 1994, eliminated the beef stocks mountain in 1994 and 1995. The production of beef for intervention thus ended, but the BSE crisis threatened to trigger intervention buying again. The underlying problem remained that consumption was falling as fast as production 'with the result that the basic imbalance in the market – a permanent surplus of 600,000 to 700,000 tonnes – remains' *Agra Europe*, 28 April 1995, p. P/1). Consumer attitudes to beef may continue to affect EU production; opportunities for exports may be constrained; and, in the longer term, the potential for increased beef production in Central and East European countries could be realised. Even before the renewal and intensification of the BSE crisis in 1996, the beef sector threatened to be a source of recurrent problems for the EU.

The BSE crisis

Against this background of difficult structural conditions, the controversy over bovine spongiform encephalopathy (BSE) and speculation about a link with Creutzfeldt-Jakob disease (CJD) depressed beef sales in Britain in 1995. Further revelations about a likely link between infected meat and a new strain of the disease in March 1996 New Variant Creutzfeldt-Jakob disease (NVCJD) provoked a major crisis of consumer confidence which also had a significant impact on the market in other EU countries. As a result of consumers giving up beef altogether, or eating less beef than they had previously used to, it was estimated that the market suffered a permanent decline of 11 per cent. The ensuing crisis badly damaged relations between Britain and other member states, and undermined the stability of the CAP at a time when it appeared to be entering a period of relative calm.

Scientific understanding of BSE and NVCJD is still far from complete, but the most likely explanation of the discovery of a new variant of a rare disease originally discovered in 1920 was that it was related to the consumption of beef from cattle infected by BSE, first identified in 1986. BSE produces microscopic holes in the brains of cattle, leading to the animals' eventual death; NVCJD is, similarly, invariably fatal. It should not be assumed that anyone who has eaten the offal of an animal suffering from BSE will then be stricken with NVCJD: it is possible that there may need to be a genetic predisposition to the disease; that there may be a cumulative effect – that is, that one would have to eat a considerable amount of contaminated meat to be affected; and that the incubation period is a long one, so that many people may die of some other condition before NVCJD becomes evident. Indeed, by the autumn of 1996, only fourteen victims of NVCJD had been identified, far fewer than the eighty or so individuals under the age of forty-five who die each year from dementia. Such considerations, however, had little impact in countries such as Germany, where public health consciousness is very high.

The mechanisms associated with the appearance of BSE are still far from clear, but the most plausible explanation is the one that follows. Britain has a large sheep population and this population has been afflicted with a disease known as scrapie for at least two hundred years. The disease was recognised clinically in 1732, but probably dates from the importation of Merino sheep in the fifteenth century (Ford, 1996, p. 33). It seems likely that BSE jumped species from scrapie-infected sheep through poorly rendered offal fed to cattle in the early 1980s. In 1981 and 1982 the meat rendering industry stopped the use of chemical solvents to extract fat from carcasses and started to sterilise them at a lower temperature. These changes were introduced for a combination of financial and environmental reasons: 'Infective agents like scrapie – which may have been inactivated by the process – would be more likely to survive a gentler form of processing' (Ford, 1996, p. 22). It has also been suggested 'that the increasing intensity of milk production and the widespread introduction in the 1980s of the Holstein specialist dairy breed [could] have played a part in the BSE outbreak' (*Agra Europe*, 2 August 1996, p. P/4).

Although much popular commentary sought to blame the EU for the harmful consequences of the BSE episode, some portion of the responsibility must be attributed to the policy errors made by the British government. The most serious error was undoubtedly made in 1988, when it was decided that there should be compulsory slaughter of cows afflicted by BSE, but with compensation for only 50 per cent of the value of the animal. This gave farmers an incentive to conceal BSE cases. Full compensation was not introduced until January 1990, with the number of BSE cases peaking at 34 370 in 1993.

From the beginning of the crisis, the key to rebuilding public confidence in beef was seen as the implementation of an effective eradication scheme through the slaughter of targeted cattle. As Franz Fischler emphasised, the slaughter programme was not intended 'by itself to eradicate the disease, but to send an important signal to consumers that we are taking effective measures to protect their health' (*Agra Europe*, 20 September 1996, p. P/2). The EU asked the Ministry of Agriculture, Fisheries and Food (MAFF) to propose such a scheme at the end of March. In mid-April, it was announced that MAFF was looking at a limited eradication scheme. By the end of April, it was estimated that 40 000 cows might have to be slaughtered under the selective cull scheme, a figure that increased to 60 000 in May, and 80 000 in June. The agreement reached with the EU in June at the Florence summit added another estimated 67 000 cattle from the 1989/90 birth cohort, giving a total likely to be around 147 000 if the selective cull was carried out. By July, the UK had already slaughtered 203 505 animals under the scheme introduced at the end of April which covered cattle over thirty months of age. One and a quarter million animals are anticipated to be slaughtered in the first year of this scheme, which was planned to run alongside that for 'cohort' calves born on the same farm as animals that subsequently developed BSE.

The validity of the culling approach was, however, called into question by a study by Oxford-based scientists released in August 1996 which showed that, given knowledge about the way in which BSE can be transmitted, it should die out by the year 2001. It was concluded 'that the most sophisticated targeting strategy available would allow progress to be made in eradicating BSE through slaughtering only 29 healthy animals for every BSE case saved, compared with 79 healthy animals per case saved under the agreed "cohort" approach' (*Agra Europe*, 30 August 1996, p. P/1). The public health damage had already been done, with around 446 000 animals entering the human food chain before the introduction of the ban on bovine offal in 1989, with a further 283 000 animals estimated to have entered the chain between 1989 and 1995: 'The implication is therefore that the main reason for this selective cull – and possibly the only one – is to make it look as if "something is being done" about BSE in order to reassure consumers' (*Agra Europe*, 30 August 1996). The British government found itself caught between farmers and its own backbenchers, who were critical of the unnecessary killing of healthy animals, and other member states, who insisted on the most stringent measures to eradicate BSE. In September 1996 the British government suspended its selective cull of cattle thought to be most at risk of contracting BSE, making the calculation that even if the cull was carried through, continental markets might not be reopened to British beef. European ministers saw the suspension of the selective cull as a breach of the undertakings Britain had given at the Florence summit. The suspension was lifted in December 1996.

The BSE episode provoked a serious crisis in Britain's relations with the European Union, leading to a further deterioration in relationships with other member states, particularly Germany. The underlying problem was the deep divisions in an electorally unpopular Conservative Party over Britain's relationship with Europe. The need to maintain a façade of unity in the Conservative Party between Euro-enthusiasts and Euro-sceptics, and the presentation of the issue in a way that would boost government popularity, often seemed to be driving the way in which the BSE issue was managed in Britain.

The episode started in March with mutual mistrust on both sides. Accusations were made in Britain that the initial single country bans of British beef exports by individual member states were driven by the countries' own commercial objectives. Certainly, member states were worried about the impact of the British BSE crisis on their own domestic beef industries. The Commission also felt that the British Government had not informed it quickly enough about the impending crisis. Franz Fischler, the EU agriculture commissioner, complained to the British agriculture minister, Douglas Hogg, that Hogg had not warned the Commission about the impending announcement on BSE at the Farm Council in March. Fischler wrote, 'If the new findings of your scientists are as troubling as they sound, then the measures you announced seemed insufficient. If, on the other hand, your findings do not add to the existing body of knowledge about a link with BSE, a more careful reaction might have been preferable' (*Agra Europe*, 29 March 1996, p. P/3). Poor communications between Britain and Brussels institutions continued to be a problem. In May there was 'frustration at the UK government's failure to give members of the Standing Veterinary Committee (SVC) a preview of its selected slaughter plans and the general unwillingness of agriculture minister, Douglas Hogg, to visit other ministers . . . and to give a preview of his proposals' (*Agra Europe*, 3 May 1996, p. M/3).

The European Commission's handling of BSE was also criticised, particularly by the European Parliament. Letters written in 1993 by Guy Legras, the top official in DG VI, seeking to limit discussion of BSE in animal welfare and public health committees, were published in the French newspaper *Liberation*. The Commission's defence was that its primary objective at that time, in the absence of any scientific evidence of a health risk to humans, had been to prevent a collapse in the beef market at a time when it was heavily in surplus (*Financial Times*, 3 September 1996). Although denying that he had tried to limit discussions on the disease or keep information out of the public domain, Legras subsequently admitted to the European Parliament that developments in BSE had been monitored badly because of staff shortages in the Commission, which only had a dozen people working in its inspection division (*Financial Times*, 2 October 1996).

The British government's decision in May to disrupt EU decision-making processes because of the lack of progress in lifting the world-wide ban on exports of British beef seems to have been inspired largely by domestic political considerations. The major imperative seems to have been to find a means of coping with divisions within the Conservative Party. It is difficult to see that the final agreement brokered at the Florence summit offered Britain much that it could not have obtained by normal processes of negotiation. The prime minister's claim that almost all elements of the European Union's ban on beef exports would be lifted by November was not enshrined in any agreed timetable. The three-week period of disruption was, however, the most serious in the EU since the French 'empty chair' episode in 1965, and led to some eighty pieces of legislation being blocked at various Council meetings. All this did was to widen the gulf between Britain and other member states: 'The residue of ill feeling left by the British tactics was everywhere apparent . . . as they look to Europe's future, others have decided they can no longer accommodate their awkward island neighbours' (*Financial Times*, 24 June 1996).

There was a particularly serious deterioration in relations between Britain and Germany, symbolised by the actions of German farmers burning the union flag. When it was revealed at the beginning of August that maternal transmission of BSE was possible, German officials demanded that the EU restore a strict ban on British beef. The environment minister for North Rhine Westphalia, Baerbel Hoehn, argued that consideration should be given to extending the ban from British beef to dairy products. The German upper house, the Bundesrat, amended a government bill to continue to ban British bull semen, which the European Commission had exempted from the export ban. The Social Democrats could use their control of the Bundesrat to block measures while presenting themselves as defenders of public health. Such a course of action, however, threatened to provoke a crisis between Germany and the EU.

The BSE crisis threw the CAP into a new phase of disarray. The budgetary cost was forecast to be around 1.5 billion ECU at a time of renewed financial stringency, while the Commission was faced with the likelihood of large stocks of beef in intervention stores, which could not be disposed of on the world market because of the constraints of the GATT agreement. Any beef that has been in storage has to be counted against the EU's subsidised export limits. The Commission agreed to contribute to any national government schemes to compensate for the costs of disposal of cattle at the rate of 70 per cent of the total cost (although in Britain this would be offset by a consequent reduction in the budget rebate). Plans announced in the summer included the slaughtering of up to one million ten-day-old calves (the 'Herod premium', thought likely to be unpopular with the public), taking another million store cattle into intervention and raising the intervention limits by over 300 000 tonnes. Despite the cost and range of the measures, 'There are real doubts as to whether the measures will go far enough to bring EU beef production to within the limits required if the building of an immovable beef mountain by the end of the decade is to be avoided' (*Agra Europe*, 2 August 1996).

The policy dilemma facing the Commission was summarised by Franz Fischler at a meeting of commissioners in July:

> The EU was facing end-of-year intervention stocks of more than 600,000 tonnes, the Commissioner warned. Given the EU's GATT commitments the Community could not dispose of the surplus on world markets. Nor could intervention solve the problem of the beef sector on its own because the Commission had already

purchased over 180,000t of beef since April but prices had continued to fall by around 15% on average across the Community. (*Agra Europe*, 19 July 1996, p. E/1)

The only apparent way out of the budgetary dilemma was to make cuts in arable aid, given that grain farmers had benefited from high world prices. These proposals met strong opposition from German farmers, however, who argued that the compensation payments had been promised to be permanent. They were also upset by the proposed removal of special derogations in the beef sector for East German farmers. There was speculation, however, that Germany would vote against the arable aid cuts, but not block the overall plan: 'Meeting the economic criteria for the single currency, with the help of unspent funds from the EU budget, is more important to Germany's political elite than the wealth of cereal farmers' (*Agra Europe*, 2 August 1996, p. P/6). By October, however, it appeared that it might be possible to fund the stabilisation of the beef market from other parts of the CAP budget.

The consequences of the BSE crisis included the diversion of the attention of EU decision-makers from other pressing problems; new tensions between member states, making consensus formation more difficult; new budgetary problems that are difficult to resolve, given internal and external constraints; a severe structural surplus problem in a key product sector; and an undermining of public confidence in modern systems of farming. All this amounts to a serious policy disaster caused by the negligent handling of policy in one member state. Despite much adverse publicity and considerable provocation, the Commission handled the crisis in a sensible and measured fashion.

The sheep that didn't baa in the night

Sheepmeat is of less central concern to the EU as production is concentrated in a relatively small number of countries. Key players in EU agricultural politics, such as Denmark, Germany and The Netherlands, have hardly any presence in sheepmeat production. There are three countries in which sheepmeat is around 5 per cent of agricultural production: Britain, the Republic of Ireland, and Spain (the figures for Greece are influenced by goatmeat): 'The United Kingdom is the largest consumer, producer, exporter and importer of sheepmeat in the European Community' (House of Lords, 1988,

p. 7). Britain has a special system of specialised sheep farming based on breeding on the hill farms, fattening lower down, and finishing lower still. Sheep are thus crucial to the hill farming economy in less favoured areas in Britain, but it has been suggested that sheep farmers have been 'regarded as essentially utilisers of marginal land or producer of marginal products in good land areas' (*Agra Europe*, 4 August 1995, p. E/4). World trade in sheep is dominated by New Zealand and Australia, with the European Union being the largest importer and consumer (European Commission, 1995, p. 88).

Reforms of the sheepmeat regime implemented in 1990 phased out over three years the variable slaughter premium paid in Britain (a form of deficiency payment), with the objective of achieving a unified regime with a single premium subject to annual limits. The Mac-Sharry reforms in 1992 took matters a stage further by introducing individual quotas for farmers wishing to claim sheep annual premium, thus introducing a quota regime in another sector. It should be emphasised that ewe quotas are not as strict a limit on production as are milk quotas. In 1995, the Court of Auditors produced a highly critical report on the sheepmeat regime, centring on the soaring cost of the system (up from 600 million ECU in 1980 to 2000 million ECU in 1995) and inadequate safeguards against fraud. According to the report, 'the amount spent on sheep and goatmeat under the regime averaged 1.7 ECU per kilo of sheepmeat produced – three times as much as the comparable amount spent on beef' (*Agra Europe*, 20 October 1995, p. P/5).

Although the sheepmeat regime does not rank in economic and political importance with dairy products, cereals and beef, it still has the capacity to cause controversy between member states. Anglo-French relations have been strained in the past by French farmers attacking lorries containing British exports. A special emergency package for Irish sheep farmers at the end of 1995 illustrates the complex interaction between domestic and European level politics in the CAP.

A crisis in the Irish sheep sector had been brewing for some time. Ireland suffers from a long-run cost disadvantage compared to Britain and France, and 'in the longer run significant proportions of the industry may be subject to competitive pressures' (Boyle *et al.*, not dated, p. 138). The crisis arrived sooner than expected, and in September 1995 5000 farmers brought the centre of Dublin to a standstill in a protest about low sheep prices. Faced with this level of domestic disquiet, Ireland threatened not to back any package of measures at the end of the Spanish presidency in December 1995 if additional ewe premium was not provided. Britain considered that any aid granted to the Republic of Ireland would lead to pressure for similar aid from their sheep farmers. At its December meeting, the Council of Agricultural Ministers announced a special emergency aid package for Irish farmers, topped up by the Irish government. Britain was less than pleased about the market distorting effects of this aid, but did succeed in ensuring that the additional premium would also be paid to farmers in Northern Ireland. At a crucial time in Anglo-Irish relations, which had already been strained by British opposition to the endorsement of additional subsidies for Irish Steel, it was perhaps as well that Britain gave way to a country where over 40 per cent of farmers' incomes derives from EU subsidies.

The underlying problems in the sheepmeat sector are familiar ones. The EU is a high-cost producer, with production costs being £84 per kilogram in Ireland and £112 in France, compared with £40 in New Zealand (*Agra Europe*, 4 August 1995, p. E/4). Production has stabilised, but consumption is declining, most worryingly in Britain, which is the key consumer country. Sheep farming is, however, the only viable form of farming in many remote and hilly areas, and its cessation would have serious landscape effects. The EU has so far managed to ensure 'reasonable returns to producers, although falling prices could put the EU budget under strain' (*Agra Europe*, 8 December 1995, p. M/3). As the Irish case shows, any particular national problem can be tackled by threatening to obstruct decisions on other issues. The decision could also be interpreted as another step towards the renationalisation of the CAP taken as an inadvertent byproduct of another decision.

Fruit and vegetables

Any critic of the CAP looking for ammunition need look no further than the fruit and vegetable sector: 'For taxpayers, the regime represents very poor value for money. Much of the expenditure on fruit and vegetables is spent financing the destruction of edible, healthy and nourishing food' (National Consumer Council, 1995, p. 92). In recent years, over a million tonnes of fresh fruit and vegetables has been destroyed annually.

The sector has been the subject of two highly critical reports from the Court of Auditors, in 1989 and 1995. The 1989 report noted that the regime was beset by fraud and the way in which it worked meant that lower-quality produce was reserved for processing, while better-quality produce was either used for animal feed or destroyed. The report presented by the Court of Auditors to the European Parliament in 1995 on the EU's 1994 accounts singled out the fruit and vegetable regime for harsh criticism. It was noted that expenditure on fruit and vegetables had more than doubled between 1988 and 1994. The dumping of withdrawn rotting produce was causing serious environmental problems, polluting surface and groundwater, and attracting insects which harmed other crops.

In order to understand why such a situation has been allowed to develop, it is important to note that Greece, Spain, France and Italy receive 92 per cent of all EU expenditure in the sector, with half of their production being withdrawn from the market. Italy and Spain alone account for 85 per cent of all citrus fruit production, nearly half of all vegetables, and 45 per cent of fresh fruit (*Agra Europe*, 5 May 1995, p. E/6). A significant producer of crops such as tomatoes is The Netherlands, but its production is glasshouse-based: 'Glasshouse producers usually are very market responsive and they anticipate changes in prices by shifting as early as possible to more profitable crops' (OECD, 1992c, p. 77). The Netherlands has pursued its concerns in direct discussions with Spain, but has not been prepared to pursue suggestions from producer organisations that it should open up a debate on the distribution of structural funds. Hence debate on reform on the fruit and vegetable sector has been strongly influenced by the concerns of the Southern member states with progress being delayed, for example, by what was stated to be the illness of the Portuguese member of the Commission.

The biggest change in the sector has been the growing influence of the large supermarket chains which enter into direct contracts with producers or packers, insisting on high quality standards. Such vertical relationships are particularly well developed in countries such as Denmark, Sweden and the UK, but are also becoming increasingly important in parts of France and Spain. Rather than accepting this as a development that might be beneficial for the consumer, the Commission has been preoccupied with strengthening the existing producer organisations into larger-scale regional or even pan-European organisations, so that they can countervail the market power of the large retailers. If the members of a producer organisation account for at least two-thirds of the producers in area, it would be able to make rules binding on other producers in relation to production, marketing and withdrawals. The reform proposals for fruit and vegetables have thus gone down a corporatist path which seems out of touch with contemporary market and political realities.

Under the reform proposals, withdrawal prices would be reduced by 15 per cent over five years, so as to reduce the incentive to produce crops for intervention: 'In terms of eliminating the waste of intervention, the proposals are less than radical and will result in only modest changes in the means of supporting producer prices' (*Agra Europe*, 22 September 1995, p. P/1). Even so, the proposal attracted some opposition from Southern member states, who were concerned that 20 per cent of the operational funds would come from member states: 'What is needed is a clear official acceptance of the fact that much of the operation of intervention for fresh produce and the subsidising of processing is nothing more than a disguised social subsidy for less favoured Mediterranean areas' (*Agra Europe*, 22 September 1995, p. P/3). Rather than trying to delay structural change in a demand-led sector, it would be better to focus on the rural development needs of disadvantaged areas dependent on fruit and vegetable production.

The reform proposals were finally agreed under the Irish presidency in July 1996. They contained the essential elements of the Commission's proposals, although 'Producer member states scored a major victory in the June Council decisions when they succeeded in removing from the proposal the requirement for the national authorities to co-finance operational funds' (*Agra Europe*, 26 July 1996, p. E/3). Details of the package – such as adding melons to the list of products eligible for withdrawal, and the provision of aid for asparagus processing and hazelnut growers – bore the hallmarks of a traditional CAP compromise. Getting an agreement on some kind of package is understandably often seen as a triumph in itself even if the need for fundamental reform is not met.

Bananas

A recurrent myth in the British press about the CAP is that Brussels bureaucrats banned curved bananas (see the *Sun*, 21 September 1994, p. 1 and leader). In fact, the EU proposed minimal quality rules for green, unripe bananas which would classify them according to quality and size in order to facilitate international trade. Nevertheless, bananas have provoked some real controversies in the EU.

Agriculture commissioner Franz Fischler commented in 1995 that 'no other market regime in the history of the CAP had been the subject of such controversy' (*Agra Europe*, 13 October 1995) as the banana regime. This much-enjoyed fruit has brought the EU and the USA close to a trade war and has produced serious divisions among member states (and inevitable corny jokes about 'banana splits'). The issues involved are, however, far from frivolous, as they go to the heart of the EU's relations with Third-World countries, regulated by the Lomé convention. The convention provides duty free access to EU markets for bananas from specified African, Caribbean and Pacific countries (ACP), most of which were formerly colonies of EU states.

In order to understand the banana controversy, it is first necessary to understand the structure of the market: 'Bananas are the fifth most important food commodity in world trade' (Farmers' Link, 1995, p. 1). EU banana production, which accounted for 21 per cent of the European market in 1990, is concentrated in the outermost regions of Europe – Crete, the Canary Islands, Madeira, the Azores and the French Overseas Departments of Guadeloupe and Martinique. Four member states thus have a producers' interest in banana issues: France, Greece, Portugal and Spain. EU production is subject to the usual special pleading for commodity regimes. It has been claimed to be 'highly sensitive in the regions of production since it usually constitutes the principal agricultural commodity, production being centred around small family holdings, providing a large number of jobs in rural regions, generating economic and social stability and representing a particular environmental feature of the landscape' (European Parliament, 1992b, p. 18).

Sixty per cent of the EU market is supplied by so-called 'dollar bananas' produced by US multinational corporations, principally Chiquita, Del Monte and Dole. Dollar bananas are mainly produced in Latin America, but some are grown in the American state of Hawaii: 'Dollar bananas are substantially cheaper at the point of production, and the dollar traders were more powerful than their ACP counterparts' (Farmers' Link, 1995, p. 7). Dollar bananas are produced on large plantations as part of a vertically integrated system of production which minimises the costs of harvesting, conditioning, packaging and transport. A report by the Association of European Banana Producers found that 'overall US multinational control of production from EU and ACP countries has increased from 6% in

1992 to 31% in 1994, partly as a result of strategic acquisitions by US firms' (*Agra Europe*, 6 October 1995, p. E/2).

Some small ACP countries have economies that are highly dependent on banana production: for example, the Windward Islands. One of the benefits of bananas is that they produce a year-round income. They require little capital to plant and can be established on steep slopes. Windward Islands marketing has been controlled by the British company, Geest, but they sold their banana division to Fyffes at the end of 1995, on the grounds that they could not make any money out of it. Their share prices tended to be affected by 'hurricanes and strange fungal diseases' (*Financial Times*, 20 September 1996). In October 1996 there were violent incidents associated with a strike by farmers in St Lucia on the Windward Islands, whose Banana Salvation Committee wanted to be allowed to sell their fruit to the American company, Chiquita Brands (*Financial Times*, 4 October 1996).

Before the creation of the single market, there were different arrangements for the importation of bananas in different member states. Germany, which consumes more bananas than any other country in the EU (double the UK level of consumption), is the principal importer of bananas in the EU and is a major customer of the multinationals. This reflects the fact that Germany is a country that lacks its own 'colonial' bananas and has imported them from Latin America. Before the Treaty of Rome could be signed, a protocol had to be agreed that allowed Germany to import as many bananas as it wanted. Thus Germany had free trade, while the UK operated an import licensing system for Jamaica and the Windward Islands. When the Berlin Wall was breached, one of the first shopping goals for Easterners travelling across was the purchase of bananas, and the new länder have proved to be a significant additional market for dollar bananas.

These arrangements were 'clearly incompatible with the Single Market programme' (Swinbank, 1993, p. 370) and led to the establishment of a banana regime in 1993. This was a very complex arrangement, with import licences being allocated in relation to the activities of primary imports, secondary imports and marketing. Dollar banana import quotas were allocated between three categories: 'It appears that part of the aim of this complex arrangement was to enable the ACP companies to cross-subsidise their more expensive ACP banana from the profits of Dollar bananas' (Farmers'

Link, 1995, p. 9). A highly critical World Bank report argued that the new banana regime was costing European consumers $2.3 billion a year in inflated prices compared with $700 million under the old regime. Most of the extra cost was in monopoly profits for the European companies which market bananas with little benefit going to the overseas producers. The study argued that the system 'severely distorts competition, encourages black marketeering, restricts the growth of the EU banana market, discriminates against efficient producers and robs inefficient ones of incentives to raise productivity and cut costs' (*Financial Times*, 20 January 1995).

In October 1994 the USA received official complaints from Chiquita Banana International and the Hawaii Banana Industry Association about the EU banana regime under Article 301 of US trade law. This eventually led the USA to file a complaint against the EU under the World Trade Organisation's dispute settlement procedures (replaced in 1996 by a second complaint backed by a number of Latin-American countries). There were those who argued that it would have been better to seek a bilateral settlement with the United States rather than to allow the dispute to escalate. Commissioner Fischler made it clear that he was not happy with the banana regime, a view supported by Sir Leon Brittan. The Spanish and Portuguese commissioners argued that the EU regime was not contrary to WTO rules, and that all the US government was doing was passing on the objections of large multinational companies (*Agra Europe*, 14 July 1995). The Commission suggested in October 1995 that agreement should be sought on increasing the percentage share of import licences for dollar bananas, while maintaining the present level of import licences for ACP countries.

No consensus was possible within the Council of Ministers. Germany wished to defend its position as a large-scale importer of low-cost dollar bananas and argued that the Commission proposals did not give enough licences to dollar bananas. Other countries without traditional links with banana producers (the Benelux countries, Austria, Denmark, Finland and Sweden) wanted a large 'dollar banana' quota for their consumers. However, the countries with ACP ripening or producer interests (France, Greece, the Republic of Ireland, Portugal, Spain and the UK) represented a formidable defence of the status quo. Spain in particular made it clear that no fundamental changes to the banana regime would be countenanced during its presidency in the latter half of 1995. The succeeding Italian presidency seemed unlikely to produce a compromise on this contentious issue. With France leading one camp and Germany the other, the Council of Ministers was deadlocked and the banana problem had to be referred back to the Special Committee on Agriculture.

The wine lake

'The European Union is the leading wine economy in the world with, on average, 60% of world production and 55% of world consumption' (European Commission, 1996, p. 80). Draining the structural surplus known as the wine lake is one of the fundamental problems facing the CAP. The basic problem is that more wine is being poured in at one end than is being consumed at the other. The EU tries to cope with the situation by siphoning wine out of the lake for distillation (for example, into vinegar), and by grubbing up vines from the vineyards on the hills around the lake. 'The problem is . . . that EU-financed distillation is a positive stimulant of over-production of largely undrinkable wine, since it maintains less efficient growers of poor quality wine who would have given up long since if it were not for the EU support system' (*Agra Europe*, 19 July 1996, p. P/1). The policy measures that have been taken have been undermined by national aids, poor enforcement and fraud. In its often trenchant style, *Agra Europe* (18 November 1994, p. P/1) has denounced the wine regime as 'a racket which has been applied in such a way as to maximise the mulcting of the taxpayer by the EU wine industry'.

In 1993 the Commission published a discussion paper on wine sector policy which provides a succinct and often pointed summary of its problems: 'The major basic problem is a *structural imbalance* of the market, inbuilt and permanent, that the [market organisation] mechanisms have failed to bring under control' (European Commission, 1993a, p. 1). The report points out that there is a continuing decline in consumption of some two million hectolitres a year, particularly marked for table wines, but with saturation of the market as a whole for quality wines. New competitors with lower production costs are appearing in countries such as Australia, Chile and Hungary. These countries are using modern technology to produce wines at a good quality-to-price ratio. The EU still dominates the market for high quality wines, but is losing ground in the expanding middle sector of the market. The area under vines is decreasing, but less quickly than consumption, and in any case this is offset by an increase in yields. The EU thus finds itself running a wine support policy that costs around 1.5 billion ECU a year, involving the 'annual destruction of an average of 20–30 million hectolitres of substandard and undrinkable wine' (*Agra Europe*, 27 May 1994, p. P/1).

Compulsory distillation is weakened by a long list of loopholes such as state aids, the exemption of musts, and the downgrading of quality wines. The sector is particularly lacking in transparency and there is 'too much use of national-level statements, manifestly distorted, for establishment of forward estimates and distillation decisions' (European Commission, 1993a, p. 3). Problems of fraud are rife and have to be dealt with by a viticultural inspection unit with a staff of two. In its 1993 annual report, the Court of Auditors criticised the Council and Commission 'for creating a wine market support regime that has resulted in subsidised distillation becoming a permanent part of the system' The mistake of creating a market based on selling into intervention has been allowed to occur in this sector as in others: 'What the Council has done . . . is to set Guide prices too high so that the actual buying-in price has been consistently higher than the market price: a positive encouragement to producers to deliver to distillation rather than to the market' (*Agra Europe*, 18 November 1994, p. P/2).

Even leaving aside the problem of the misappropriation of funds, the substantial sums of money spent on abandonment of vineyards has not achieved its objective of reducing production. In the five-year period up to 1993, 1.2 billion ECU was spent on grubbing up vineyards, but the production of table wine increased by over 20 per cent (*Agra Europe*, 18 November 1994, p. P/2). Two-thirds of the vineyards in the EU are less than one hectare in extent, and they account for less than 20 per cent of the commercial output (*Agra Europe*, 27 May 1994, p. P/1). The closure of vineyards of this type under the abandonment programme can easily be offset by efficiency gains in larger operations. Abandonment is in any case open to environmental and social criticism as it 'carries risk of depopulation and desertification of certain areas, particularly hill areas, and of pockmarking the countryside with waste ground' (European Commission, 1993a, p. 3).

The Commission's discussion paper made it clear that the wine regime was far too complex, and that if matters were left as they were, the structural surplus would be 39 million hectolitres by 1999/2000: 'The Commission wishes to stress that the only option that appears to it to be ruled out is continuing with the status quo. If present policy is not rapidly changed the market situation for wine will rapidly become untenable and the regional wine economies will continue to weaken' (European Commission, 1993a, p. 12).

The Commission therefore proposed the creation of 'multiannual regional viticultural adjustment programmes', although it should be noted that compulsory distillation would remain the cornerstone of the system. Apart from measures to reduce yields, such as harvesting unripe grapes, wine production quotas would be introduced with over-quota production resulting in compulsory distillation at a very low price. The proposals would, however, still leave the EU heavily involved in the sector and engaged in the wasteful storage and disposal of surplus product: 'Even if there were no further concessions to producer States, 'the Commission proposals would still mean that close to 20 million hectolitres of surplus wine would have to be disposed of each year. With wine consumption continuing to fall, this surplus will increase, even if the quotas are agreed and properly applied at the proposed level' (*Agra Europe*, 27 May 1994, p. P/1).

In terms of the underlying politics of the sector, Mediterranean countries are significant producers of wine, although Greece ranks only sixth among EU producers. A number of areas such as Southern Italy and Central Portugal are essentially producing for intervention. France is the second largest producer and would face a 30 per cent reduction in supported production under the Commission's proposals, which by itself guarantees that they are unlikely to survive unmodified. A significant difference from the fruit and vegetable sector is that Germany is a significant producer, because it finds itself at odds with the Mediterranean producers as it has to add sugar to its wine to make it palatable, a need that does not arise in the same way in the sunnier producing countries.

It is very doubtful whether the Commission's stated clear objective that an 'overall balance on the wine market, must be achieved by the end of the century' (European Commission, 1993a) was ever attainable, even on the basis of the Commission's proposals before their inevitable modification. What is clear is that the rapid change in the policy that the Commission called for was not achieved. By the spring of 1996, the reform package was still being bounced around in Council working groups. The main hope for progress was that the Irish presidency starting in July 1996 would be able to resolve the problem by some trade-off between Northern and Southern interests. Viticulture is very important in some regions of the EU, but the wine sectoral policy is not the best way of solving rural social problems, and it clearly fails to serve the interests of consumers and taxpayers.

The sugar regime: less than sweet

The sugar regime illustrates two of the political problems associated with the CAP: the tensions that exist between the defenders of agricultural interests and second stage food processing industries, and the political difficulties of securing even the most minimal reform. The sugar regime combines 'an extremely high support price, a rigid quota system and state control of the relationships between beet growers and sugar factories' (Marsh and Tangermann, 1996, p. 19). It should be emphasised that the regime relates to beet sugar; preferential arrangements exist for the import of cane sugar from Lomé convention countries. From the point of view of the farmer beet sugar is an attractive crop:

> In many beet producing regions, sugarbeet today is one of the most profitable major crops grown. In addition, its contractual nature provides safe, stable revenues and, for soil restoration purposes, it is an excellent crop to rotate on land which will grow cereals. It is, however, a very technical crop, requiring high direct costs per hectare. (Chätenay, 1996, p. 5)

As a consequence there is an over-supply of sugar which has to be disposed of on the world market, depressing the world market price and pushing up the level of export aid required. The sugar market 'boasts the greatest surplus of all the common agricultural markets . . . The truth is that sugar beet sowing in the Community could be reduced by a minimum of 20% at no risk to the internal market supply' (Court of Auditors, 1991, p. C290/45).

Setting up the sugar regime proved to be difficult: 'The Commission had proposed free competition within the Community market, which would have promoted a shift of production from high-cost areas (notably Italy but also Germany) to lower-cost areas in northern France and Belgium' (Tracy, 1989, p. 265). What was established was a three-tier system of quotas. The A tier of quotas, allocated to the factories and transferred by them to the farmers in terms of guaranteed quantities and prices, is supported by intervention prices. Factories pay a levy on production beyond their A quota but within their maximum B quota, so that the system is self-financing. The original idea of the B quota was that it would be produced for export or to compensate for a poor harvest in regions where it was economically profitable to do so: 'The fact is that the institutional price is so generous that B sugar is produced even in the regions which are least suited to sugar beet production . . . B sugar can be produced with almost the same confidence as A sugar' (Court of Auditors, 1991, p. C290/45). C quota sugar, of which almost half is produced in France, can only be sold outside the EU. The effect of export refunds, reinforced by cross-subsidisation of exports as a result of the higher internal price of sugar, 'has been acutely felt by third world countries, many of them dependent on sugar sales for most of their external income' (National Consumer Council, 1995, p. 72). The Court of Auditors maintains that (1991, p. C290/16).

> The history of the system of production quotas for sugar shows that it has been used as an instrument designed for satisfying the industrial and national interests that are at stake in the market, rather than as a means of guiding production . . . The various adjustments to and extensions of the system have resulted in the preservation and maintenance of vested interests.

One crucial interest is that of the influential sugar refiners. From their point of view the existing arrangements are defensible: 'the European sugar regime has delivered a safe supply of high quality sugar . . . at reasonable prices . . . It has been, overall, a remarkable market management system which operates extremely smoothly and which represents a complex balance of interests' (Châtenay, 1996, p. 2). However, although the cost of the disposal of surplus product is, uniquely among commodity regimes, met by the producers, this additional cost is reflected in the price of sugar and is hence indirectly charged to the consumer. In the ten years preceding the 1991 Court of Auditors report, the world price for white sugar was 53 per cent of the Community intervention price. The notion that the system is self-financed is, in the view of the Court of Auditors, an illusion. It is simply that the cost is borne by the consumer rather than the taxpayer.

The first stage sectors of the food processing industry, those 'near the farm gate', are often well-disposed to the CAP. They have a mutual interest with farmers in ensuring security of supply and excluding competition from outside the EU. The second stage food processing industries, who see their raw material supplies being forced up by the CAP, often take a very different view. Over two-thirds of the sugar produced in the EU is used in the production of biscuits, cakes, soft drinks, confectionery, ice cream and so on, which do not have market protection. The sugar users are represented by the EU's Committee of Industrial Users of Sugar (CIUS) and their perspective is that farmers and sugar processors have combined to lobby effectively to preserve a system which is highly beneficial for them. They receive support for their stance from the Union of EU Soft Drinks Associations (UNESDA), which has explained the politics of the situation in terms of a transference of market power into political power. Sugar processing requires substantial investment in technologically advanced plant and this entry barrier is reflected in an oligopolistic structure, with four companies controlling about 50 per cent of the EU market (*Agra Europe*, 1 December 1995, p. E/4). In Olsonian terms, they are therefore able to function as a 'privileged' group.

The EU felt impelled to make some changes in the sugar regime to ensure that it could meet its GATT commitments, but proposed the minimum changes necessary, 'To comply with the GATT obligations, provision will be made for the possibility of a cut in budgetary amounts spent on sugar export subsidies – by reducing the quotas for supported production – for one or several marketing years' (*Agra Europe*, 20 January 1995, p. P/1). The Commission did propose to eliminate storage aids for C sugar, but this proposal was resisted by a number of member states, and storage aids were retained with some modifications. Despite the very limited nature of the adjustments proposed, bickering developed among the member states (sometimes referred to as the 'hot-beet syndrome'). The final agreement required a series of compromises and six hours of bilateral discussions. Finland was allowed an increased import quota of raw sugar, while Sweden was allowed to assign a proportion of its quota to the island of Gotland.

A minimalist set of proposals was thus watered down even further. The end result is that 'after prices for cereals, oilseeds and protein crops were cut by around one third under the MacSharry reform, the unchanged price for sugar beets now stands out of the overall level of crop prices like a towering rock island from a low sea' (Marsh and Tangermann, 1996, p. 5). An influential group of arable farmers and an oligopolistic industry, when combined with national and regional interests, represent a formidable obstacle to significant change. The situation thus remains essentially as the Court of Auditors described it in 1991 (C290/44):

> After 22 years of common organization of the markets in the sugar sector, it must be concluded that the experiment of organizing these markets on a Community basis has failed. The way the system has developed has run counter to the very concept of the common market . . . and several of the essential objectives assigned to the Common Agricultural Policy . . . As things stand currently, the European market in sugar is anything but a common market: it is no more than the sum of the individual national markets.

Other Southern products

Rice has produced a classic North–South conflict within the EU, with Northern states wanting a more market-orientated regime, and Southern states wanting to maintain existing supports as far as possible. Italy accounted for around 60 per cent of EU output in 1994, followed by Spain with 17 per cent and France, Greece and Portugal with between 5 and 7 per cent each. Some change was inevitable because the GATT agreement will lead to increased import competition as a result of import charge limits agreed with the United States. The Commission thus proposed cutting the intervention price but introducing simultaneously compensatory subsidies which would double the cost of the commodity regime. Critics of this policy see it as extending 'the long term dependency of yet another major sector of EU farming on what are clearly production linked subsidies' (*Agra Europe*, 21 July 1995, p. P/1).

In the cotton sector, the task of reform was perhaps made easier by the fact that there are only two producer countries – Spain and Greece. Commission reform proposals ended special aid measures for small producers and sought to tighten controls on fraud. Final agreement was reached in June 1995 when Greece was given a 84 000 tonne rise in its quota (*Agra Europe*, 23 June 1995, p. E/6).

In contrast, all the Southern countries, including France, are involved in olive oil production, and agreement on reform has been more difficult to achieve. Reform proposals were eventually brought forward in September 1996, involving a shift from market support to producer support, with intervention and consumption aid being replaced by direct payments to growers: 'Like reform of the arable aid regime . . . the new scheme is likely to prove more expensive, especially in the initial stages' (*Agra Europe*, 13 September 1996, p. E/ 3). In what might be seen as another gesture towards policy renationalisation, member states are allowed to top-up payments by up to 50 per cent. Provision is made to limit the maximum number of trees that may benefit from aid in each member state. This will involve the setting up of an olive geographical information system by member states to keep a track of olive groves. The old system was beset by fraud and serious administrative problems: 'The Commission is clearly conscious of the likely problems it will face in implementing and policing the new system, especially given the rather poor track record of some of the Mediterranean states in managing EU finances' (*Agra Europe*, 13 September 1996, p. E/3).

Tobacco was included in the MacSharry reforms. Intervention buying and export refunds were abolished, being replaced by quotas and premium payments, leading to a 17 per cent fall in production in 1993. Nevertheless, 'Tobacco is the most heavily subsidised CAP crop per hectare. Average annual funding for the Europe Against Cancer Campaign for the period 1990/94 amounted to . . . one thousandth of the CAP support expenditure' (National Consumer Council, 1995, p. 98). Defenders of subsidies to tobacco growers have produced the usual mix of arguments: it is important in less favoured regions, it is environmentally friendly because it requires few inputs and is grown on small plots which require hedges, and it has even claimed that it provides a basis for investment in 'green' tourism (*Agra Europe*, 28 April 1995, p. N/3). The decision-making atmosphere of the CAP does not encourage special interests to exert much quality control over their arguments.

Given all these special arrangements for Southern products, it is something of a surprise to learn that their total share of CAP spending has declined:

> An undisputable fact is that spending of the southern producers has not only declined absolutely over the last ten years, but also significantly in terms of the proportion of the total agricultural support budget. This fact is all the more remarkable in that during this period two important producers of Mediterranean commodities became full members of the European Union . . . As a proportion of total EAGGF expenditure, the Mediterranean group share has never risen above its 1985 level of 20.2% and in 1995 is likely to have fallen back to 13.5%. (*Agra Europe*, 16 June 1995, p. P/2)

This pattern reflects the increased spending on cereals and meat following the MacSharry reforms. It gives the Southern states a motive to be even more resolute in the defence of what they have, thus making reform more difficult. It is worth noting that the admission of Malta and Cyprus would make little difference to the situation, as agriculture accounts for only 3 per cent of GDP in Malta, and 5.4 per cent in Cyprus (*Agra Europe*, 22 March 1996, p. E/3). It would, however, provide some redress for a shift in the political centre of gravity in the EU following the admission of Austria, Finland and Sweden.

Conclusions

A view often voiced in the late 1990s was that after the conclusion of the Uruguay Round there would be a period of stability in the CAP, a 'lull' until the next phase of trade negotiations in 1999, followed by the probable admission of the first Central and East European countries. During this lull, incremental reform of those CAP regimes not covered by MacSharry could proceed so that a reshaped policy would be in place by the beginning of the twenty-first century.

As this chapter has shown, the cereals reform has been more generous to farmers than intended because of unanticipated changes in the world market situation, which remains volatile. The dairy regime is going to require further consideration as not all problems have been solved and the future of quotas will have to be reviewed as the year 2000 approaches. However, a measure of progress has been made in these important sectors, although new and serious problems have arisen in one of the MacSharry sectors: beef. In sugar, a totally inadequate 'reform' has been put into place which does not address any of the problems of the sector, reflecting the particular balance of forces in the sector and its low profile compared to cereals or dairying. In a number of sectors where Southern producers predominate – fruit and vegetables, wine, olive oil – progress has been agonisingly slow. The precedent of the rice sector suggests that any eventual reform will be bought at a budgetary cost. The proposals for fruit and vegetables in particular display a lack of commitment to modernisation and a determination to interfere with existing trading structures, which could drive some wholesalers out of business.

In the commodity regimes, member states are vigorous in defending their own particular national interests. Given that governments are answerable to national rather than European electorates, this is not surprising. Hence, in order for any agreement to be reached, complex deals have to be struck in which trade-offs are made between different sectoral, national and even subregional interests (such as the sugar beet growers of Gotland). In order to understand this complex, multilevel pattern of bargaining, it is now necessary to look at the ways in which decisions are taken in the EU about the CAP before returning to the reform debate at a macro level in Chapter 6.

6

Decision-Making and the CAP

The focal point of decision-making on the CAP is the Council of Agriculture Ministers. Here, the interests of the various member states have to be reconciled in a complex process of intergovernmental bargaining. Three crucial sets of actors have an input into this decision making process: DG VI, the agriculture directorate-general of the Commission; the agricultural lobby; and the member states. Other actors, such as the European Parliament, are more marginal actors.

The overall configuration of the decision-making process has changed over the years. The early years of the CAP were based on a Franco-German bargain in which the central relationship between the Commission and the Council of Ministers was augmented by a close working relationship with the agricultural lobby: 'The Luxembourg Accord . . . forced consensual decision-making on the Council and encouraged DG-VI to develop the expertise and contacts necessary to finesse proposals through the system. DG-VI, in collusion with COPA, thereby enjoyed unmatched power during the 1970s' (Phillips, 1990, p. 50). Discussion centred around the fixing of prices using something called the 'objective method' introduced by Commissioner Lardinois in the 1972–3 price review. This was an attempt to increase prices in such a way as to keep farm incomes in line with non-farm incomes. Against a background of inflation, it became increasingly difficult to maintain the objective method, which was eventually abandoned in 1982. The 1980s saw an increasing preoccupation with controlling the budgetary cost of the policy, but policy 'remained largely a monopoly preserve of DG-VI and the

Agricultural Council until the special summit in Brussels in 1988' (Phillips, 1990, p. 51).

In recent years, the circle of actors involved in agricultural policy formation in the EU has widened, while traditional core participants, notably the farm lobby, have become marginalised. This has largely been a consequence of the inclusion of agricultural policy within the Uruguay Round, which has both drawn in other directorates-general within the Commission to the policy process, notably DG I, and has also led to crucial interventions by heads of government, notably Chancellor Kohl of Germany. Issues other than supply and price, such as quality, health and environment, have also come to play an increasingly important role, and this trend has also widened the circle of relevant decision-makers. DG VI has, however, sought to defend its territory vigorously from incursions by other directorates-general whenever possible: note, for example, its vigorous response to the publication of a report on the CAP by the economic affairs directorate in 1994.

Nevertheless, agricultural policy still remains remarkably insulated for a policy that consumes half of the EU budget. Policy proposals from the Commission are not routed through COREPER, but through the Special Committee on Agriculture. Agricultural policy making is highly compartmentalised, although in that respect it is no different from the United States (Moyer and Josling, 1990, p. 201). The very complexity of the CAP means that there is a high political entry barrier into the policy community. The only independent criticism of the CAP has come from consumer organisations, which have been largely marginalised; from environmental groups, who have to tackle a range of other issues apart from the CAP; and from agricultural economists, who, whatever their analytical skills, often lack political acumen. Indeed, one of the characteristics of the agricultural economics literature is that it either ignores the decision-making process altogether, or uses a public-choice approach which, although it may explain why vested interests are strong and consumer interests weak, does not suggest how the balance of forces might be changed.

An analysis which centred on the farm lobbies themselves would be inadequate. It is also necessary to take account of, for example, coalition politics in member state governments, and the institutional mechanisms at the European level. The analytical perspective adopted here is therefore similar to that of Moyer and Josling (1990, p. 203): 'The major farm policies survive because of the particular sets of institutions involved in the setting of the policy and the structure of the decision framework in which they operate, as well as the pressures from interest groups.'

The Commissioner makes a difference

It does matter who is the member of the Commission responsible for agriculture. An effective Commissioner can play a more central role in the decision making process:

> When the Commissioner is assertive (as was Frans Andriessen from 1985–8), he can dominate the process along with his Cabinet. When the Commissioner is less assertive, (as was his predecessor, Poul Dalsager), the locus of policy formation is centred much more on DG-VI. (Moyer and Josling, 1990, p. 31)

With the exception of Carlo Scarascia-Mugnozza, who was commissioner in 1972 after Sicco Mansholt, had unexpectedly become president of the Commission, the agriculture commissioner has always been drawn from one of the smaller northern member states. Indeed, for the first thirty years of the European Community, the post was always held (apart from the Mugnozza interregenum) by a commissioner from either Denmark or The Netherlands. He (a woman has never held the post) had not always been agriculture minister in his home country, although the last three commissioners have been (see Table 6.1).

When the post falls vacant, the pool of candidates depends on nominations for commissioner by the member states. In the autumn of 1994, with Rene Steichen having to stand down to make way for Jacques Santer as Commission president, initial attention centred on Bjoern Westh from Denmark, who had the three key qualifications of being 'a man with considerable agricultural experience from a small northern country' (*Agra Europe*, 30 September 1994, p. P/3). However, Denmark nominated a woman, Ritt Bjerregaard, as its commissioner. Another possible candidate, Arlindo Cunha from Portugal, was also not nominated by his government. The new Greek commissioner, Christos Papotsis, was also suggested, but an informal meeting of the agriculture Council 'threw up strong resistance to a Greek taking on the job' (*Agra Europe*, 30 September 1994, p. P/4). Given

TABLE 6.1

Commissioners responsible for agriculture

Term of office	Name	Country	Served as agriculture minister?
1958–72	S. Mansholt	Netherlands	Yes
1972–3	C. S. Mugnozza	Italy	No
1973–7	P. Lardinois	Netherlands	No
1977–81	F. Gundelach*	Denmark	No
1981–4	P. Dalsager	Denmark	Yes
1984–9	F. Andriessen	Netherlands	No
1989–93	R. MacSharry	Ireland	Yes
1993–5	R. Steichen	Luxembourg	Yes
1995–	F. Fischler	Austria	Yes

Note: * Died in office 13 January 1981.

the success of Ray MacSharry in the post, attention then centred on the Irish social affairs commissioner, Padraig Flynn. He was apparently under some pressure from Dublin to take the job, as it was thought in Irish interests to have someone in this key position at a time when further reform of the CAP was anticipated. However, Flynn's friends apparently pointed out to him, that taking the job might undermine his future political prospects in Ireland.

Austria had indicated its interest in the agriculture portfolio. There were misgivings about giving such a key portfolio to a new member state, and about placing a German speaker in a largely French-speaking directorate. There was speculation in the Danish press that Santer offered the Austrians the job if they would appoint a non-social democrat, to tip the balance within the Commission in favour of a non-socialist majority (Personal communication, Carsten Daugbjerg, 24 April 1996). Whatever the reasons for the appointment, Austria's agriculture minister, Franz Fischler, was nominated and, as will be discussed later, the choice turned out to be a very astute one. The post of agriculture commissioner requires considerable political skills. Success requires a clear vision of what is to be achieved, but also a willingness to make compromises that satisfy the interests of particular member states:

> The Agriculture Commissioner, the key actor in the Commission process, must maintain the confidence of a number of often conflicting constituencies, which include the other Commissioners,

the Agriculture Council, the farm lobby and DG-VI. This implies he must first establish his credibility by showing he is in control of agricultural policy and can get things done. Since power is divided in the EC, this requires skill at political persuasion. (Moyer and Josling, 1990, p. 53).

The experience of the last three commissioners illustrates how the political skill of the commissioner can have an impact on the policy process. MacSharry steered through a reform of the CAP which, although modified from what he had originally wanted, did set a new direction for the policy. He had to give way to pressure from the British among others on providing compensation payments for larger farmers, but 'MacSharry's success in pushing his reform plan through in an extremely short period of time was overwhelming' (Tangermann, 1996, p. 12). Other commissioners had produced reform documents: Lardinois had issued an 'Improvement' paper in 1973 and a 'Stocktaking' paper in 1975. Gundelach issued a 'Future Development' paper in 1978 and a 'Reflections' document in 1980. The reforms of the 1980s had been driven by budgetary pressures, but as the Commission's 1991 Reflections paper made clear, they had not solved the underlying problems of the CAP.

The GATT Uruguay Round provided a new context for the reform debate. It brought intensified international pressure on the EC to initiate real reform, and it also brought a wider range of actors into the debate within the European Community. However, Ray MacSharry played an important role in converting these pressures into a sustained reform impetus. MacSharry's skills included a grasp of the complexities of his brief and a canny personality which mixed an undemonstrative nature with considerable determination and, when necessary, aggression: 'Brought up in one of the toughest schools of politics, the Fianna Fail party which has dominated Ireland since independence, Mr MacSharry is no stranger to the black arts of political street-fighting' (*Financial Times*, 14 November 1992).

While denying that the GATT negotiations had any impact on his reform proposals, Mr MacSharry astutely used international developments to exert pressure for change within Europe while making sure that he retained the acquiescence of the member states. His 'normal negotiating tactics' were described as 'a mixture of poker and horse-trading' (*Financial Times*, 14 November 1992). Tangermann has constructed a hypothetical but plausible story of how MacSharry made reform possible. According to this account, MacSharry realised that CAP reform had to precede a GATT agreement:

> Hence there was only one strategy he could adopt at the Brussels meeting of the GATT in December 1990. He had to let the negotiations come as close as possible to a compromise, so as to show the Commission's negotiating partners that there was, in principle, the possibility of a successful conclusion of the Uruguay Round. But he then had to break the negotiations, sharply before the point where success was in reach. This would show the heads of state in the EC that a serious effort was required on their side to convince their ministers of agriculture that they had to give in, in order to allow a conclusion of the overall negotiations . . . At the same time MacSharry had to convince EC ministers of agriculture that he was firmly on their side, so that they trusted him to work out a satisfactory solution. (Tangermann, 1996, p. 10).

An optimistic atmosphere developed in the negotiations when it appeared that a text from the Swedish chair of the agriculture negotiating group might provide a basis for a settlement. But at a dramatic moment in the negotiations, MacSharry stated that he could not exceed the negotiating mandate given him by the member states. The talks broke down. MacSharry then issued his Reflections document, taking care 'to make no more than one step at a time' (Tangermann, 1996, p. 12). The broad principles of the reform were discussed before the member states saw any figures which quantified the likely impact on their national agriculture.

When it came to a later stage of the negotiations in the Uruguay Round, MacSharry again showed his ability to think several moves ahead. Early agriculture commissioners had had to deal with relatively weak presidents. Jacques Delors was an activist president, and he was also sensitive to French national interests. He believed that MacSharry was going too far in seeking to reach an agreement with the United States, and both Delors and the French government accused MacSharry of going beyond the mandate he had received from the Council of Ministers. Mr MacSharry responded by calling the president's bluff and resigning in November 1992 from all responsibility for the Uruguay Round negotiations, complaining that his efforts to secure a breakthrough were being undermined by Mr Delors. No one had engaged in a public confrontation with a Commission president in this way before. The effect was to create a temporary Anglo-German alliance against the French. In little over a week, Mr MacSharry was back on the negotiating team with a broad negotiating mandate, while Jacques Delors was left with an undermined reputation and damaged authority.

Mr MacSharry was a hard act to follow. He had achieved CAP reform and the basis for a GATT agreement on agriculture, leaving his successor to implement the programme. René Steichen, a French educated lawyer from Luxembourg, was seen in some quarters as 'a Trojan Horse for France' (*Financial Times*, 10 February 1993). His defenders argued that his more emollient personality compared to the more abrasive Mr MacSharry made him more suitable to make reform work. Based on an interview with Steichen, *Farmers' Weekly* (15 January 1993) reported, 'René Steichen promises the stubborn style of his predecessor Ray MacSharry is in the past and that contact, conciliation and consultation will be his way of working with the farming industry.'

Steichen was certainly able to work more effectively with the trade commissioner, Sir Leon Brittan, bringing the agricultural portion of the Uruguay Round to a successful conclusion. Although not as beholden to France as had been forecast, 'he was certainly not as firm with Council as his predecessor, but the work programme has not really demanded such political rigour' (*Agra Europe*, 20 January 1995, p. P/5). Although he might have hoped for a longer period of office, Steichen was 'a patient caretaker, seeing the CAP reform through its initial stages' (*Agra Europe*, 20 January 1995, p. P/4).

Fischler started his period of office very cautiously. He emphasised that his task was to implement the 1992 reform. No judgement could be made about whether it had achieved its objective until 1996. In the meantime, he was in favour of 'sequential progress' (*Agra Europe*, 27 January 1995, p. P/1). He emphasised that he saw no need to tamper with the overall direction of reform, declaring 'Reform of reform is not on my agenda' *Agra Europe*, 3 March 1995, p. E/7). There were early signs, however, that it was not business as usual. Fischler resisted attempts to ease French set-aside penalties for domestic reasons, *Agra Europe* (13 April, 1995, p. P/3) commenting: 'It is unlikely that his predecessor, René Steichen, would have been quite so clear in closing the door on diluting the set-aside rules'. Fischler showed himself as willing to take on the Germans as the French. In May 1995 he issued an unusually strongly-worded statement rebuffing criticisms made by the German agricultural minister, which noted that 'The Commission is dismayed by the unwarranted aggressiveness and lack of objectivity shown by the German agriculture minister' (*Agra Europe*, 26 May 1995, p. E/4). In July he had the temerity to tell the annual congress of German farmers that farmers become more efficient and look for sources of income outside agriculture, remarks which brought his speech to a halt amid a cacophony of cat calls and cow bells. At the end of his first six months in office, he could look back on a productive period which had seen agreements on the agrimonetary system and animal welfare, and which also saw most of the implementation rules for the GATT agreement promulgated.

Having established himself, Fischler started to define his own agenda. In a speech in Bonn in October 1995, he noted that improving competitiveness was the decisive challenge for the future. Moreover, the EU should go further in the direction of a separation of market policy and income support. This was such a remarkable speech that it produced the unusual event of a signed article in *Agra Europe* by one of Europe's leading agricultural economists, Stefan Tangermann, calling Fischler's remarks 'breathtaking':

> A few years ago, it would [have] been hardly conceivable that a speech like that could have been given by a Farm Commissioner. Until well into the Uruguay Round negotiations, a significant reduction of export subsidies for farm products was considered completely unacceptable by EU policy makers . . . By contrast, today the EU Farm Commissioner can stand up and say the EU should change the CAP such that export subsidies are no longer needed – and remain in office. (*Agra Europe*, 20 October 1995)

Tangermann has subsequently suggested that Fischler's apparent change of attitude in 1995 was influenced from within DG VI, and in particular by the French director-general, Guy Legras. Tangermann hypothesies that Legras has been influenced by the views of the 'elite' French farmers who want to maximise production and export on world markets without restraints imposed by price support (House of Lords, 1996, p. 145). There is probably something in this hypothesis, although it may underplay the extent to which Fischler is his own man.

Fischler still wants to protect farm incomes, but he wants to achieve that goal in a more transparent way. In particular, 'Farmers must be rewarded for the positive environmental role they play and be encouraged to go further in the services they provide for the rural communities and society as a whole' (Fischler, 1996, p. 7). He has also stressed new ethical concerns, arguing that 'If agriculture is to continue to be successful, it must accept the new yardsticks used by consumers, based on questions of ecology and ethics, as quality criteria for the future' (Fischler, 1996, p. 10). One has not heard his predecessors talk in the way he has about animal welfare, referring to 'taking into account both the economic needs of those involved in the trade in animals as of the animals themselves' (Fischler, 1996, p. 11). In Fischler's view, animals have needs which are a legitimate concern of agricultural policy.

Fischler has explicitly rejected renationalisation of the CAP, arguing that it would undermine cohesion as well as environmental and rural development policies. He has, however, expressed a commitment to the decentralisation of the CAP and has opened up an entirely new and intriguing institutional possibility, the regionalisation of some aspects of the CAP. In Fischler's view, 'Not everything should be ruled from Brussels in a community that stretches from the arctic regions of Finland to the Aegean Islands of Greece' (*Agra Europe*, 13 October 1995, p. E/1). Fischler has posed a set of questions to which there are no easy answers but which merit further debate (for example, is he talking just about subregions of nation states or would he include cross-border regions?):

> Should there be a voice for the regions in how Agricultural Policy is administered? And if so, would such a move be compatible with the single market or would it lead to an increase of distortions between rich and poor regions? Are there safeguards which could be built into such a system, such as a strong community framework in which regions are given a measure of autonomy? How would Member States react to such a move? (Fischler, 1996, p. 4)

Despite his disavowal of renationalisation, Fischler's approach has some similarities to it, although it also reflects the argument put forward by the Bavarian agriculture minister, Reinhold Bocklet, who has argued for a role for subnational governments in making payments to farmers. Fischler appears to envisage that 'member states would have more executive control over subsidy payments to the farming sector. Under this de-centralised approach, the Commission would set the guidelines . . . and member states would be responsible for topping up the payments as they saw fit' (*Agra Europe*, 1 March 1996, p. P/3).

Commission services: DG VI

Excluding the DGs dealing with personnel and administration and with science, research and development (which employs scientific researchers), DG VI, the agriculture directorate-general has the largest staff in the Commission: 826 in 1991 (Page and Wouters, 1995, p. 194). For operational purposes, the directorate-general is subdivided into directorates and then into units. Three directorates (C, D and E) are concerned with commodity-specific market organisation. Thus, for example, Directorate C is concerned with crop products and has units concerned with cereals, rice, oilseeds and protein plants; animal feed, non-feed uses, cereal substitutes and dried fodder; sugar; and olive oil, olives and fibre plants. Two directorates (F1 and F2) are concerned with rural development. One directorate (G) deals with the Guidance and Guarantee Fund, covering fraud as well as general financial management. There are three directorates concerned with horizontal functional issues: agro-economic legislation, including quality policy (B.I); quality and health relating to crops and animal nutrition, including veterinary legislation (B.II); and co-ordination, simplification and promotion (F). Two directorates deal with external relations: A with the Parliament and the Economic and Social Committee (this directorate also covers statistics and information); and H with international affairs.

From 1997 it is expected that the veterinary office of DG VI will be reconstituted as an independent Veterinary and Phytosanitary Inspection and Control Agency operating from Ireland. The agency would operate as a specialised autonomous body responsible for the protection of public, animal and plant health. The European Parliament has pressed for an independent European Food Agency which would have a higher profile and broader role.

DG VI has the reputation of being a directorate general with a strong French influence: 'French civil servants were always appointed to the key bureaucratic jobs within DG-VI that controlled cereals policy' (Phillips, 1990, p. 51). Even in the 1990s, it was possible to refer to DG VI as 'an outpost of the Paris farm ministry' (*Financial Times*, 10 February 1993). All member states are, of course, represented in the staff of DG VI. The director-general (senior official) of DG VI in 1996 was a French citizen, Guy Legras. Regardless of its national composition, there are reasons why DG VI may tend towards maintaining the status quo within the CAP:

Normally so overwhelmed with the complex tasks of managing the various market regimes, they really do not have much time to consider new ideas which would change the CAP. Besides the possibility always exists that a proposal for change would further complicate the already difficult administrative burden, or shift the balance of power in an unsatisfactory way between different departments of the Directorate-General. (Moyer and Josling, 1990, pp. 52–3).

In order to manage the reform process during the MacSharry period, a small think tank of five people was set up within DG VI (Daugbjerg, 1996, p. 15). A more enduring source of proposals for change within the directorate is the Cabinet appointed by the commissioner. With little commitment to existing policies, they can explore new ideas for reform, paying 'more attention to political feasibility than the problems of policy implementation' (Moyer and Josling, 1990, p. 53). The choice of cabinet members is one of the more important decisions made by a commissioner at the start of his period of office, and concerns were expressed that Fischler's cabinet drew too much on (often young) Austrians with little knowledge of Brussels politics. It was felt that what some commentators saw 'as a relatively weak cabinet may not be in a position to form a counterbalance to senior figures in . . . DGVI' (*Agra Europe*, 9 December 1994, p. E/7). These concerns do not seem to have been borne out by Fischler's subsequent performance.

DG VI's relations with other directorates-general

In the 1960s and 1970s, DG VI had little competition from other directorates-general in its policy domain. In this period, 'Non-agricultural directorates . . . never had much influence on farm policy' (Phillips, 1990, p. 51). However, the picture changed as new directorates-general were created, such as those for the budget and the environment. In the 1980s, 'The evidence from the milk quota and stabilizers debates shows the EC Budget Commissioner as an increasingly important actor in CAP formulation' (Moyer and Josling, 1990, p. 209).

The reforms of the 1990s have been driven largely by international trade negotiations, so DG I (external affairs) has become a more central actor. The relationship between DG I and DG VI was not, however, always an easy one during the negotiations. This is not surprising when one considers that 'DG-VI is the only sectoral branch of the Commission "placed in the driver's seat in the actual conduct of negotiations." The directorate general for external affairs exercises this responsibility for all areas except agricultural trade' (Keeler, 1996, p. 137). Nevertheless, the external affairs directorate did have some input into the reform process:

It analysed reform papers prepared by the Agricultural Directorate to ensure that they did not violate the External Affairs Directorate's interest in concluding the GATT negotiations. The fact that the External Affairs Commissioner, Frans Andriessen, was the former Agriculture Commissioner and generally had a strong position within the Commission probably helped to ensure some influence of the External Affairs directorate. (Daugbjerg, 1996, p. 15).

Nevertheless, the underlying tensions between the missions of the two directorates re-emerged during discussions over implementation of the Uruguay Round, with DG VI emphasising the letter of the agreement, and DG I 'more anxious not to offend the US . . . sticking more closely to the spirit of the agreement (*Agra Europe*, 31 March 1995, p. P/4).

The Uruguay Round agreement also brought to the surface disagreements between DG VI and DG III, which looks after the food industry. The CAP covers first stage but not second stage food processing industries, the former being defined in Annex II of the Treaty of Rome, so that second stage processing is often referred to as 'non-Annex II products'. This came to the surface in 1995 in an argument about who should control the issue of non-Annex II export licences. This may appear to be nothing more than a bureaucratic turf fight, but in fact it has important implications for the operations of multionational companies. In order to compensate food companies for having to buy raw materials at high CAP prices, their products qualify for export refunds, and the EU was obliged to impose a limit under the GATT rules. However, processed food exports have increased substantially since the GATT base period of 1986–90. DG III argued that therefore these refunds should be kept under tighter control, while DG VI wanted to maintain the administratively convenient method of relating them to the cost of primary products. The removal of refunds for some high-value-added products 'would prompt multinational food companies to disinvest from the EU and seek cheaper raw materials in other countries, such as the Central and East European countries' (*Agra Europe*, 15 September 1995, p. E/1). The underlying issue here is that the administrative arrangements reflect the fact that there is a CAP rather than a common food policy which takes account of the importance of the food processing industry in the European economy.

The environment directorate, DG XI, has senior officials specifically concerned with agricultural questions, but remains a more peripheral actor in the formation of agricultural policy, reflected in the fact that agri-environmental programmes only account for 3 per cent of agricultural spending. Relations with DG XI may, however, change under Fischler, given his emphasis on environmental policy. At a conference on agriculture and the environment in 1995, Fischler was reported as being 'upbeat about the possibility of co-operation with DGXI, the Commission department with responsibility for environmental policy. It is widely accepted that there has been little such co-operation in the past (*Agra Europe*, 5 May 1995, p. E/7).

The college of commissioners

In general, the European Commission does not have such well-developed horizontal linkages between its different directorates-general as traditional national bureaucracies have between their different ministries. Although contacts are better developed than they were in the past, policy is still to a large extent formulated within the directorates-general, leaving differences to be resolved at a higher level. Sometimes it is possible for problems to be resolved at the meetings at chef de cabinet level. Conflicts between member states cannot, however, always be resolved at this level. In February 1996, a controversy over whether the label of feta cheese should be reserved for traditional regions of Greece, a major issue for the Danish dairy industry, led to a ten to nine vote in favour of the Commission proposal. The Greek chef de cabinet of Commission President Jacques Santer stayed away from the meeting. It was suggested that this because 'the Commission wanted to avoid a potentially embarrassing political snub at senior officer level. If the vote had been tied at 10–10 the proposal would automatically have been discarded and a new one drawn up' *Agra Europe*, 16 February 1996, p. E/5).

Although commissioners take an oath of office to serve the Union as a whole, in practice they seek to protect their national interests. The annual 'clearance of accounts' in the spring always causes some difficulties, as commissioners seek to reduce fines imposed against their national governments for various irregularities. A classic example occurred in the spring of 1996, when a fine imposed on Ireland for irregularities in the beef sector was reduced from 116 million to 86.9 million ECU: 'Franz Fischler had been opposed to any reduction, but faced pressure from at least seven of his fellow Commissioners to make some concession' (*Agra Europe*, 29 March 1996, p. E/5).

National bargaining does surface within the College of Commissioners, but not to the extent or with the intensity that it does in the Council of Ministers. Progress in the budget stabilisers debate in the late 1980s was made possible by an informal alliance between the President (Delors), the Agriculture Commissioner (Andriessen) and the Budget Commissioner (Christophersen). When this 'inner circle' agreed, 'other Commissioners could not easily demur, particularly since it represented most of the budgetary and agricultural expertise in the Commission and included the dossiers potentially most affected by reform' (Moyer and Josling, 1990, p. 87). There can be little doubt that 'The greatest problems in subordinating narrow interests have come at the level of the Council of Agricultural Ministers' (Moyer and Josling, 1990, p. 210). Before considering the work of the Council itself, it is necessary to consider the two main influences on the Council when it considers policy proposals from the Commission: the member states themselves and the farm lobby.

Member states

A general reform coalition can be discerned within the Council of Agricultural Ministers. Its most enthusiastic members are Britain and Sweden, but they can sometimes win support from Denmark and The Netherlands which have commercially-orientated agriculture. This is clearly, however, not a winning coalition. The positions of the other small Northern member states – Austria, Finland and the Republic of Ireland – are constrained by the high number of marginal farmers present in these countries. The Southern states, as was apparent from the discussion on commodity regimes in Chapter 5, have their own particular agendas to pursue. Italy's effective participation is often limited by the upheavals that occur frequently in the country's domestic politics. The two pivotal member states in the politics of the CAP are therefore France and Germany, and it can be argued that the single most important actor is Germany. As happened in the GATT round negotiations, Germany can exert influence on France to shift its position on agricultural policy issues. The consequences of unification also open up the possibility of change in Germany's traditional stance on agricultural policy matters. Particular attention will therefore be paid to Germany in the following discussion.

Any general model of the role of member states in the politics of the CAP needs to take account of at least three political variables (which have to be considered in the context of the economic structure of agriculture in the country concerned): the electoral system; the nature of intragovernmental, especially coalition, politics; and the relationship between the government and the farm lobby.

The electoral system

Two variables are important in relation to the electoral system: the frequency of elections, and the method of election used. Frequency of elections is an important variable because it is evident that an impending election constrains reform initiatives on agriculture. For example, uncertainty caused by the German election in the autumn of 1994 delayed a number of decisions in the Council of Agriculture Ministers on matters such as agrimonetary reform and the welfare of animals in transport. In 1995, care was taken not to schedule any meetings of the Agricultural Council until the French presidential elections had been held.

It might be asked why the attitudes of those engaged in agriculture should be regarded as significant in an election given that, in most member states, farmers are a small proportion of the total electorate. It is a common error to equate the 'farm vote' with the number of farmers, or even their families. Within rural economies, there is a range of providers of goods and services whose prosperity is dependent on the economic success of the farming community: for example, suppliers of inputs such as machinery, fertilisers, agrochemicals and seeds; auctioneers; and veterinary surgeons. First stage food processing facilities such as abbatoirs and dairies have close economic and personal links with the farming community. Even those businesses not directly engaged in the supply of agricultural services derive a considerable proportion of their income from the farming community. In those countries where industrialisation has been relatively recent, many families still have relatives living in the countryside, or can recall, often with a sentimental glow, their own rural origins: 'In

France, active farmers comprise only 4 per cent of the electorate, but one scholar has calculated that fully 17 per cent of the electorate possess a "strong agricultural attribute" . . . While the specific numbers differ across countries, this demographic multiplier effect is obviously politically relevant throughout the European Community' (Keeler, 1996, p. 130).

As far as the frequency of elections is concerned, the German system is of particular relevance. Land elections are held at regular intervals and are important not just because they can affect the composition of the provincial level of government, but also because they can influence control of the upper chamber, the Bundesrat. They are also seen as an indication of government popularity and may affect the internal balance of power within the coalition government. Germany's use of the veto on cereal prices in 1985 appears to have been influenced by 'the imminent *Land* elections in Bavaria in 1986' (Hendriks, 1991, p. 107). 'Particularly before elections, political decision-makers dreading demonstrations and protest actions by farmers have preferred strategies of conflict avoidance' (Heinze and Voelzkow, 1993, p. 29). The fact that there are sixteen länder ensures that there is no 'post-electoral moment' in Germany.

Of the different forms of electoral system used in Europe, the STV system in the Republic of Ireland attunes candidates to the concerns of particular blocs of voters. Candidates who support CAP reforms may be punished by the electorate, particularly in the west of Ireland, as the president of the Irish Farmers' Association found to his cost after he had backed the MacSharry reforms. A senior Irish civil servant commented in interview that the electoral system produced predominantly rural deputies representing particular interests whose concern was with the preservation of rural stability.

Coalition and intra-governmental politics

At any one time the majority of governments in the European Union are likely to have either coalition governments or governments that rely on tacit agreements with minor parties to sustain them in office. The principal exceptions to this pattern are Britain and France, and in the latter case there is always the possibility that the president may be from a different party than the majority in the legislature. Parties with an agrarian base, although small in terms of popular support or the number of seats held in the legislature, may be crucial to coalition formation. It should also be noted that eastern enlargement would increase the number of countries in the EU in which agrarian parties are politically significant, for example, Hungary, Poland.

The Free Democrats in Germany have been kept in existence by the list portion of the dual electoral system: 'German governments have been largely dependent on the decision of the FDP to form a coalition with one or other of the main parties' (Hendriks, 1991, p. 125). As part of its survival strategy, the FDP placed a greater emphasis on the farm vote, hoping to attract support from farmers who gave their constituency vote to the CDU or CSU. When the SDP/FDP coalition was formed in 1969, the FDP's 'right wing asked for a "price" in return for its support, which above all was favourable treatment for agriculture. The post of Minister of Agriculture was given to Ertl. He had been a key factor in enabling the FDP in Bavaria to keep above the crucial 5 per cent level of voters' support needed for parliamentary representation' (Hendriks, 1991, p. 129). He remained in office until 1983 and, as a consequence, came to exert a dominant influence in the Council of Agricultural Ministers (Swinbank, 1989, p. 305). Apparently, he was strongly disliked by the Danish farm commissioner, Finn Gundelach (Jenkins, 1989, p. 334). 'Even in public . . . Ertl, seemed often to be pursuing an independent line at odds with his Cabinet colleagues, even his fellow FDP ministers in the coalition government' (Swinbank, 1989, p. 304).

Ertl was succeeded by another Bavarian, Ignaz Kiechle, a member of the CSU (the Bavarian ally of the CDU) who remained in office until 1993. A dairy farmer, 'Kiechle, in his turn . . . proved just as tenacious as Ertl in protecting the interests of German farmers' (Swinbank, 1989, p. 306). In 1985 he used the Luxembourg Compromise to veto an increase in cereal prices, even though it was open to question how far such an action, welcome though it was to agricultural interests, fitted in to Germany's broader European objectives.

In 1993, Kiechle was replaced by Borchert, the first non-Bavarian to hold the agricultural portfolio for over twenty years and seen as 'more supportive of liberal CAP reforms' (Keeler, 1996, p. 144). Although Borchert placed a new emphasis on objectives of efficiency and competitiveness in a statement entitled 'Der küntifge Weg' ('The Future Way') issued when he took office, political realities meant that he also had to be ready to mount a traditional defence of German agricultural interests. In a speech in December 1995, admittedly directed at a domestic farm audience, Borchert set himself against the reform consensus in the Council of Agricultural Ministers by declaring that further reform of the CAP was not necessary to meet the twin challenges of eastern enlargement and the liberalisation of agricultural trade.

Nevertheless, the structural changes in German agriculture resulting from unification may in time lead to a change in the balance of German domestic interests and hence Germany's stance in the Council of Ministers. As an agriculture ministry official told Malhan, 'the whole discussion about the structure of agriculture all over Germany is increasing again as a result of German unification' (Malhan, 1996, p. 251). Malhan concludes that unification has produced continuity rather than change in Germany's stance on issues such as CAP reforms:

> The old structures governing agricultural policy-making have continued to exert influence over policy decisions and the traditional protectionist stance propounded by these structures has continued after unification. The advent of a new CDU Agricultural Minister, Jochen Borchert, has not altered that path either. The tradition that farmers have a special position in society and need to be aided and protected is one which transcended many turbulent changes in agriculture: unification has not upset that tradition. (Malhan, 1996, p. 265)

However, as Malhan recognises, the debate about the nature of agriculture has changed, as it is no longer possible to insist that a normal family farm is about 20 hectares or that one cannot farm with more than eighty cattle. At the moment, this debate is principally at an expert level. Tangermann has drawn attention to the existence of this expert debate, noting that 'It is often the case that what the farmers' union says later becomes the position of the Federal Government on agricultural policy' (House of Lords, 1996, p. 144). Tangermann notes that the Deutsche Landwirtschaft Gesellschaft (the German Agricultural Society) which 'represents the more managerial and entrepreneurial farmers, usually the larger ones' has issued 'a very strong statement about the inadequacy of the Common Agricultural Policy' (House of Lords, 1996, p. 145).

As Tangermann emphasises, 'The official position of the German Government is pretty traditional and conservative when it comes to changes in the CAP' (House of Lords, 1996, p. 144). One of the political blockages to change is the strength of the CSU, which ensures that the particular interests of Bavarian farmers are protected carefully. While the Bavarians no longer hold the agriculture ministry, it is difficult to see it being held by someone from one of the new länder. Tangermann notes that 'As long as the undercurrent of new thinking does not get to the level where it can change the mind of the Bonn Government, it is unlikely to be effective when it comes to making decisions on the [CAP]' (House of Lords, 1996, p. 145). In the longer run, however, the changes in the structure of German agriculture might start to influence Germany's position on the CAP.

The continuities in the domestic politics of German agriculture are illustrated by the fact that over a period of nearly thirty years, Germany had just three farm ministers. In the two years to 1995, Britain had four agriculture ministers (Gummer, Shephard, Waldegrave and Hogg). In part, this reflects a high rate of ministerial turnover in Britain's single-party governments than in most coalition governments. It also reflects the fact that the agriculture ministry under Conservative governments has often served as a way station for ambitious ministers. No minister wants to stay there too long, because like the Home Office, it is a ministry where sudden crises can develop from which it is difficult to derive much credit. Three of the four Conservative ministers were members of the so-called 'East Anglian mafia', with constituencies in the large scale and prosperous arable farming areas, a factor which may have some influence on British government attitudes towards issues such as modulation. Labour ministers have been drawn from more peripheral rural areas in the west and north of Britain.

Farm organisations at the member state level

Only a few member states have organisations representing farmers which come close to enjoying a representational monopoly. The clearest example is Sweden:

> Without exaggeration, the Federation of Swedish Farmers can be described as the most encompassing interest organization in Sweden. It includes all categories of farmers among its union membership, as well as people who identify with the countryside. It also represents the entire farmers' cooperative movement. Thus, as the peak organization for farmers, it has influence over food production from seeds, to soil, to wholesalers, and through a large part of the food processing industry. (Micheletti, 1987, p. 178)

In Germany, the Deutscher Bauernverband (DBV) achieves structural unity by functioning as an umbrella organisation for both Land level bodies and functionally specialised organisations: 'There is no doubt that the DBV is one of the most powerful interest groups in West Germany. Demands and objectives articulated by the DBV have effectively determined crucial decisions taken by the Federal Government and influenced its position . . . at European level' (Hendriks, 1991, p. 144). The threat of rapid structural change seems to have enhanced the DBV's cohesion, maintaining its monopoly of representation in the face of the emergence of as yet small competing organisations (Heinze and Voelzkow, 1993).

In Britain, the representational hegemony of the National Farmers' Union, and the associated farmers' organisations in Scotland and Northern Ireland, has been eroded to some extent by the development of a separate organisation in Wales which is particularly strong in Welsh-speaking areas, and the emergence of a Tenant Farmers' Association. An alternative small farmers' association, the Northern Ireland Agricultural Producers' Association, was set up in 1975 after the fall of the Stormont regime (Greer, 1996, p. 114). In general, however, the strength of the principal farmers' organisations has rested on their close, if sometimes contentious, working relationship with the agriculture departments in London, Edinburgh and Belfast. Britain is, however, the only member state (apart from Italy under the Prodi centre–left government) where there has been discussion of dissolving the separate agriculture ministry or at least reconstituting it as a Department of Rural Affairs with a broader mandate. Prime Ministers Thatcher and Major gave assurances that this would not happen under their governments, but the idea might be revived by a future Labour government, with profound implications for the influence capacity of the farmers' organisations.

In most member states, however, farmers' organisations are divided. Farm organisations are differentiated in terms of militancy (France), partisanship (Greece) and confessional affiliation (The Netherlands), but the most pervasive division is that of farm size, particularly in those countries where marginal farms have not been squeezed out of existence. Spain has three national associations affiliated to COPA. ASAJA represents large and middle-sized farms; COAG is a federation of middle-sized and small farms found in modernised and intensive farming areas such as the Catalonian coast; and UPA represents small farmers in less-favoured areas such as Galicia, and part-time farmers with working class backgrounds.

ASAJA is linked to the Spanish employers' organisation, and some of its smaller members have broken away to form a fourth organisation (Iniciavita Rural) because of this link. UPA, in contrast, is the agricultural branch of one of the two main Spanish trade unions, while COAG also leans to the left (Estrada, 1995, pp. 351–2). Similarly, in Portugal, the organisation representing large and middle-sized landowners is linked to the parties of the right and left, while the organisation representing smaller farmers is connected to the left (Estrada, 1995, p. 352).

These partisan links can also be found in Italy. Of the two small farmers' organisations founded after the war, Coldiretti was linked to the Christian Democrats, while Confoltivattori (later CIA, Conferdrazione Italiana Agricoltori) was linked to the left. The interest of large-scale landowners was looked after by Confagricultura. However, as Italian politics has changed in the post-Cold War era, the tensions between the organisations have lessened and they have started to have joint meetings of their executives. Thus, 'the three agricultural organizations remain autonomous but they tend to present themselves to the outside world with a unanimous line of action' (Capo, 1995, p. 306). In Greece, the close integration of the two principal farmers' organisations with the parties of the right and left meant that 'the co-operatives monopolised the conduct of the formal relations between the farmers and the State for a long period of time' (Goussios and Zacopoulou, 1990, p. 35). Hence, the federation of co-operatives has a more central role in the representation of farmers' interests than in other member states.

In Denmark, a historical cleavage between farmers and smallholders led to the formation of different organisations for the two groups. However, they are integrated into an Agricultural Council which also organises agribusiness associations and some more specialised bodies (Just, 1990). In the Republic of Ireland, the Irish Farmers' Association is the leading representative organisation but its representative monopoly is challenged by the Limerick based Irish Creamery Suppliers Association. There is quite a strong rivalry between the two bodies (Collins, 1995).

French farmers have drawn on a tradition of *jacqurie* (or peasant revolt) which goes back to the fourteenth century. A close corporatist relationship between the main farm organisation, the FNSEA and successive French governments (Keeler, 1987) has co-existed with a tradition of militant demonstrations. In 1991, however, Co-ordination Rurale broke away from FNSEA, complaining it was too moderate. In the view of Co-ordination Rurale leaders, the FNSEA was 'the government's lackey' and its demonstrations amounted to the 'equivalent of "taking tea with the local (government) prefect"' (*Financial Times*, 20 September 1993). One underlying cause of this split was that some farmers in the French wheat belt had borrowed heavily to invest in the farms on the basis of CAP support prices and then found it difficult to service their debts. Co-ordination Rurale spearheaded French opposition to the MacSharry and GATT reforms, seeking to draw support from all sections of the rural community, not just farmers. In September 1993 it organised a 'blockade' of Paris which, however, caused only marginal disruption to transport routes. The French Government gave Co-ordination Rurale 'the cold shoulder, partly because of its occasionally violent tactics and partly in deference to the mainstream FNSEA . . . which fears CR eating away at its membership' (*Financial Times*, 20 September 1993).

In The Netherlands, the three farmers' associations organised around the country's religious–ideological 'pillars' came together in a corporatist Board of Agriculture (the *Landbouwschap*). Recent developments in Dutch agriculture have, however, undermined this overarching structure of unity. These developments have a significance beyond The Netherlands, given the transformation elsewhere of farmers' cooperatives into agribusinesses. Frouws and Ettema point out (1994, p. 106): 'it is the farmers' relations to the co-operative and private agribusiness which, to a large and increasing extent, are determining their interests. Traditional, horizontal farmers' unions have always neglected these relations'. By organising their own political lobby, the large co-operatives have undermined the co-ordinating role of the *Landbouwschap*.

Saturated markets and limited budgets have intensified competition, and conflict between different sectors of agriculture in The Netherlands has led to the formation of separate organisations for arable farmers and pig producers. Frouws and Ettema argue that such isolated sectoral lobbies would be weaker than general farmers' unions. The small scale of most farming enterprises and their location in a regional context are unifying factors. Hence, they envisage a matrix form of organisation in which there is more scope for product based interest representation within general horizontal organisations. Such a pattern seems likely to develop in the Northern member states, but in the Southern states, conflicts between different sizes of farm and contrasting partisan linkages still have to be overcome. In France, militancy is likely to continue to be a way of life for farmers as long as they enjoy a high level of support from domestic public opinion.

Farmers' organisations at the European level

The Commission assisted the formation of the European farmers' organisation, Comité des Organisations Professionnelles Agricoles (COPA), which works closely with the federation of agricultural co-operatives, Comité Genéral de la Coopération Agricole des Pays de la Communauté (COGECA). Young farmers' organisations are influential in some member states and they are organised through the Committee of European Young Farmers (CEJA), which is represented on the COPA praesidium. Small and family farmers are organised through the Coordination Paysanne Europeene (CPE). COPA is by far the most important of these organisations: 'It currently employs a full-time staff of forty-five, while most Euro associations get by with one or two officials' (Keeler, 1996, p. 134).

Although the influence of the farm lobby is part of the legend of the CAP, most analysts are agreed that its influence has declined since the 1970s, when it was consulted about price packages even before they were submitted to the governments of member states (Gray, 1989, p. 220). This reflects both the increased strain placed on the CAP as its budgetary cost became unsustainable, and the increasing divergence of the interests of COPA members as new member states joined. It thus became difficult to maintain internal cohesion with COPA as the organisation sought to respond to a series of CAP reform proposals. In order to maintain its influence with the Commission, COPA could not simply dismiss reform proposals, but it then had to justify its stance to its member organisations, who were in turn under pressure from their more militant members. Perhaps earlier successes had engendered a sense of complacency, with Gray reporting (1989, p. 223) that 'Some Commission officials feel that COPA "has stood on its laurels far too long" and no longer deserves to be regarded as a success story'. Phillips (1990, p. 72) goes so far as to argue that COPA 'was pushed to the margins of the European debate'. An internal report in autumn 1996 was highly critical of the organisation's effectiveness.

In the summer of 1994, André Herlitska, secretary general of COPA since 1958, was replaced by Daniel Guengen, who came from an agribusiness background as director general of the European Committee for Sugar Manufacturers. His appointment was followed by efforts to revitalise COPA in an attempt to dispel its 'lacklustre and rather negative reputation' (*Agra Europe*, 9 June 1995, p. E/5), relaunching itself under the presidency of Sir David Naish, formerly president of the English and Welsh NFU. Naish questioned whether the requirement of unanimity in internal decision-making was feasible in an enlarged Europe. COPA also declared that it would make a more constructive effort to influencing policy. This was clearly necessary given the flawed logic of some COPA statements. On the agrimonetary system, COPA declared that farmers should not have to live with the vagaries of the currency markets as did all other industrial sectors, because green rate revaluations had an immediate price-cutting effect (*Agra Europe*, 13 April 1995, p. E/5). This overlooked the fact that the reason they had such an effect was the reliance of many farmers on sales into intervention, an option that motor manufacturers, for example, do not have. On eastern enlargement, COPA stated that it 'must in no way put the current level of agricultural support in the EU in question' (*Agra Europe*, 21 April 1995, p. E/3). Such statements suggests that much not had changed since the 1980s when Commission officials considered 'that COPA has its hands tied by its members . . . For many officials, COPA's arguments have remained unchanged and do not show how they are dealing reasonably with the reality of oversupply, budgetary crisis and the demand for lower prices for agricultural raw materials' (Gray, 1989, p. 223).

The continuing difficulties faced by COPA were reflected in the surprise resignation of the secretary-general, Daniel Gueguen, in March 1996. No reasons were given, although it was confirmed that his contract was due for renewal in the summer of 1996 (*Agra Europe*, 1 March 1996, p. E/6). A demonstration by around a thousand farmers in Luxembourg over the BSE crisis in June 1996, in which thick black smoke was produced by the burning of tyres as farm ministers ate their lunch, provoked arguments about whether it was organised by COPA or the French Union (*Farmers Weekly*, 28 June 1996). In any event, it was mainly French, German and Italian farmers who turned up, Scottish farmers claiming that Luxembourg was a difficult place to get to, illustrating the difficulties of mobilising farmers from across Europe.

Nevertheless, COPA remains more influential than the economically more significant agribusiness lobby. For example, at a meeting with Franz Fischler in September 1995, the European Agrifood Trade Association, CELCAA, asked the EU to hold consultations with the agrifood trade and involve them more in the formation of EU agricultural policy (*Agra Europe*, 15 September 1995, p. E/4). The chair of the trade and economic committee of the European Dairy Association complained that Commission officials were not prepared to listen to its arguments, and that key points were only accepted by the Commission after interventions in the Council of Ministers (*Agra Europe*, 27 October 1995, p. E/2).

One of the principal weaknesses of the agribusiness sector is its heterogeneity. Even if one leaves aside the various input industries such as machinery and agrochemicals, the first stage and second stage sectors of the food processing industry have different interests relation to the CAP. The Confédération des Industries Agricoles et Alimentaires (CIAA) has not been strongly resourced and is relatively uninfluential.

If there is one grouping of individuals that has had a greater influence on policy formation in recent years it has been the agricultural economists. They may not have caused the paradigm shift in approaches to CAP reform, but their ideas were available when new approaches were needed, while organisations such as COPA were seeking to defend the ancient regime. Although Tangermann, one of the most influential agricultural economists in the EU, argues, no doubt correctly, that academic arguments had little direct influence on the policy process 'they may have found their way into actual policy considerations through the activities of the OECD'. The OECD work showed that price support 'was less effective in supporting farm incomes than agricultural policy-makers had tended to believe, and that a mutual and balanced reduction of support in all countries would be less harmful for farm incomes than what politicians might have thought' (Tangermann, 1996, p. 7). In the context of the Uruguay Round negotiations, the message that policy change with less pain than was expected might be possible was a welcome one, and tended to be more influential than the defensive posturings of the farm lobby.

The Council of Agricultural Ministers

All these pressures come to bear on the Council of Agriculture Ministers, where the various national concerns emerging from domestic politics have to be moulded into a series of tolerable compromises. Such a process of intergovernmental bargaining in response to domestic political pressures invariably produces suboptimal policies and at times of crisis it has been necessary for matters to be referred upwards to the European Council of heads of government for resolution.

Meetings of the Council of Agriculture Ministers are prepared for by the Special Committee on Agriculture (SCA), the agricultural equivalent of COREPER made up of senior permanent officials from the member states plus a Commission representative. The SCA sets up 'a whole series of specialist committees . . . to examine the detailed technical issues that inevitably arise in examining Commission proposals. Thus dozens, if not hundreds, of national civil servants regularly commute from their national capitals to Brussels to serve this committee structure' (Swinbank, 1996a, p. 12). In practice, a 'close informal working relationship usually exists between the SCA and the Commission' (Moyer and Josling, 1990, p. 34). Matters may be considered by specialist working parties before the SCA attempts to reach a consensus. The SCA seeks to ensure that as many points as possible on the crowded agenda are 'A' points, which can be adopted formally by the Council. Matters on which it is not possible to reach agreement in the Council may be referred back to the SCA.

The Council of Agriculture Ministers is distinguished from other councils by the frequency and length of its meetings, which often extend into the early hours of the morning. A Council that starts on Monday afternoon can last until Thursday. It has to make more legislative decisions: more than twice as many as any other Council in the period from December 1993 to March 1995. Many compromises taken by 'exhausted farm ministers after days and negotiations at a marathon Council' (*Agra Europe*, 23 June 1995, p. E/11) often turn out to be a nightmare to implement. For example, increased spending on dehydrated fodder has helped Southern states, but has to led to arguments about the definition of sun-dried and dehydrated material (if fodder spends some time in an oven is it still sun dried?). Northern states have attempted to redeem their losses by classifying grass cut from airports, road verges and golf courses as dried fodder.

Swinbank argues (1989, p. 304) that the Agriculture Council is more of a 'club' than the other councils, although as the EU grows in size, this feature is likely to diminish in importance. Nevertheless, 'for "core" CAP business I think it could still be claimed it is the Council *for* Agriculture' (Personal communication, Alan Swinbank, 11 April 1996). Particularly difficult issues may be tackled at informal dinner discussions or in special restricted sessions (minister plus one adviser). Despite the use of various mechanisms to reach agreement, the Agriculture Council exhibits a greater propensity to vote than any of the other major Councils. Of 114 legislative acts adopted by the Council between December 1993 and March 1995, just under a quarter were adopted on the basis of a qualified majority vote: ten with abstentions only, and seventeen with votes cast against (European Council, 1995, p. 53).

On one occasion, it appeared that it might be necessary to invoke the Ioaninna Compromise. This was a concession secured by Britain over voting rights in the enlarged EU, when it was proposed to raise the blocking minority threshold in the Council from twenty-three to twenty-six. Under the compromise, if there are between twenty-three and twenty-six votes in the minority, a member state can call on the presidency to continue discussions on the matter for a 'reasonable time'. Britain invoked the compromise in October 1995 when it found itself forming a minority of twenty-four votes with Sweden and Italy in opposition to a proposal to allow member states to compensate their farmers for currency devaluations. The Commission agreed a concession under which it would review payments after a year to see if they were still necessary. As a consequence, Sweden withdrew its objection and the UK changed its position to abstain.

The then Spanish president claimed afterwards that the 'Ioaninna compromise had worked as an institutional mechanism as it had secured a compromise among member states' (*Agra Europe*, 27 October 1995, p. E/5). However, other member states thought it was inappropriate to invoke the compromise over a matter that had already been agreed as part of a larger package, while Commission sources suggested that the concession won by the UK was a minor one. However, the very existence of this measure does make securing compromises within the Council an even more delicate and difficult task.

A crucial role in securing agreement is played by the presidency of the Council, which rotates among member states every six months. It is generally thought more advantageous to be president in the first six months of the year, which is not interrupted by the August holiday break, and when the annual price package has to be settled. Presidencies tend to be evaluated in terms of their technical competence in chairing meetings and discharging business, and, even more important, their ability to broker compromises between different political interests.

Some presidencies are more successful than others, and chairing and co-ordinating the wide range of committees and working parties can be more of a strain for smaller states. In the case of Belgium, domestic political tensions can affect the operational effectiveness of a Belgian presidency: 'Although a wide package of measures was finally tied up at the December 1993 Agriculture Council [at the end of the Belgian presidency], this took an awfully long time and was achieved at the cost of considerable expense in "sweeteners" to every member state. Belgium . . . singularly failed to achieve the principal aims of its presidency' (*Agra Europe*, 30 June 1995, p. N/6). The Italian presidency in the first half of 1996 was rated as 'unimpressive in the agricultural sector, but this has mainly been due to the change of government in the middle of the six-month term, which brought policy developments more or less to a standstill' *Agra Europe*, 28 June 1996, p. P/8). Italy came close to abolishing its agriculture ministry under the Prodi government, but decided to retain it because of the need for a strong presence in Brussels. The Irish presidency in second half of 1996 was anticipated favourably because of its skill in brokering compromises in the agricultural arena, a reputation quickly justified by its resolution of the impasse on fruit and vegetable reform. Member states will, of course, seek to use the presidency to advance their own agendas. Hence, the Spanish presidency in the second half of 1995 emphasised fruit and vegetable reform, but was thought to have given a low priority to eastern enlargement (*Agra Europe*, 3 November 1995, p. P/5).

As Nugent observes (1991, p. 351), 'Of all the Councils, the Agriculture Council is the one most reliant on issue linkages and package deals for conducting its business.' Every member state, even Luxembourg, wants something from the Council, and has to be prepared to make concessions elsewhere to secure what it wants. Given the weakness of the reform coalition in the Council, progress in terms of changing the nature of the CAP really depends on the assent of France and Germany, and sometimes on Germany exerting pressure on France. Germany thus has a pivotal role in the Council, but that does not mean it always gets its own way. Of course, what amounts to an acceptable outcome for a member state is not always easy to judge. German farmers were angry when, in 1995, both the Agriculture and ECOFIN councils rejected their government's plans to compensate farmers for income losses through the VAT system. However, 'Like other farm ministers, Borchert is also keen to blame politically unpalatable decisions on Brussels even when, as in the case of the VAT request, it was clear from the outset that the German proposal would never be acceptable' (*Agra Europe*, 8 December 1995, p. P/4).

Atkin argues (1993, p. 70) that, even discounting the effects of domestic political pressures, one should not expect good decisions from the Agriculture Council. Policy benefits are received by farmers in the member state, while the costs can be passed on to consumers or overseas producers. The Council of Agriculture Ministers still works to a large extent in an insulated decision-making process, but one whose assumptions and policies have been subject to increasing challenge, both from within and outside the EU. Hence, 'business as usual' in the form of elaborate compromises has continued in parallel with efforts to achieve systematic reform.

The European Parliament

The European Parliament is one body that one might expect to represent Third-World, consumer or more general public interests in relation to agricultural policy, and indeed it tries to do so. It is, however, a relatively marginal player in the decision-making process on the CAP. As Gardner comments (1996, p. 11):

> With its presented limited role in the legislative process, the Parliament can . . . have little direct effect on the development of policy. The consultation process introduced under the Single Act does allow it to delay measures which it does not like, but the airing of criticisms of the development of policy within the agriculture and other committees is a far more important influence on the decision-makers.

Specialist agricultural publications such as *Agra Europe* devote considerable space each week to the activities of the management committees, but mention the European Parliament relatively infrequently. At the heart of its lack of influence is the way in which the agricultural budget is decided. As a report from a group of MEPs notes:

> EU expenditure is divided into two categories: compulsory
> expenditure (CE) and non-compulsory expenditure (NCE). The
> European Parliament has little or no say over compulsory
> expenditure and until now could not even decide what constitutes
> or does not constitute CE. Agricultural spending, which accounts
> for 50% of the Budget, is compulsory. This effectively means that
> the EP has no say over 50% of the Budget other than to reject the
> Budget as a whole. (Land Use and Food Policy Inter-Group, 1995,
> p. 13)

It is on matters that lie outside agricultural policy as conventionally defined where the Parliament may be able to exert the greatest
influence. The biotechnology industry suffered a major setback in
March 1995 when the European Parliament rejected draft legislation
on the patenting of new plants and genetically altered animals. This
was the first time the Parliament had used its Maastricht treaty
powers to reject a compromise text agreed by representatives from the
Parliament and the Council of Ministers under the co-decision
procedure. The MEPs directly involved thought they had achieved
an acceptable compromise, but it was voted down 'following heavy
lobbying from environmental and animal welfare groups' (*Agra
Europe*, 3 March 1995, p. P/5).

Within the Parliament, farming interests are well represented on
the Agriculture, Fisheries and Rural Development committee whose
recommendations may be influenced by national electoral considerations. They are, however, often counter-balanced by those of the
budgets committee. For example, in 1995, the European Parliament
preferred the advice of the budgets committee over that of the
agriculture committee, which had recommended that all agricultural
prices should be increased by 1 per cent, complaining that agriculture's share of the budget was 'only' 49 per cent.

The weakness of the European Parliament in relation to the CAP
reflects a lack of democratic accountability in the decision-making
procedures of the EU as a whole. An experienced food industry
lobbyist commented, 'once something gets into the decision-making
procedure, such as the CAP, it escapes the normal political influencing factors and becomes the province of the experts (especially the
officials) and the Ministers who . . . all want something from the
system so horse trade up the spoils' (Anonymous personal communication, 9 May 1996).

Management committees

Management committees exist for each of the principal farm product groupings (see Table 6.2). The need for such committees arises from the fact that the day-to-day implementation of the CAP is delegated from the Council to the Commission. The Commission is obliged to consult them in areas where responsibility has been delegated to it: for example, export refunds. Just what should be delegated may become the subject of dispute. For example, in 1995 the Commission suggested that future decisions on the rate of set aside should be taken by the management committee, an option that would maximise Commission influence on the matter. Member state representatives in the Special Committee on Agriculture took the view that fixing set aside should continue to be treated as a political rather than a technical decision, a view endorsed by the European Parliament.

DG VI services and chairs the management committees, which are made up of civil servants from the member states, exercising the same number of votes as the member state would have in the Council of Ministers. Servicing the management committees 'represents a major portion of the workload of the officials employed in the commodity divisions in DG VI' (Swinbank, 1989, p. 316). This rather demanding

TABLE 6.2

Management committees in agriculture, 1996

Name of committee	Frequency of meetings
Agrimonetary	As required
Beef	Monthly
Cereals	Twice a month
Dairy	Twice a month
Dried fodder, peas and beans	As required
Fruit and vegetables*	Monthly
Non-Annex II products	Monthly
Olive oil	Monthly
Pigmeat	Monthly
Poultry	Monthly
Sheepmeat	Once or twice a month
Sugar	Twice a month

Note: Meeting frequencies are subject to variation, but the two most important committees (cereals and dairy) generally meet twice a month.
* There are separate committees for fresh and processed fruit and vegetables, but these generally meet jointly.

administrative chore is, however, important to DG VI's control of its organisational turf: 'This "control" of the management committee procedure tends to strengthen the hand of DG VI in CAP policy implementation, in comparison to other DGs with legitimate interests' (Swinbank, 1989, p. 317).

National interests come to the surface in management committees just as in other parts of the decision-making process. The author has had an opportunity to observe this tendency as the UK representative on a minor management committee in an area other than agriculture. Various devices may be used to secure desired outcomes: for example, claiming that the German text on a proposed decision is fuller than an inadequate English one, on the assumption that the UK representative will not be able to read German. Many of the matters discussed in the agriculture management committees do raise matters of national concern, albeit in a limited sphere.

For example, at a meeting of the fresh fruit and vegetables committee in March 1996, a draft proposal to impose import licences on apples, pears and tomatoes from third countries was the subject of intense discussion. Tomatoes were deleted from the draft, as a product that was not available for twelve months of the year, while lemons were added at the insistence of the Italians and the Spanish. The committee delivered a 'no opinion' vote by a majority of forty-one votes to twenty-six, with twenty abstentions (*Agra Europe*, 29 March, 1996, p. P/ii). Unless there is a negative opinion from a committee, in which case the matter has to be referred back to the Council, the Commission can approve such draft regulations through its internal procedures and publish them in the Official Journal to bring them into force.

What happens in the management committees is of more direct interest to food processors and traders than to farmers, who are more concerned with the general level of support prices and compensatory payments. Table 6.3 contains a sample of decisions taken by management committees in March 1996. Matters such as import licences, destination codes and export refunds are highly technical, but they also have a direct impact on the profitability of food processors and traders: 'Timely knowledge of forthcoming changes to export refunds . . . can be of significant value to the recipient' (Swinbank, 1989, p. 318). From the perspective of the second stage food processing and trading sectors, the operation of the management committees is another example of the way in which the decision-making process is biased in favour of the concerns of farmers, and, to some extent, first

TABLE 6.3

Examples of decisions taken by management committees, March 1996

Cereals and oilseeds
Bids accepted for open market export tenders to third countries.
Historical yield figures used in calculating arable aid payments were changed for three member states and one German Land.

Dairy
Butter intervention reopened in the Republic of Ireland.
Aids for the private storage of Greek cheese set.

Fruit and vegetables
Committee voted on procedures for issuing refund certificates for subsidised exports.
Germany called for a higher quota for canned mushrooms.

Olive oil
Export refund levels were set.
Committee voted to amend the regulation relating to the import of olive oil from Tunisia.

Poultry
Destination code for boneless turkeymeat was changed to exclude the former Soviet Republics as well as the USA and East/Central Europe.
Inconclusive discussion on simplification of egg sizes.

Sheepmeats
Tariff quotas increased for Australia, New Zealand and Chile.
Discussion on fraudulent import of sheep and goats that are not pure bred, to evade higher rates of duty.

Sugar
Export tender awards accepted.
Production levies for 1995/6 set.

stage processors, which are often the instrument of agricultural policy. More generally, 'the existence of the committees does mean that the member states have a direct input into, and ultimately a control over, all but the fine details of agricultural policy and the management of that policy' (Nugent, 1991, p. 355).

Court of Justice

'Literally hundreds of cases concerning the CAP, and trade in food and agricultural products, go before the Court; and lawyers specialising in the CAP are in heavy demand' (Swinbank, 1996a, p. 20). One of the most famous cases to come before the Court of Justice, the Cassis de Dijon case of 1979, concerned a foodstuff. It produced a ruling that any product lawfully produced and marketed in any one member state must, in principle, be admitted on the market of any other member state, subject only to narrow exceptions justified objectively, such as public health. When the UK government asked the Court to lift the ban of exports of British beef, the Court ruled against the UK on the grounds of the paramount importance of the protection of health. Given that British Euro sceptics see the Court as the institution which most actively promotes the 'federal' character of the EU, there was a certain irony in the UK government seeking its protection.

When the normal political bargaining processes within the Commission and the Council of Ministers produce an outcome that member states find unacceptable, they may resort to the Court of Justice. In June 1996, the European Commission adopted a regulation designed to offer trademark protection to a list of agricultural products, many with a traditional association with particular geographical areas. In particular, it was decided that countries other than Greece producing feta cheese could no longer market it under that name. Denmark is traditionally a major producer of feta cheese, while it is also produced by France and Germany. These three countries took the matter to the Court in September 1996. In parallel, the Danish Dairy Board and MD Foods, along with a number of German feta producers, challenged the Commission's decision in the Court of First Instance under Article 173 of the Treaty which covers matters of direct or individual concern affecting a natural or legal person (*Agra Europe*, 20 September 1996, p. E/3). Whether or not the two matters are combined, a ruling is not expected before 1998.

As with other aspects of EU policy, decisions that have been carefully negotiated, both within the EU and outside it, may be overturned by the European Court of Justice. For example, under the Blair House agreement between the EU and the United States, corn gluten could be imported into the EU duty free. France challenged this decision in the Court of Justice on highly technical grounds and the Court found in its favour, also ruling that the Commission had acted incorrectly in amending a Council regulation on technical definitions of corn gluten under its own authority.

'Not for the first time, Commission officials have been presented with a major policy headache as a result of a Court of Justice ruling'

(*Agra Europe*, 15 December, 1995, p. P/3). The agreement on corn gluten was a key element in the Blair House agreement which made possible a Uruguay Round settlement on agriculture. The USA saw the ruling as further evidence of EU protectionism, while COC-ERAL, the organisation of European feed and grain traders, saw the decision of the Court as posing great problems for its members. The Commission was thus faced with working out a new solution on the issue, which, although technically possible, would have to satisfy the French, the Americans and the Court of Justice. Decisions by the Court of Justice can thus add an additional element of uncertainty to an already complex and unpredictable decision-making process, although a counter-argument is that the Court offsets the unpredictability and possible unconstitutionality of the Commission and Council.

Conclusions

If one asks the question 'Who benefits from the EU's decision-making processes on the CAP?', then the clear answer in budgetary terms is France, followed by Germany. France received just under a quarter of EAGGF spending in 1994, nearly eight billion ECU in total, followed by Germany with 5.17 billion ECU. However, both these countries are net contributors to the EU budget, notably Germany, whose net payments exceeded receipts by 13 637 million ECU in 1994. Spain is the third largest beneficiary from EAGGF, and a net beneficiary overall, but, as noted in the previous chapter, the Southern member states have not done as well from the CAP as they might have hoped. The Republic of Ireland has done rather well, with EU aid accounting for an average 41 per cent of farm incomes (*Agra Europe*, 3 November 1995, p. N/3). The Northern states with efficient farm sectors, such as Britain, Denmark, The Netherlands and Sweden, have less interest in the CAP as it is constituted at present, but cannot, by themselves, secure reform. Indeed, Denmark has traditionally been a supporter of the CAP and is not a net contributor to the EU budget as a whole. This differentiates its position from The Netherlands, which is becoming increasingly concerned at the steady rise in its EU net budget contributions, by far the largest for a small member state. A report from senior officials in the Dutch Finance, Agriculture and Foreign Affairs ministries called for farm subsidies to be abolished and to be replaced by direct income aids for farmers, ideally paid for by the member states themselves (*Agra Europe*, 19 January 1996, p. E/4).

France and Germany are unlikely to consent to any changes in the CAP, which threaten their interests fundamentally. France continues to exert a substantial influence within DG VI, but MacSharry and Fischler have shown what a skilled commissioner can achieve in terms of reorientating policy. In the longer run, it is Germany's position that is crucial. Both its broader manufacturing trade interests, and the change in its internal agricultural structure after unification, may edge Germany in the direction of a policy that is more orientated towards efficiency and competitiveness in agriculture.

7

The Reform Imperative: Eastern Enlargement, Trade and the Environment

Although the MacSharry reforms represent the first real progress towards significant revision of the CAP since its inception, the policy remains substantially unreformed. More than half of the total OECD transfer of resources to agriculture in 1994 occurred in the EU, estimated at some $80 billion. While subsidy levels in other countries, such as the United States, have fallen slightly, the Producer Subsidy Equivalent (PSE) in the EU has continued to rise. The percentage PSE is now five times the level in Australia (see Table 7.1). The OECD's 1996 report on agricultural policies noted that in 1995 the European Union was paying out an average subsidy of $21,000 to every full-time farmer in the EU: 'Despite CAP reform and the Uruguay Round, this figure represents a 75% increase on the $12,000 average for the years 1986–88 for the EU-12' (*Agra Europe*, 31 May 1996, p. P/1).

The budgetary costs of the CAP account for a very large share of EU spending, although agriculture accounts for a small and declining share of the EU workforce. After falling back from 64.2 per cent in 1988 to 53.2 per cent in 1992, the EAGGF share of total EU expenditure rose once again to 55 per cent in 1994 (*Agra Europe*, 8 December 1995, p. P/5). The net cost of the CAP rose from 26 318 million ECU in 1990 to a forecast level of 42 752 million ECU in 1996, an increase of 62 per cent. The cost per head in the EU rose

TABLE 7.1

Producer subsidy equivalents for EU and selected countries

	1979–81	1989–91	1994*
Australia	8	10	10
EC/EU	36	45	50
United States	15	22	21
OECD average	29	40	43

Note: * Provisional figures.
Source: OECD, *Agricultural Policies, Markets and Trade in OECD Countries, Monitoring and Outlook*, 1995.

from 76.6 ECU in 1990 to a provisional level of 101.7 ECU in 1995 (European Commission, 1994b, 1996). Even though spending was kept within budget in the mid-1990s, it remains questionable whether this level of spending represents a good use of scarce resources at a time when public expenditure is under pressure and the EU faces a range of problems in such areas as deficiencies in infrastructure, long-term unemployment and more general problems of social exclusion. One of the least attractive aspects of the policy is its high adminis-trative cost. Farmers have to use their time filling in elaborate forms, while in terms of government costs the level could be 5 per cent of the value of arable compensation payments and as much as 25 per cent of the value of livestock payments (Josling and Tangermann, 1995, pp. 9–10).

In many respects, however, the real burden of the CAP falls not on the EU budget but on consumers who have to pay more for their food than they would have to do in the absence of the CAP. For example, Munk estimates that of total transfers to farmers of 64 billion ECU in 1990, 50 billion ECU could be attributed to consumers rather than the budget (Munk, 1993). Because poorer families spend more of their income on food, the general effect is regressive. A number of attempts have been made to estimate the additional cost to a typical family. In Britain, it was estimated that the CAP adds £10 to the weekly shopping bill of a family of four (National Consumer Council, 1995, p. 2). A study in The Netherlands found that the costs of the CAP for consumers were at least $430 per capita in 1993, meaning that for a household of four people, the costs of the CAP amount to around 7 per cent of disposable income (Kol and Kuijpers, 1996, p. 101).

While it is clear that the CAP does impose a burden on consumers which has been little reduced by the reforms of the 1980s and 1990s, as import protection levels remain high, such figures need to be treated with some caution. If the CAP was abandoned, many farmers would go out of business, and the EU would import more food, thus pushing up world market prices, so that many of the benefits of eliminating the policy would be offset. The assumption of immediate abandonment without transitional adjustment measures is, however, an unrealistic one, and there is no doubt that the net losses to consumers are substantial.

The farmers do not benefit as much as one might expect from the CAP. Of the funds available, a significant proportion is spent on administration; another slice goes to traders, financiers and the providers of storage for surplus crops; while a significant amount is fraudulently diverted, sometimes by criminal organisations. During the period between 1975 and 1989, despite ever-increasing expenditure on the CAP, and a 35 per cent fall in the Community's agricultural population, there was little improvement in the per capita spending power of those engaged in agriculture (European Commission, 1991, pp. 2–3). The real beneficiaries in financial terms of the CAP are the suppliers of goods and services to farmers, with perhaps as little as 11 per cent of the total costs of the CAP being retained as net farm income (Johnson, 1995, p. 31). Much of that increase has come in the form of increased return to land, with one of the main effects of the CAP being to force up the price of agricultural land, perhaps by as much as by 40 per cent above the level that would apply in the absence of the policy. This raises entry barriers for new entrants, and has no apparent social benefits, although it helps to explain why so many banks have devoted considerable resources to increase their share of the agricultural lending market (Grant and MacNamara, 1995).

The stark realities of the situation are well summarised by Josling and Tangermann (1995, p. 7):

EU agriculture is not currently competitive. Yields are high because of high use of purchased inputs encouraged by high prices. As a result the value of output at true market prices (i.e. prices on international markets) is barely enough to cover input costs. The agricultural sector itself is generating virtually no income for its labour and capital . . . and relies on transfers from taxpayers and consumers.

This is clearly not an acceptable situation from a social perspective, but one also has to ask whether it is really in the interests of farmers? Do they necessarily want to engage in high input forms of intensive farming for artificial markets? Would there not be a case, as agricultural economists have suggested, for buying farmers out from their subsidies with bonds that could be used as a transitional form of income, or as a capital basis for a new business enterprise?

Defenders of the CAP have drawn attention to the significant reductions in surpluses in storage, combined with a rise in farm incomes, since the MacSharry reforms. The virtual disappearance of the butter mountain, along with other stored surpluses, is, of course, a welcome development, but overlooks the favourable world market conditions that have prevailed in the 1990s. Climatic changes could affect the world supply and demand balance, while the BSE crisis in beef shows how unanticipated factors can upset the budgetary balance of the EU. The CAP is also very sensitive to fluctuations in the dollar/ECU rate, as a number of production aids and almost all export refunds are fixed in terms of the gap between Community prices in ECUs and world prices in dollars. The consequences can be explained as follows:

> Put simply, and starting from the premise that EU prices are significantly higher than world price levels: when the dollar rises, the gap between the high EU price expressed in ECU and the world price closes and the export subsidy declines; when the reverse happens, the export subsidy increases as the world price falls. (*Agra Europe*, 27 January 1995, p. P/5)

In the 1995 financial year, depreciation of the US dollar against the ECU increased the EAGGF guarantee section expenditure by 543 million ECU (*Agra Europe*, 5 January 1996, p. E/3). Such an increase was sustainable because trends in the agricultural economy produced a budget underspend, but a more substantial depreciation could occur in less favourable circumstances.

With no trade negotiations until 1999, and relatively favourable world market conditions, the late 1990s appeared to offer a period of relative stability (the BSE affair aside) in European agriculture. The director of international agricultural affairs in DG VI has argued that the EU 'should take advantage of a "window of stability" over the next three years to take far-reaching decisions about the future shape of its agricultural policy' (*Agra Europe*, 9 February 1996, p. E/6).

Although is encouraging that the Commission is preparing a new Reflections paper for 1997, a window of stability may not be a window of opportunity. Indeed, it may slow down the reform impetus, creating a mood of complacency in which reform becomes more difficult. Certainly, there has been some evidence that that is the case from the difficulty experienced in dealing with the unreformed commodity regimes. Commissioner Fischler seems to see stability as a value in itself: 'Farmers, the world order, need stability in order to plan ahead and compete successfully' (Fischler, 1996, p. 7).

Stability is, however, likely to be disturbed by the accession of countries from East and Central Europe. Fischler notes that in some quarters there is 'anticipation that any future enlargement will spell the end of the CAP altogether . . . I do not share this fear or this hope!'. Equally, 'There is no question of simply extending the old CAP to new members' (Fischler, 1996, p. 5). The remainder of this chapter will consider the challenge presented to the CAP by eastern enlargement, and the renewed challenge likely to result from a second round of agricultural trade negotiations, concluding with a review of the developing but still weak links between agricultural and environmental policy.

Eastern enlargement

Enlargement of the European Union to the east is driven by broad policy considerations which must ultimately outweigh the claims of the CAP. Given the prospect of a resurgent Russia, security considerations demand that the countries of East–Central Europe should be integrated as effectively as possible into the European system. This requires sustaining their economic reform and growth and consolidating their democratic stability, both objectives that can be achieved more effectively within the European Union. Given its location, Germany is particularly interested in both the political stability of the countries of East–Central Europe and the opportunities these countries offer for German investment and exports. The countries that are most threatened by eastern enlargement, particularly in the area of agriculture, are those with substantial areas of marginal production, notably the Southern member states and the Republic of Ireland.

The agriculture structures of Central and East European Countries (CEECs) differ considerably (see Table 7.2). In some countries, agriculture is of central importance in the economy, whereas in others it is of more marginal importance. In the period after the removal of the Communist regimes, agricultural output slumped as domestic incomes fell, generous consumer subsidies were withdrawn, and price competitive imports flooded into previously largely self-sufficient markets. In general, 'The decline in aggregate gross agricultural output in the region probably stopped in 1993' (OECD, 1995b, p. 13). However, growth since then has not very been rapid and has been stagnant in key commodities, such as milk, in a number of countries. The important point as far as future policy is concerned is that the CEEC have considerable potential for the expansion of output. As Brian Gardner has noted, 'the arable area of the CEEC-10 amounted to well over half that of the EU-15 . . . but the current value of total agricultural production was less than one-tenth of the EU figure' (*Agra Europe*, 10 November 1995, p. E/3).

Any assessment of the likely impact of the CAP on the admission of CEECs to the EU has to take account of the political reality that admission is likely to be a phased process, and is not going to happen

TABLE 7.2

Agriculture in the economy of CEEC 10, 1993

	Agricultural production as a percentage of GDP	Agricultural employment as a percentage of total employment
Visegrad Four		
Czech Republic	3.3	5.6
Hungary	6.4	10.1
Poland	6.3	25.6
Slovak Republic	5.8	8.4
Other possible early entrants		
Estonia	10.4	8.2
Slovenia	4.9	10.7
Other countries		
Bulgaria	10.0	21.2
Latvia	10.6	18.4
Lithuania	11.0	22.4
Romania	20.2	35.2

Source: Derived from M. Hartmann, 'Implications of EU East Enlargement for the CAP', CREDIT conference, Nottingham, 1996.

until the early years of the twenty first century, for even the most suitable candidates. Apart from Cyprus and Malta, the first wave of negotiations is likely to include the Visegrad Four (the Czech Republic, Hungary, Poland and Slovakia), plus Estonia and possibly Slovenia. Sweden, Finland and Denmark have close trading relationships with the Baltic States and are keen to see them become members. They will therefore be prepared to act as 'sponsor states' for these prospective new entrants, although they appear to realise that Estonia is a more plausible candidate than Latvia or Lithuania. Similarly, Austria and Italy are likely to press for the inclusion of Slovenia. Bulgaria and Romania are likely to be much later entrants, which is just as well given the centrality of agriculture in their economies.

Of the likely early entrants, agriculture is not a major part of the economies of the Czech Republic and Slovakia. Agriculture is somewhat more important in Estonia and Slovenia, but their economies are a fraction of the size of other potential entrants. The two key potential entrants are Hungary and Poland; Hungary because of its agricultural strength, and Poland because of its agricultural weaknesses. Indeed, estimates by Dutch agricultural economists (*East Europe Agriculture and Food*, January 1996, p. 2) indicate that around half of the accession costs imposed on the CAP as a result of entry to the EU by the 'Visegrad Four' would emanate from Poland.

Poland has worse natural conditions for agriculture than most other European countries, so a normal market adjustment of Polish agriculture, even if there were no structural weaknesses, would imply a much smaller farming sector than at present. Polish land is predominantly arable, but land quality 'is among the poorest in Europe' (Kowalski, 1991, p. 57). Soils are predominantly light, leading to a susceptibility to drought: 'Poland's climate is intermediate, somewhat between the maritime climate of Western Europe and the continental climate of Eastern Europe. This leads to frequent weather vagaries and important changes from one year to another' (Kowalski, 1991, p. 57).

Poland developed its agricultural structure in a different way from other state socialist countries: 'Alone among the CMEA partners, Poland in the 1950s aborted its collectivization programme and opted for the continuation of small-scale private farming, circumscribed by centrally planned targets for compulsory deliveries . . . 76 per cent of land remained in private ownership and production suffered from the proliferation of small fragmented farms with around 2.7m holdings

divided among 17m individual parcels, with no strategy for rearran-
gement of holdings' (Répassy and Symes, 1993, p. 83). A category of
worker peasants was created, who combined an industrial job with
working their smallholdings. Since the end of the Communist regime,
many jobs in heavy industry have disappeared, so that there is a large
peasantry attempting to eke out a living on holdings with an average
size of 7 hectares (OECD, 1995b, p. 65). These peasants exert
significant political influence through their own political party, so it
is no surprise that, after an initial period of liberalisation, policy
became more interventionist in the mid-1990s. The PSE is still low,
however, at around 15 per cent, although this does not include social
security payments to farmers.

The EU has no need of agricultures dominated by large numbers of
marginal farmers reliant on income support. Optimistic forecasts by
the Polish government that their numbers will reduce considerably by
the year 2000 do not seem well-founded, given economic conditions in
Poland. The problems of farm structure in Poland are compounded
by weaknesses in the distribution and food processing sectors:
'Although fully privatised, wholesale activity remains very undeve-
loped and inefficient, causing something of a bottleneck in the system'
(OECD, 1995b, p. 61). 'Studies also suggest that, at least at the end
of the centrally planned period, the food industry was less competitive
internationally than the rest of Polish industry; in particular, food
processing had negative value added when measured at world prices'
(GATT, 1993, p. 123).

Substantial progress has been made with the privatisation of the
food processing industry, and there has been some inward investment,
although not on the scale experienced in Hungary. There are areas in
which it would be possible for Poland to make a significant impact on
the European market. For example, in pig production, it is possible to
build up large-scale and efficient units without too great a capital
investment, particularly given low labour costs and low rents for land
and buildings. Some analysts consider that by the years 2005 to 2010
there will be a US-style corporate pig-keeping system in Poland and
Hungary, posing a major challenge to more costly production elsewhere in Europe (*Agra Europe*, 23 October 1994, p. M/6).

Hungary is much more favourably situated for agricultural production than is Poland, and this is reflected in a long tradition of food
exports to other parts of Europe. Much of the country is a plain;
although there are some problems of environmental degradation, the
soil is generally fertile; and the continental climate favours a wide

range of agricultural production. Productivity levels in wheat were 85 per cent of the EU level in 1994, and 88 per cent in milk; the corresponding figures for Poland were 59 per cent in each case (Hartmann, 1996, table 6). 'This is a country that could give our arable farmers a real run for their money in the very near future' *Farmers Weekly*, 27 August 1993. Hungary, however, shares the structural problems found in other countries in East–Central Europe: 'On the structural side, difficult decisions have been made with considerable pragmatism on very complex issues such as compensation, privatisation and collective farm reforms; yet actual progress has so far been slow . . . However, the degree of adaptability of Hungarian policy-making to the unfolding situation is particularly striking' (OECD, 1994c, p. 26).

Although the state socialist regime in Hungary initially ignored the food industry, it underwent intensive development in the 1970s, with the objective of attaining domestic self-sufficiency and increasing food exports to help the balance of payments. Managers in food companies were given an increasing measure of freedom, certainly greater than that enjoyed by their counterparts in other state socialist countries, although they complained to the author in discussions towards the end of the socialist regime about their inability to reinvest profits. Investment decisions often seem to have been taken haphazardly, so it was possible to see in one plant a state of the art, computer-controlled production system for salami using imported Western equipment located next to old-fashioned labour-intensive methods of production. Over 50 per cent of exports went to other socialist countries organised in COMECON, principally to Russia, which took 90 per cent of the grain crop. The virtual disappearance of this market caused serious problems at the beginning of the 1990s. Like other former socialist countries, Hungary was unable to take full advantage of the import quotas awarded to it by the EU under the Europe Agreements.

Since the end of the socialist regime, the Hungarian food processing industry has seen a substantive infusion of inward investment involving lead West European companies, for example, Nestlé and Unilever: 'In autumn 1994 the share of foreign capital in the privatised companies of the food processing industry made up about one third of total invested capital. Foreign investors have acquired dominant positions in the vegetable oil, sugar, brewing, confectionery and tobacco industries' (OECD, 1994c, p. 52). This level of investment is a vote of confidence in the potential of the Hungarian food economy. It also points to the economic impact Hungary could have within the European Union.

The impact of eastern enlargement on the CAP

There have been very wide variations in the estimates of the likely budgetary impact on the CAP of admitting countries from East–Central Europe to EU membership. Hartmann notes a range from 3.7 billion ECU to 40.5 billion ECU in annual budgetary costs (Hartmann, 1996, p. 11). These variations are not so surprising when one considers the many simplifying assumptions that have to be made before producing a forecast: how many countries would be admitted; when they would be admitted; what further reform of the CAP would have been undertaken by the time of entry; what would be the nature and length of the transition period; what would the level of world market prices be at the time of entry; how would GDP, and hence domestic demand, grow in the period up to entry; and what changes would occur in agricultural productivity before entry. One of the most recent estimates, by the Dutch Agricultural Economics Institute, suggests that if the Visegrad Four countries were admitted in the year 2000, agricultural spending might grow, in the worst case scenario, by 7.6 billion ECU, or 18.7 per cent of the 1996 EAGGF Guarantee Fund. This lower estimate 'results from the fact that the earlier studies assumed marked increases in productivity in the 1995–2000 period, especially in the livestock sector, and assumed that the bulk of the extra production would have to be sold on the world market with subsidy' (*East Europe Agriculture and Food*, 1996, p. 2).

Estimates of this kind do cast some doubt on earlier claims by British ministers that 'I think it would be impossible on budgetary grounds to bring these eastern European countries into the European Union with the common agricultural policy in its present form. Put crudely, I think that it would probably bankrupt the European budget' (House of Lords, 1994b, p. 122). However, even if eastern enlargement does not produce a cataclysm within the CAP of the kind hoped for by some of its critics, even a 20 per cent increase in an already large budget is unacceptable. Moreover, without policy changes, the costs would rise as more countries joined and their agricultural sectors recovered.

There are four broad options that could be pursued in terms of handling the impact of eastern enlargement on the CAP. One option would be to have some kind of two-tier CAP, with the new eastern member states kept at a lower price level. Policies in the CEECs traditionally relied on substantial subsidies to consumers, and although the subsidies have largely disappeared, price levels for producers have not risen in compensation in the transition period. The main drawback of this approach is that it would involve the regulation of cross-border trade and is completely at odds with the notion of a single market. However attractive notions of a multi-speed Europe may seem to be, it is not feasible to admit countries to an organisation and then exclude them from the policy which accounts for over half the budget.

A second option is to have a very long transition period, say fifteen years, for the new entrants. This option has won some support within the EU because it is the kind of fudge that appeals to both member states and officials. It delays difficult decisions on reform for as long as possible, and supporters can point to the precedent of Spain and Portugal, both of which had transition periods of ten years. However, this precedent is open to misinterpretation. As the Spanish minister of agriculture has pointed out, 'the agricultural sectors in Spain and Portugal were much closer to those of the EU-10 when they acceded in 1986 than those of the CEECS are at present' (*Agra Europe*, 1 December 1995, p. P/1). As Tracy notes (1996, p. 22), 'The main reason for their transition period was to enable the EC to maintain restrictions on their exports of sensitive products (fruit, wine, vegetables). It is true that it did also give them time to make structural adjustments, but the arrangement was more in the EC interest than in that of the new Member States.'

There is also a practical problem in that previous transition arrangements were based on balancing payments known as accession compensatory amounts paid at the border between the entrants and the rest of the Community. When Northern enlargement took place in 1995, 'this no longer proved possible because the Union had meanwhile established the borderless single market. In the absence of border controls, accession compensatory amounts [can] no longer be implemented' (Marsh and Tangermann, 1996, p. 14). Hence, with the Northern enlargement, prices had to be aligned on the day of accession. Some way would have to be found of overcoming this practical difficulty. A transition period will be necessary, but its length and nature will have to be scrutinised carefully by reformers.

A third option would be the imposition of various quantitative controls on the new member states. However, 'this would be merely

replacing the state controls of the old communist command economies with the state controls of the Brussels bureaucracy' *Agra Europe*,
27 October 1995, p. P/2). Nevertheless, if dairy quotas still existed,
they could be applied at self-sufficiency levels in these countries,
rather than allowing for exports.

The fourth option would be to admit the Central and East
European countries into the CAP without any transitional period
or special arrangements. This would depend on first eliminating the
arable aid compensation payments, which would be expensive to
apply to these countries: paying them for Poland alone would cost 2.2
billion ECU a year (*Agra Europe*, 29 March 1996, p. P/6). Indeed, it
has been suggested that, as they have low PSEs, and as the payments
were intended to compensate producers for lower prices, there is no
need to apply them where lower prices have in any case prevailed.
Fischler has stated that the potential entrant countries have prices
below EU (and, in some cases, world) levels. Prices would rise when
they joined, so 'There is nothing that actually requires compensation'
(*Agra Europe*, 1 March 1996, p. P/2). This is an attractive but
unacceptable argument, because to make compensatory payments
to some farmers and not to others would create serious distortions of
competition within a supposed single market.

When the Commission initially started to draft a policy on eastern
enlargement, conflicts appeared between DGI and DGVI, with each
directorate-general sponsoring its own expert reports. Four reports
commissioned by Sir Leon Brittan in his capacity as commissioner for
external trade were rejected speedily by the outgoing agriculture
commissioner, René Steichen. The reports were not particularly
helpful in so far as the range of accession costs they suggested varied
between 13.5 and 32 billion ECU, but this was far above Steichen's
own estimate of 4 to 5 billion ECU. Steichen's successor, Fischler,
complained that these 'radical recipes for change' lacked political
realism and were not helpful, commenting that 'Over stretching
oneself had never been a good strategy' (*Agra Europe*, 7 April 1995,
p. P/6).

However, the Commission was eventually able to come up with a
coherent and consistent line on eastern enlargement. Part of the
approach adopted has been to emphasise the desirability of the EU
supporting structural reform in East–Central Europe, rather than
reproducing existing support levels under different conditions. It is
evident that there is still much to be done in terms of improving
distribution systems, and food processing and marketing in these

countries. Another urgent need is for a proper system of agricultural credit, which is generally lacking in these countries and which has played a key role in the development of agriculture in countries such as France. However, the proper functioning of such a system depends in turn on settling still unresolved questions of property title. Priorities for structural reform are 'a functioning land market, mortgage legislation, rural banking, the development of education and extension services with an emphasis on management skills, and the building of an efficient marketing infrastructure and its supporting institutions' (OECD, 1994b, p. 18).

The Commission's Agricultural Strategy Paper adopted in November 1995 accepts that further reform of the CAP beyond that anticipated in the MacSharry proposals will be necessary. The impetus comes from an anticipated additional budgetary cost of at least 12 billion ECU of admitting ten countries from East and Central Europe, but, even independently of enlargement, rising yields and the likely restrictions on subsidised exports would make further reform necessary. Undertaking a major reform after enlargement would be difficult and costly. However, the Commission paper rejects radical reforms that would phase out market support and introduce decoupled and degressive compensatory payments. The report does, however, recognise that a 'natural economic selection of farm types' will occur in the CEECs, edging away from 'an earlier tendency to stress the merits of family farms – sometimes equated with "small" farms' (Tracy, 1995, p. 19). Although the paper as a whole is rather general in character, it does represent a further stimulus to the reform process and is an acknowledgement of the likely importance of enlargement in bringing about further significant reform over the next ten to fifteen years.

Some analysts consider that it is unlikely that any CEECs would be admitted before the year 2005, followed by a five-year transition period. The Commission is certainly envisaging a negotiating period longer than the three years taken for the EFTA countries. Within Germany, the elite consensus in favour of enlargement is not shared in farming circles. Farm minister Borchert has argued that the CEECs should not be allowed to join the EU until they can compete on an equal footing, which he interprets as meaning large-scale reductions in the labour force of the kind that occurred in East Germany (*Farmers Weekly*, 19 January 1996). There are dangers, however, in a 'wait and see' approach which delays membership for too long. Such an approach 'might increase resistance in these countries against an EU membership, given the fact that growing nationalism can be notice already' (Hartmann, 1996, p. 13). Just as the particular problems of agriculture were not allowed to prevent the Uruguay Round negotiations being concluded, they must not delay an enlargement of the EU which serves broader and more important economic, political and security objectives.

Liberalising agricultural trade

Analysts are generally agreed that the impact of the Uruguay Round on agricultural trade 'may prove to be modest' (OECD, 1995c, p. 58) in the period up to the year 2000, although more effects are likely to be felt in the dairy sector than in cereals, with export-orientated countries such as Denmark being particularly affected. One of the key changes in agricultural trade rules introduced by the agreement was the conversion of non-tariff barriers into tariffs which have to be reduced significantly over a five year period up to the year 2000. The principle of tariffication introduces greater transparency and predictability into agricultural trade, but the way in which it was implemented in the agreement undermined its effect. Not only was the base period chosen (1986–8) one in which support levels were high, but the tariffs that countries set in their schedules were higher than the gap between domestic and world market prices in the base period, a practice known as 'dirty tariffication'. Even after the 36 per cent tariff cut scheduled in the Uruguay Round had been implemented in the year 2000, average tariff levels in the USA and the EU will be higher than in the 1989–93 base period (*Agra Europe*, 24 November 1995, p. E/5). Therefore, 'much needs to be done in future round[s] of multilateral trade negotiations in order to achieve substantial and real reductions in agricultural protection' (Ingco, 1995, p. 51).

The GATT negotiations provided the impetus for the MacSharry reforms because the consequences of a complete breakdown in the economic relationship with the United States were too serious to contemplate. What was needed was to get an agreement on agricultural trade which offered enough concessions to the US position to make it acceptable to the Americans, but still protected the essential objectives of the EU. This was what was achieved, so that one had an agreement that was suboptimal in terms of permitting efficient producers to serve consumers, but was politically optimal in preventing a breakdown of international economic relations. By securing consensus on new measures of the level of agricultural support, it also provided a basis for future progress.

For the period of implementation, however, the pressure for reform from agricultural trade liberalisation was reduced substantially. Admittedly, a number of disputes on specific issues such as beef hormones continued to provide a focus for trade friction between the USA and the EU. It was also possible to argue that 'Towards the end of the implementation period . . . the mutually reinforcing effects of the new rules and disciplines will begin to exert significant pressure for policy reforms' (OECD, 1995c, p. 58). Much in practice would depend on such uncertain factors as exchange rates and world prices. In general:

> there seems little in the [Uruguay Round Agriculture Agreement] to enforce rapid or radical CAP reform. Given the exemptions, and the prospects for stronger world markets than appeared likely a few years ago, there seems quite enough scope in the Agreement itself to enable the Commission to avoid even changing the CAP on this account, except in relatively minor administrative ways, at least until well into the next decade, when CEEC enlargement will loom. (Thomson, 1996, p. 11)

Article 20 of the Agreement on Agriculture does, however, recognise explicitly that 'the long-term objective of substantial progressive reductions in support and protection resulting in fundamental reform' is an ongoing process. It is agreed that negotiations for continuing the reform process will begin in 1999 one year before the end of the implementation period (2000). Quite what form these negotiations will take remains to be seen. In any event, it is unlikely that they would lead to agreement on further changes in agricultural trade until some years into the twenty-frist century. Proposals, such as those by the Cairns Group to bring to an end the 'blue box' arrangement in the Uruguay Round would be opposed by the USA, which would want to maintain deficiency payments, and the EU, which would wish to continue to use compensatory payments not fully decoupled from production.

However, the context in which the post-1999 discussions take place will be influenced substantially by the 1996 US Farm Bill (H.R. 2854, the Federal Agriculture Improvement and Reform Act). In order to understand the significance of this measure, it is first necessary to sketch in some of the background of the development of

US agriculture over the past quarter century. The ideological justification for farm support in the United States has, as in Europe, been couched in terms of supporting the family farm. Such farms still exist in significant numbers in the United States, particularly in the dairy sector in the upper Midwest and in the north-east. However, there are also many farms that are large-scale corporate businesses, while there has also been vertical integration with the agribusiness sector. Such large-scale corporate farming is characteristic of California, where it is dependent on supplies of irrigated water from federal and state projects made available at well below its economic cost.

Up to the 1970s, US farm policy focused on providing domestic stabilisation of markets, with exports arising as by-products of surplus management. However, balance of payments problems led to a new emphasis on a commercial exports strategy that suited the interests of large-scale export-orientated producers and the multinationals which provided them with inputs and traded their products. However, the USA found itself with increased competition from the EU in world grain markets, and in particular from France. The 1985 Export Enhancement Programme was a deliberate attempt to counteract EU competition in the world grain markets by increasing the economic and political costs of subsidised EU exports, thus setting the scene for the Uruguay Round negotiations (Libby, 1992). All these policy shifts reflected the considerable political displacement of food processing and trading companies in the United States, in part reflecting the dependence of American politicians on donations to wage their lengthy and expensive re-election campaigns.

There have thus been two policy corners in the United States. Family farmers have insisted that agricultural prices should cover the cost of production and provide a fair return: 'The opposite policy corner, usually occupied by large agribusiness firms, grain companies, fertilizer and equipment manufacturers and banks, advocates setting prices as low as possible to encourage agricultural exports' (Le Heron, 1993, p. 107). In practice, it is the larger farms that have been the beneficiaries of federal policy. Five per cent of farms, 'mainly large corporate farms with incomes over $300,000 or more, get 40% of government aid' (*Farmers Weekly*, 20 November 1995). Very often this aid has been for 'buying air', not planting crops or disposing of herds. For example, a farmer in the San Joaquin valley received $8.2 million under the dairy herd buyout programme (*Sacramento Bee*, 13 September 1995).

A Republican Congress determined to cut the federal budget advanced the concept of the 'freedom to farm', which would severely cut set-aside programmes and other subsidies. Although their original proposals were modified, President Clinton signed the bill somewhat reluctantly because he believed that the bill failed to provide an adequate safety net for family farmers: 'The Bill is seen as a victory for grain buyers and input suppliers who fought to reduce the government's ability to restrain acreage, and a defeat for advocates of the traditional "supply management" style of farm supports that have characterised US farm policies for some 60 years' (*Agra Europe*, 5 April 1996, pp. N/5–6). Arable farmers will receive fixed payments for a seven-year period, while the support price for milk is to be reduced. Many smaller enterprises could be squeezed out of business.

President Clinton is determined to restore a farm safety net, but what is more significant is the area of agreement between the President and the bill's Republican sponsors. The chairman of the Senate agriculture committee commented, 'The important thing about this bill is the unleashing of American agriculture to make more money' (*Financial Times*, 4 April 1996). Similarly, President Clinton expressed his satisfaction with the trade-related aspects of the bill, stating that his administration would use existing and new export programmes 'to expand upon the record levels of agricultural exports we have achieved. This will ensure that America's farmers continue to take advantage of the growing opportunities in the world market' (White House press statement).

In other words, with greater planting flexibility, US farmers will be producing more product for world markets. There is certainly scope for them to do so. For example, in the dairy sector, 'there are enormous dormant production reserves in the US' (*Agra Europe*, 15 December 1995, p. M/6) in states such as South Dakota. There is also further scope for cutting costs, given that Californian farmers have shown what can be achieved in terms of milk yields per cow in herds as large as two thousand. On the arable side, Dr Martin Abel of Produce Studies, which has researched the Farm Bill, has forecast, 'The US will be able to change its crop mix in response to market forces far quicker than before. In the next year we will see a rise in the corn and spring wheat acreages, a rise in soya bean plantings but probably a fall in cotton and rice' (*Farmers Weekly*, 19 April 1996). As American farmers larger-scale increase production, they will demand greater access to world markets. One can thus expect the United States to press hard for further liberalisation in agricultural trade in

1999, supported by the Cairns Group of medium sized agricultural exporters. The EU is already anticipating these pressures in the work it is carrying out for its new 'reflections' document on the CAP (see Chapter 8). In the first years of the twenty-first century, a new reform impetus may thus emerge as a consequence of the challenges posed by eastern enlargement, reinforced by demands for a more effective liberalisation of agricultural trade.

Environmental policy

Another potential pressure for reform comes from the growing link between agricultural and environmental policies. The 'environment' is something of a portmanteau term and in this discussion it is used in the broadest possible sense. It is, however, important to distinguish between a number of different environmental impacts of agriculture, not only because the problems themselves differ not only in character, but also in terms of the associated patterns of politics. Although the notion of 'the environment' implies an ecological system in which, if a natural equilibrium is no longer possible, political intervention may be necessary to offset the undesirable consequences of modern agricultural practices, relatively few environmental activists take such a broad perspective. Most of them are concerned with particular problems, such as landscape effects, or the impact of agriculture on bird life.

Broadly speaking, there are six areas of impact of modern agriculture that have given rise to concern. One of the areas of greatest concern has been the significance of agriculture as a source of water pollution. Runoff from livestock and arable farming operations may not only lead to the aesthetic deterioration of rivers and damage to marine life, but the entry of pesticides and nitrates into drinking water may be perceived as having an effect on human health. How great the risk is to human health is a matter of some controversy, but the nitrates directive is the one action taken by the EU so far that is likely to have a significant impact on the pattern of farming in member states. It is therefore discussed more extensively below.

There is considerable concern about the landscape effects of modern agriculture. Of course, if agricultural activity was to cease in, for example, upland areas, the consequent landscape changes would lead to a deterioration in visual beauty from the viewpoint of most observers. However, farming practices which, for example, involve the grubbing up of hedgerows produce landscapes which are generally thought to be less attractive than more traditional forms of farming. 'Prairie farming' may also make the countryside less accessible to walkers: tensions between ramblers and farmers are a recurrent problem in Britain. Modern farm buildings may use materials and be on a scale that makes them more intrusive in the landscape than traditional building using local materials.

Intensive forms of production can lead to soil damage: 'Erosion is a particular problem in Spain, where 17% of farms experience serious difficulties and a further 28% moderate problems' (Ockenden and Franklin, 1995, p. 41). Soil erosion is not, however, the leading feature of debates about agriculture and the environment that it is in the United States. Although straw burning has been a problem in the past (it was banned in Britain in 1992), air pollution is more of a problem associated with manufacturing industries and motor vehicles than with agriculture. However, it can be a problem associated with very intensive forms of farming. For example, in The Netherlands, 'In spring when animal slurry, stored all winter, is spread, or as is now decreed, injected into the land, the smell across wide areas of the country is unpleasant' (*Financial Times*, 26 April 1994). Smells associated with farming activities may be one of the sources of tension between a traditional rural population and urban dwellers moving to country areas.

The maintenance of biodiversity and the protection of species from extinction is another area of concern. Extinction of species of animals does not affect humans directly in the way that global warming does, but humans may be concerned about biodiversity for ethical, aesthetic or utilitarian reasons (List and Rittberger, 1992, p. 88n). No fewer than ten species of birds have declined by more than 50 per cent in the UK in the past twenty-five years, a rate of decline paralleled elsewhere in Europe: 'Birds are considered good indicators of environmental health, and the loss of so many birds from the farmed landscape has been paralleled by a general decline in biodiversity' (RSPB, 1995, p. 7). Changes such as the increased use of pesticides and fertilisers, the loss of mixed farming systems and the shift from spring- to autumn-sown crops, which has led to the loss of winter stubbles, have all influenced the ability of birds to survive: 'These changes were stimulated by the CAP arable regime, which . . . has encouraged farmers to strive for higher yields with detrimental effects on farmland habitats' (RSPB, 1995, p. 7). Another consequence of the intensification of production has been the loss of wetlands.

Animal welfare may not conventionally be regarded as an environmental issue, but it is certainly becoming a more central agenda item for the CAP. This is illustrated by the disputes over animal transportation and the rearing of calves in veal crates. Further controversy is anticipated over a Commission report on battery cages in poultry production, which is thought likely to recommend that chickens should have more space. Agriculture commissioner Fischler has emphasised animal welfare issues in his public statements in a way that his predecessors have not done. Attitudes towards animal welfare issues do, of course, vary considerably between member states, with public opinion in Britain paying particular attention to them. The Conservative government called for a commitment to animal welfare to be written into the Treaty of Rome as part of the Intergovernmental Conference, while the Labour Party went further, in calling for animals to be treated as 'sentient beings' rather than agricultural products.

Underlying all these issues is the tension between the intensification of farming that has resulted from the productionist emphasis of the CAP and the more recent emphasis on the importance of environmental goals. Intensification can be measured in terms of 'quantity of physical inputs per unit of land' (Winter, 1996, p. 4). As Winter emphasises, knowledge structures are important and good management can ensure that environmental values are secured. Nevertheless, although each farm is different, and sensitive management can achieve a great deal, 'it is probably fair to say that in aggregate terms increasing intensity can be associated with a decline of environmental value or, at the very least, should give rise to concern' (Winter, 1996, p. 5).

Another underlying tension, particularly found in more urbanised Northern states such as Britain, is that between city and rural dwellers. City dwellers may tend to perceive the countryside as primarily a recreational asset, which they are entitled to use by virtue of the subsidies paid to farmers. Indeed, in the worst cases, farming becomes very difficult in urban fringe locations because of vandalism, crime and the use of the countryside to dump litter, which represents a danger to animals. As city dwellers become more affluent, and the range of recreational pursuits becomes more diversified, new sources of tension may arise: for example, harm to livestock and damage to crops caused by hot air balloonists. More generally, 'The debate on sustainable agriculture is open to the challenge that it reflects a middle-class, town-based view of requirements which should be inflicted on agriculture, when there is only limited evidence of a willingness by these same people to pay the higher price for food that would inevitably result from the imposition of such requirements' (*Agra Europe*, 21 June 1996, p. N/3).

From the perspective of the farmer, he or she is attempting to conduct a business on land which should be respected as private property, not treated as a public asset. Of course, the polarity of perspectives is not necessarily as marked as has been implied. Farmers can earn good money by providing accommodation for city visitors, selling them farm produce, or even turning the farm into a golf course or country park. Diversification has been encouraged in the UK, where over 40 per cent of agricultural holdings undertake some form of non-farming business (Country Landowners' Association, 1994, para. 103).

Formulating a satisfactory agri-environmental policy is not, however, just a matter of reconciling the often contradictory perspectives of urban and rural dwellers. Broadly speaking, farmers and environmentalists favour two divergent approaches to agri-environmental policy. Farm interests are increasingly seeing environmental policy as a means of retaining subsidies to agriculture. If farmers are not to be paid for producing surplus products, then perhaps they can be paid for looking after the countryside. On the whole, farmers would prefer to run a business rather than be countryside wardens, but what is most important is to retain public financial support for agriculture. It is just this possibility that concerns those who want to reform the CAP. As a British agriculture minister, Douglas Hogg, has commented, 'it will be important to avoid creating a new class of subsidy-dependent farmers under the guise of environmental or structural policy' (Hogg, 1996, p. 9).

Many environmentalists, on the other hand, would like to see a wholesale change in farming to a more extensive, sustainable form. For example, they would argue that organic farming should be encouraged through subsidy. Opponents of such an approach argue that food security would be endangered and food prices would rise. The advocates of a market approach would maintain that, if consumers are prepared to pay the premium required by organic products, then the market will respond. More generally, however, advocates of a market approach to agriculture find themselves on difficult ground when dealing with environmental problems. Pollution problems can be dealt with through the price mechanism by the use of taxes, but the advocates of a market based approach are concerned that subsidies will reappear under a new guise as environmental payments.

The development of agri-environmental policy

'When the UK joined the EEC in 1973, the CAP paid little regard to the environment' (Country Landowners' Association, 1994, para. 59). European environmental policy has been driven by three vanguard states: Germany, Denmark and The Netherlands. Their role helps to explain the relative lack of progress in adjusting agricultural policy to give a greater weight to environmental concerns. Both Denmark and The Netherlands have too many interests bound up with intensive agriculture. Germany remains a key actor and receives 20 per cent of all the EU funds available for agri-environmental programmes (*Agra Europe*, 16 August 1996, p. E/4). However, the orientation of the new länder to larger-scale, and hence more intensive, farming introduces new contradictions into its role as an environmental vanguard state.

Agri-environmental measures do not, in general, have a significant effect on trade between member states. Hence, many of the first initiatives were taken at member-state level and reflected the distinctive problems and priorities of each member state. This did lead to considerable variations in policy:

> At present, there are great variations between Member States in the degree to which environmental measures are applied to agriculture. The scope, rigour and economic significance of environmental measures is far from uniform, varying from a sophisticated assembly of policy instruments in several northern countries, such as Denmark and the Netherlands, to more limited interventions, particularly in Mediterranean regions, where intensive agriculture is on a more limited scale. Even within northern Europe, there are contrasts. (Baldock and Mitchell, 1995, p. 18)

Agri-environmental policy in Britain has reflected a concern for the appearance of the countryside and the extent to which it provides a habitat for birds and other wildlife with an emphasis on approaches that involve co-operation rather than compulsion: 'Initial UK responses to concerns over the impact of agriculture on the environment involved a combination of stricter protection for valuable sites and advisory work to foster the belief that intensive farming and wildlife conservation could exist side by side' (Country Landowners' Association, 1994, para. 61). Capital grants for ploughing-up land, draining land and removing hedgerows were ended in 1984. In 1987 the launch of ALURE (Alternative Land Use and Rural Economy) represented 'the first ever major inter-Departmental exercise designed to show an integrated approach to policies for the countryside' (Country Landowners' Association, 1994, para. 62).

Environmental schemes developed in Britain have abided 'by the British tradition of voluntarism which reinforces the view that solutions to environmental problems should be decided at the level of the individual farm' (Allanson *et al.*, 1994, p. 29). Of course, more is likely to be achieved with the active co-operation of farmers, and the particular circumstances of each farm do differ. Nevertheless, the philosophy exemplified by Farming and Wildlife Advisory Groups, 'that nature conservation and commercial farming can happily co-exist may have confirmed some farmers in their belief that effective conservation need not involve making hard choices that demand some personal costs' (Cox *et al.*, 1990, p. 177). Planting trees and creating ponds may be desirable activities, but they do not represent a solution to the general problems of the relationship between farming and the environment. Schemes such as that run by MAFF for Environmentally Sensitive Areas (ESAs) 'remain marginal in terms of the fraction of agricultural land they encompass' (Allanson *et al.*, 1994, p. 29). They are also vulnerable to defections from farmers. It was suggested that at least a third and perhaps a half of farmers in the Pennine Dales Environmentally Sensitive Area scheme might leave when the five-year contracts expired in 1997. From the farmers' perspective, 'The ESA payments are just not sufficient to compensate for losses caused by stringent management prescriptions' (*Farmers Weekly*, 23 February 1996).

Of all the member states, it is perhaps in The Netherlands that the conflict between intensive agriculture and the environment has been most apparent. The combination of intensive agriculture, a considerable portion of land below sea level requiring elaborate systems of drainage, and a high population density has produced particularly acute agri-environmental problems. The country has faced a manure crisis because there is such a high stocking density of animals eating imported feed that it is difficult to dispose of their wastes: 'Indeed critics have suggested that some areas in the east and south of the country are like a gigantic sewage farm' (*Financial Times*, 26 April 1994).

Because knowledge and information about farming practices was dominated by the Dutch agricultural policy community, 'pollution by agriculture only became an issue of public and political concern in the 1980s' (Frouws and van Tatenhove, 1993, p. 228). A series of targets were set, which required a considerable reduction in agricultural pollution. In order to maintain competitiveness, a considerable emphasis was placed on the deployment of new environmental technologies such as the industrial processing of liquid manure or the recirculation of waste water in glasshouses (Frouws and van Tatenhove, 1993, pp. 229–30).

The biggest single problem, however, remained the manure surplus, which it was estimated could reach 7.5 million tonnes by the year 2000. In 1995 the Dutch government launched a plan to establish a manure fund to buy up phosphate manure quotas from farmers. The plan led to demonstrations by farmers, who were concerned that lower yields would result, leading to a fall in incomes.

In general, there has been much less progress in the implementation of agri-environmental measures in Southern member states. National administrative capacity in environmental policy is often deficient. Greece and Italy suffer from a diffusion of environmental functions and deficient co-ordination. Italy has been particularly affected by bureaucratic lethargy or *lentocrazia* ('slow-ocracy') (Weale *et al.*, 1996, pp. 267–8). Progress in implementing the EU's Agri-environmental Regulation appears to have been slow (Povellato, 1996). In Spain, 'the public debate on the possible polluting effects of agriculture as a diffuse source of pollution did not exist before Spain entered the EU' (Garrido and Moyano, 1996, p. 95). The debate appears to be gaining pace, but is complicated by the heterogeneity of production systems: 'The implementation of agri-environmental measures in Spain has been remarkably slow compared with other European countries' (Garrido and Moyano, 1996, p. 104).

At the European level, the Single European Act which amended the Treaty of Rome in 1987 required that 'environmental protection requirements shall be a component of the Community's other policies'. The Commission's 1991 Reflections paper acknowledged the problems that resulted from the encouragement of intensification: 'Where intensive production takes place nature is abused, water is polluted and the land empoverished' (European Commission, 1991,

p. 2). The paper recommended that 'Measures should be taken to encourage farmers in the use of methods less damaging to the environment' (European Commission, 1991, p. 15).

The introduction of compulsory arable set aside promised the possibility of some environmental gains. Areas set aside can provide winter feeding and nesting habitats for birds, although the benefits gained depend on management methods, particularly spring weed control. They were also offset by the permissibility of using set-aside land to grow industrial crops. The RSPB concluded that more fundamental reform to encourage extensification would be required to enhance the limited environmental benefits derived from compulsory set aside:

> The available evidence does not suggest that the reforms have reduced the intensity of arable farming in areas which remain cultivated. There is no evidence of reductions in the intensity of use of chemical fertilisers of pesticides by cereal growers . . . The reforms have also effectively fixed the area devoted to arable production, maintaining specialisation of farm systems and discouraging a shift back towards mixed farming systems. (RSPB, 1995, p. 33)

The MacSharry reforms included a package of 'accompanying measures' on the environment which required member states to introduce a package of agri-environmental schemes. The implementing Regulation (2078/92) allows 'Member States very considerable freedom to set their own environmental objectives . . . which can then be implemented with Community co-finance or as purely State-aided measures' (Wilkinson, 1994, p. 28). Permissible schemes include those that reduce the use of fertilisers or agrochemicals; support organic farming; lead to more extensive forms of production; reduce stocking densities; maintain the countryside or landscape; rear rare breeds; provide for the upkeep of abandoned woodland; set aside farmland for environmental purposes such as reserves; and manage land for public access and leisure. Schemes introduced in Britain include a Meadowland Scheme; a Habitat Improvement Scheme; an Organic Aid Scheme; a Moorland Scheme; and Countryside Stewardship (Tir Cymen in Wales): 'Although the list is impressive in its range and diversity, the total spend adds up to little more than 2–3% of total agricultural support spending. Several of the schemes have had a very low take-up to date' (Winter, 1996, p. 17).

According to the then EU environmental commissioner, Yannis Paleokrassas, Britain and Germany were among the countries that had applied the agri-environmental measures in a responsible fashion. However, he 'criticised the relative lack of progress made in adjusting agricultural policies to environmental requirements' (*Agra Europe*, 14 October 1994, p. E/3). Agri-environmental measures account for a little over three per cent of the CAP budget:

> While the agri-environment measures have great potential, at the levels of funding currently envisaged, they will never be major influences on the agricultural landscape and the wildlife and historic features which it supports, or the recreational opportunities which it offers. At these levels of funding, they will always represent a missed opportunity. The major influence on the environment in rural areas will continue to be the mainstream market support measures which absorb by far the greatest proportion of the available funds and which still show only limited concern for the environment. (Country Landowners' Association, 1994, para. 80)

Franz Fischler, as agriculture commissioner, has placed a greater emphasis on the environmental dimension of the CAP. He sees it as part of a multifunctional agricultural sector which does not just produce food but serves society as a whole by promoting rural culture and protecting nature (*Agra Europe*, 17 November 1995, p. E/5). In Fischler's view, agricultural policy 'cannot lead a life apart from environmental policy or concerns such as animal welfare' (Fischler, 1996, p. 7).

Nevertheless, the debate about CAP is still dominated by concerns about farm incomes and the international competitiveness of European agriculture. Key papers by reform orientated economists such as Josling and Tangermann (1995) make no reference to environmental issues. Environmentalists favour an approach based on cross-compliance, which would attach environmental conditions to agricultural support policies. For example, a specified percentage of the farmed area could be required to be used for approved conservation purposes, or farmers could be placed under a general obligation not to remove landscape features and habitats, David Baldock, of the Institute for European Environmental Policy, has argued that 'cross-compliance should not just involve some minor extra requirements but should positively encourage extensive production, while set aside should be "targeted" – for example towards setting higher rates for low-yielding regions and areas such as the South Downs in England, which are vulnerable to soil erosion' (*Agra Europe*, 21 June 1996, p. N/ 3). Although some elements of cross-compliance were introduced in the MacSharry reforms, there is generally little political support for such an approach in the EU. Baldock and Mitchell (1995, p. 79) argue that there is a reluctance to impose new burdens on farmers in the wake of the MacSharry reforms, and that the incremental nature of policy-making in the EU (in contrast to five-year reviews in the United States) makes major new policy proposals difficult to introduce.

Economists are also uneasy about cross-compliance because, as Tangermann has explained, such an approach violates the 'Tinbergen rule': 'that if you have more than one objective in your policy you need more than one policy instrument, because only in very rare and coincidental cases does it happen that the same instrument has the desired effect on two, three or perhaps four objectives' (House of Lords, 1996, p. 147). They question whether farming activities are necessarily the best way of maintaining a preferred environment, and whether there might be a more cost-effective way of securing desired environmental objectives. They are concerned that environmental policies might 'become a route whereby governments of rich countries give their farmers unfair advantages in competition with others within the EU' (Marsh and Tangermann, 1996, p. 42). This is clearly a risk, given that 3 billion DMs in agri-environmental aid are anticipated to be available to German farmers from EU, federal and Land sources in the period 1993–7 (*Agra Europe*, 16 August 1996, p. E/5). Economists may, however, place too much faith in the ability of cost–benefit analysis to measure the intangible benefits associated with environmental measures.

The relationship between the CAP and environmental policies is likely to be a persistent agenda item in the reform debate. Of all aspects of the CAP, it is the one that most engages public opinion, if only because it is more readily comprehensible and has stronger value-related, even emotional, undertones. It also raises difficult distributional issues. Wealthier members of the population may be comfortable with paying more for food that is organically produced or is based on production methods that are environmentally friendly and protect animals. Less well-off members of the population, for whom food represents a larger proportion of their budget, may give a greater priority to cheap food. Although it clearly has had harmful environmental consequences, the postwar productionist food system has delivered a secure food supply at reasonable prices. In any event, it seems unlikely that environmental concerns will provide a major impetus to the overall reform debate. Nevertheless, EU environmental policy initiatives can be expected to have an increasing impact on farming practice, as has already happened in the area of water pollution.

The nitrate directive

The application of the EU's nitrate directive from 1999 is likely to have considerable impact on agriculture in a number of member states. If the directive were to be applied without modification, 'then the impact on the output of the EU livestock sector could be significant: an estimated 12% reduction in pig production, a 10% fall in egg and broiler production and an 8% fall in milk production' (*Agra Europe*, 25 August 1995, p. P/2). According to a report issued by the United States Department of Agriculture, 'it could reduce exports of pigmeat by more than 10% and change the EU from an important exporter to a net importer of pig products' (*Agra Europe*, 5 August 1994, p. P/4). The effects would be felt particularly in countries with intensive livestock regimes such as The Netherlands, Denmark and Belgium, but there would also be a substantial impact in the UK (especially England) and northern Germany. Given the scale of impact, it would seem likely that some derogations from the directive will be allowed. Nevertheless, it remains the most striking example of a direct impact of EU agricultural policy on farming practice.

Water pollution was an early area of EU environmental activity. The 1980 Drinking Water Directive specified a maximum allowable concentration of 50 parts per million of nitrate in drinking water supplies. Concern about rising levels of nitrate in water was stimulated by a possible link with human health, specifically the 'blue baby' syndrome and stomach cancer. However, there is no credible scientific evidence of such a link. Another area of concern is eutrophication: increased nitrate run-offs to watercourses increase the nutrients available for algae production.

These plants use CO_2 to grow, but when they putrefy they use oxygen, using up the oxygen supply in the water and leading to fish deaths. Eutrophication is seen to have a particularly damaging effect in estuaries, by destroying fish and vegetation.

Nitrate pollution of water can arise from both the application of 'artificial' nitrogen to the land and the use of animal manure. On the whole, the major problems arise with livestock farming, because arable farmers use nitrogen in a way that minimises run-off. One of the complications in this policy area is that it can take a considerable time for nitrates to leach into the water supply, so there is a delay between applying new policy measures and assessing their effects. Nevertheless, efforts to blame the problem on the ploughing of land in wartime for the current problem 'stretch credibility . . . the slowest percolation rates of surface water to aquifers (in chalk) are around forty years, whereas some of the highest nitrate concentrations are found in limestone aquifers where the rate of percolation is estimated at less than ten years' (Seymour, Cox and Lowe, 1992, p. 93). It has also been argued that more extensive organic farming would lead to an increase in nitrate problems. Organic systems rely on the use of farmyard manure or 'green crops' ploughed into the land: 'As such green material and farmyard manure decompose . . . they are liable to lead to uncontrolled flushes of nitrates leaking from soil' (*Financial Times*, 25 January 1991).

The 1991 Nitrates Directive was designed to reduce the level of nitrate entering the water supply in those areas considered to have a nitrogen content above the acceptable level. In England, the directive was implemented initially through a Nitrate Sensitive Areas scheme, which qualified as part of the EU's agri-environmental programme. Farmers joined voluntarily for a period of five years. In its basic form, it placed limits on the amount of nitrogen that could be used on the farm. The premium scheme, which had a good uptake, provided for the conversion of arable land to grassland. Thirty-two Nitrate Sensitive Areas were established, varying in size from a few hundred to several thousand hectares. Each was chosen because it was a key water source that was above or near the nitrate drinking water standard.

By 1999, land in Nitrate Vulnerable Zones (NVZs) will be subject to mandatory good-practice measures. In Denmark and The Netherlands, the whole countries have been designated as NVZs, but the British government selected particular areas. There are sixty-eight NVZs in England and Wales, affecting around 8000 farms and 12 per cent of arable land. The NVZs are concentrated in eastern England and the Midlands: for example, a large triangle roughly bounded by Aylesbury, Bedford and Leamington; a large area of Essex north of Chelmsford; and a large area on the Norfolk–Suffolk border. In the NVZs, the use of chemical nitrogen is banned between September and February unless there is a specific crop need, and tightening limits are placed on the use of organic fertilisers such as slurry and poultry manure. Field-by-field records of nitrogen use will be compulsory. Farmers will be able to claim a 25 per cent grant of up to £85 000 per business for expenditure on such items as waste storage and handling, but there is no compensation for loss of income.

Small dairy farmers are particularly likely to be affected by NVZs, with additional costs of up to £100 a cow eating into their margins. They are likely to have to reduce herd sizes to reduce their stocking rate, and to export slurry off the farm to meet the NVZ requirements. Smaller farms tend to compensate for their size by maintaining higher stocking densities and applying nitrogen at levels in excess of 250kg a year, compared with the NVZ limit of 210kg a year, reducing to 170kg after four years. Thus, a farmer with eighty cows in a NVZ has estimated that his herd will have to be reduced to sixty-seven cows, representing a loss of £22 450 a year in milk returns (*Farmers Weekly*, 2 February 1996).

The NVZ scheme has caused considerable resentment among British farmers, who criticise the UK government both for voting for the 1991 directive and for enforcing it too strictly. The National Farmers' Union has argued that the 50mg limit should be treated as an average measurement rather than a maximum. The Chairman of the new Environment Agency commented that 'A lot of money has been spent through the nitrate legislation, which has taken away valuable reserves for other important problems' (*Farmers Weekly*, 9 February 1996). The rather unpredictable nature of the EU's decision-making process may mean that the problems tackled are not necessarily those which should have first priority.

The limits of agri-environmental policy

The terms of the debate about agricultural policy have changed, to place a new emphasis on the environmental consequences of modern farming practices. In the measured language of the EU's environmental action programme, 'it is not only environmentally desirable, but it also makes sound agricultural and economic sense to seek to strike a more sustainable balance between agricultural activity and the natural resources of the environment' (European Commission, 1993b, p. 70). Using blunter language, a group of MEPs argues that 'intensive farming, driven in part by product based subsidies and in part by technology, has actually done significant damage to the land

and rivers it holds in trust for society – damage that would not be tolerated from a chemical factory' (Land Use and Food Policy Inter-Group, 1995, p. 6).

It is difficult to escape the conclusion that what has happened in the CAP so far is that some token concessions have been made in the direction of incorporating environmental policy considerations. If nothing else, the balance of budgetary expenditure makes that clear. An incremental approach is not wholly undesirable, as it allows experiments to take place with a range of policy measures. However, an approach based on seeing what initiatives come forward at member state level leads to a certain incoherence and divergence in policy. The underlying economic forces that sustain intensive farming remain in place: large-scale farmers, supported by subsidies and readily able to borrow funds because the CAP inflates land prices, are encouraged by input suppliers to maintain a style of farming that emphasises the maximisation of output.

If environmental policy objectives are really important, then the objectives of the CAP need to be changed, a theme which will be returned to in Chapter 8. One should not attempt, however, to overlook the fact that this is an area in which there is considerable variation in the attitudes of EU citizens, both between and within member states. Vegetarians, for example, more common in Northern member states, are likely to have particular views on farming practices. While all EU citizens would presumably want to have water that is safe to drink, and food that is safe to eat, there is much more variation in views on animal welfare issues. For example, the author finds bull-fighting and fox-hunting repugnant. However, bull-fighting is deeply embedded in Spanish culture and is not a matter on which other member states can or should pronounce. Rural dwellers could claim that the urban population does not and cannot understand the place of fox-hunting in country life. In discussing the relationship between environment and agriculture, one is not just looking for policy mechanisms that achieve their stated goals efficiently (as one might, for example, with milk quotas). Fundamental issues are being raised, not just about agriculture, but also about the type of society in which we want to live, and whether we regard animals as being a part of that society.

8

The Possibility of Radical Reform?

The analysis presented in this book suggests that the politics of the CAP are such that truly radical reform of the policy is very difficult to achieve. Exogenous shocks to the system have produced significant changes in policy, and the impact of CEEC membership may produce such a shock in the future. However, these policy changes have often been diluted during the process of implementation, or their effect has been offset by changes in the world market situation, as happened with the MacSharry reforms. A single member state cannot block policy change completely, but a small group of states adversely affected by a proposed shift in policy can dilute it to such an extent that its impact is muted. Britain is as capable as any other member state of acting to protect its particular interests, as it did with its opposition to modulation during the MacSharry reforms.

In this chapter, three radical policy options are considered. Renationalisation would involve the partial dismantling of the CAP in the form in which it has existed for approaching forty years. Converting the CAP into a common rural policy would involve a substantial reorientation of the objectives of the CAP. Finally, it is argued that real reform of the CAP requires a rewriting of its treaty objectives. It could be that such a development would be the final recognition that radical reform had taken place, rather than being a means of achieving reform. One cannot, however, dismiss rewriting the treaty objectives as merely a symbolic action, because symbolism is at the heart of any political process (Edelman, 1967).

Renationalisation

The CAP has coexisted throughout its history with national payments to farmers made by member state governments. The highest level of support has been paid in Germany, which introduced VAT rebates for farmers worth several billion DMs following the agrimonetary reforms of 1984–5. The less wealthy countries such as Spain, Greece and the Republic of Ireland are less able to provide assistance to their farmers, although Italy has been relatively generous. These countries have been among the leading critics of any drift towards the renationalisation of the CAP. Countries with relatively efficient agriculture and a reform orientation also see dangers in renationalisation. The permanent secretary of the Danish Ministry of Agriculture has commented:

> As two-thirds of Danish agricultural production is exported, it is impossible for Denmark to compete in granting national subsidies. Therefore, it is essential for Danish farmers that there should be a strict set of Community rules to regulate national subsidies. (Bernstein, 1994, p. 36)

It is one thing for member states to give what can be represented as social aid to farmers, or to support agri-environmental schemes permitted under Council Regulation 2078/92. Deliberate renationalisation of the CAP, however, would undercut market unity and has proved to be a highly controversial topic. This is not surprising when one considers that renationalisation may be defined 'as a process whereby sovereignty is transferred from EU institutions to Member States' which leads to decision-making, implementation and/or financial responsibility being 'partly or totally transferred from the supranational to the national level' (Kjeldahl, 1994, p. 16).

The scene for the debate on renationalisation was really set by two developments within the EU. The introduction of partial decoupling of payments to farmers by the MacSharry reforms opened up the potential of significant change in the nature of the CAP. If one is making degressive payments to farmers to support their incomes in a period of transition from high levels of subsidy based on the support of production, such payments do not necessarily have an effect on trade between member states. Hence, they could be made by member state governments, or on a shared basis between the EU and national governments, taking into account the circumstances of farmers in each country. At a more general level, the debate about subsidiarity provided a context in which it was considered proper to consider which tasks might better be discharged at member-state or even regional level. Berkhout and Meester (1994) argued that talking in terms of subsidiarity rather than renationalisation would lend greater legitimacy to the debate.

The debate on renationalisation was stimulated by two reports issued in 1994. The Danish Institute of Agricultural Economics published a volume based on a conference held in Copenhagen in 1993, which brought together a number of practitioners and leading commentators on the CAP (Kjeldahl and Tracy, 1994). In his introduction to the volume, Tracy argued that differences in natural and socioeconomic conditions and different priorities might justify greater differentiation in agricultural policy measures. However, 'too much national financing could be contrary to the spirit of solidarity and could threaten the cohesion of the EU' (Tracy, 1994, p. 3).

Rather more attention was attracted by a report issued in the autumn of 1994 under the auspices of DGII of the Commission. This was drafted by a group of agricultural economists chaired by Arne Larsen, head of the Danish Institute of Agricultural Economics, and well-known as a former *chef de cabinet* to one of the best-known agricultural commissioners, Finn Gundelach. However, it was more commonly known as the 'Munk Report', after one of the rapporteurs, Knud Munk, who then worked for the Commission's Economic Service. This report attracted strong criticism from DGVI, no doubt in part because it represented an attempt by DGII to break DGVI's grip on the debate about the CAP. A senior Commission official was quoted as stating that the report was a 'really hot potato' and there had been a 'very painful debate' about whether to publish it all (*Financial Times*, 28 September 1994). DGVI wasted no time in denouncing the report. The Director-General for Agriculture, Guy Legras, called the report 'dangerous and irresponsible', and said that it would 'kill everything that has been achieved at EU level' (*Agra Europe*, 28 October 1994, p. E/8).

The report suggested that there should be further cuts in agricultural support prices and the elimination of quantitative restrictions. As the need for compensation for decreases in prices would vary from one member state to another, the responsibility for direct income support could be devolved to the member states, provided it was implemented in a way that did not distort competition. In order to ensure that the ground rules on state aids were adhered to, member states would be required to seek EU approval for multiannual plans for direct income support to farmers (European Commission, 1994, pp. 34–5).

Although there continued to be some academic discussion of the report (Grant, 1995), matters might have ended there, and the report would have joined all the others on the CAP that attracted attention in the media when first published but were subsequently left to gather dust on the library shelves. As representatives of one of the member states with a keen interest in reform, the UK government showed little interest in the renationalisation proposal, in part because of a concern that they would be under pressure to make more payments to farmers at a national level without seeing any significant decline in the net British contribution to the CAP. The Minister of Agriculture made it clear, 'Renationalising agricultural policy would not serve the interests of either the EU or the UK. I have no intention of going down that road' (Hogg, 1996, p. 3).

The agrimonetary system has always been one of the main mechanisms by which member states have protected their farmers while subscribing to the ideal of a common agricultural market. The changes in the agrimonetary system in 1995 upset the existing balance of interests and created a pressure for a *de facto* renationalisation of the CAP. It was agreed that member states would be allowed to compensate farmers where it could be shown that there had been 'considerable' income losses because of currency movements in other EU countries. Although limited in itself, this change was seen as the first step 'towards allowing national governments the means of maintaining support of parts of agriculture in the face of a now inevitable – if long-term – scaling down of the Common Agricultural Policy' (*Agra Europe*, 14 July 1995, p. P/3). Although the European Parliament subsequently approved the measure, MEPs 'were concerned that the measure risked in effect renationalising the CAP' (*Agra Europe*, 13 October 1995, p. P/5). Such decoupled payments do provide a very convenient means of continuing support to farmers outside GATT constraints.

As the EU becomes larger, and its agriculture becomes more diverse, the task of maintaining a common policy is becoming increasingly difficult. One of the by-products of the BSE crisis was that consumers opted for local beef, leading to 'an increasing renationalisation of the markets' (*Financial Times*, 16 September 1996). However, any abandonment of the attempt to maintain a common policy would undermine the EU as a whole, as well as leading to the re-creation of barriers to trade between member states. National payments can act as a shield for inefficient farmers; for example, the French fruit, vegetable and wine sectors that have suffered from Spanish competition. Nevertheless, there does need to be more fine-tuning of the policy to take into account the considerable variations in farming conditions and structures within the EU. As noted in Chapter 6, Fischler has suggested that there might be a voice for the regions in the CAP, although it is difficult to see how this might be done, given that some countries have better developed regional substructures than others. One might also question whether one wanted, for example, Bavaria to have a greater say in the CAP.

A really radical solution would be to create regional structures which cut across the boundaries of member states. It is arguable that in terms of production methods and efficiency, the cereal farmers of eastern England, northern France and Schleswig-Holstein have more in common with each other than they do with the crofters of Scotland, wine producers in southern France, and small-scale dairy farmers in Bavaria. Such a proposal is, of course, completely utopian at the present stage of development of the EU. Even contemplating such a development reminds us how much the CAP is shaped and constrained by national interests, and how it is necessary to offset the costs of a reform for any one member state by side payments.

It is therefore not surprising that questions are asked about whether it might be more appropriate to determine and fund some payments to farmers at the national level. If the EU is seen as having some of the characteristics of a federation, then it is worth recalling that in Australia, Canada and the United States, farm policies operate at both the federal and state/province level. A mature federation retains some measure of central direction and control with autonomy to meet local conditions. But then the EU is not a mature federation, and some member states do not want it to be, so it is not surprising that agricultural policy is incoherent. The paradox is that the EU cannot really develop without properly reforming agricultural policy, but agricultural policy reform depends in part on the maturation of the EU: for example, economic and monetary union.

A common rural policy?

If the real purpose of the CAP is to achieve a higher level of economic and social development for the rural areas of the EU, then the CAP is a strange way of going about it. Agriculture is only one economic activity in rural areas, and the way in which the CAP operates tends to direct funding towards those areas of the EU that are already prosperous. Building on a 1988 Commission paper on the future of rural society, Merlo and Manente (1994) distinguish four main types of rural area in the EU:

1. *Northern–Central regions* characterised by rural areas under the pressure of modern life, such as south-east England, northern Germany and the Po valley. These are areas with large-scale productive farming that has benefited substantially from CAP funds. This type of farming often has what are perceived by nearby urban dwellers to be harmful landscape effects, but the practical alternative might be further urban sprawl. Any lack of rural services and job opportunities is offset by the presence of nearby urban conurbations.

2. *Central–Southern regions*, such as southern France and southern Germany. These are also areas with high general levels of economic development, but agricultural incomes are lower than in the first category. Farm sizes are rather small, so that one has a weak agriculture in the context of a modern, diversified economy.

3. *North Atlantic regions*, which Merlo and Manenete (1994, p. 140) characterise as intermediate 'in that they are not particularly subjected to the pressures of modern life and at the same time cannot be considered to be declining or marginal'. Examples are the west of England and Brittany. Agricultural income is close to the EU average, but these rural economies are particularly dominated by agriculture, in part because of their distance from urban centres.

4. *Southern regions and the Republic of Ireland*, where average farm sizes are relatively small. Many of these areas are mountainous, and climatic factors also make farming difficult. Nevertheless, there is a high level of dependence on agriculture, with considerable underemployment. It is in these areas that there is 'a worsening dualism between rural areas and the rest of the regional economy, concentrated in urban centres' (Merlo and Manenete, 1994, p. 141).

In the first type of area, successful farming should be possible with declining levels of support. Diversification away from farming – for example, into various types of leisure-related activity, is feasible, given the proximity of the urban population. The fourth type of area poses particularly difficult problems for rural policy. Assistance to farmers through the CAP may simply perpetuate outdated structures, but the removal of such assistance could well provoke complete economic collapse. Diversification into alternative enterprises is relatively difficult, given the distance from urban centres and the age and skill structure of the population.

Merlo and Manente (1994, p. 135) distinguish three phases in the development of EU rural policy. In the first phase from the foundation of the common market to the early 1970s rural development, was equated with agricultural development. Agriculture's general social function was seen to be keeping the outmigration from rural areas at acceptable levels. From the 1970s to the 1980s there was an emphasis on integrated rural development within the context of a rural policy, using the EC's structural funds. A third, more recent, phase has seen a greater emphasis on environmental issues and an increasing recognition of the limits of achieving a solution to the problems of remoter rural areas through the CAP.

Nevertheless, rural development policy continues to be a significant aspect of the EU's activities. Objective 1 assistance covers regions whose development is lagging behind and whose GDP is less than 75 per cent of the EU average. This covers the island of Ireland, Portugal and Greece, 60 per cent of the population of Spain, and over a third of the population of Italy. Objective 5b covers those rural areas in difficulty which do not come within the scope of Objective 1. As well as a low level of socioeconomic development, the areas selected must meet other criteria, such as the total share of population accounted for by agriculture, the level of farm income, and population density. The leading beneficiary is France, and France and Germany between them account for 59 per cent of the population covered.

One study has questioned the conventional link between rural policy and agriculture, arguing that 'the economic vitality of rural areas does not depend on agricultural production, since manufacturing and services are shifting to smaller communities' (Kol and Kuijpers, 1996, p. 124). Pointing to an alternative policy approach, Kol and Kuijpers argue (1996, p. 29):

> The equation of rural with agricultural has been a major fallacy in thinking about the long-term future of rural communities . . . rural development depends less on agriculture than is often thought. If manufacturing and services are as important to rural areas as is

agriculture, it may be more efficient to foster rural communities through improved infrastructure for transportation and communication rather than through agricultural policy support.

These comments offer a healthy corrective to an automatic association between 'rural' and 'agricultural' and point to other ways of helping rural areas. Nevertheless, the arguments presented are open to challenge on economic and other grounds. Excluding those rural areas that are in the shadow of major urban centres, a healthy rural economy still relies to a considerable extent on the sale of goods and services to the farming population. Those involved in providing specialised services (which largely have to be made available at the point of delivery) far outnumber those actually working on farms. Many of the industries in rural areas are likely to be closely linked to agriculture; for example, first stage food processing plants. Indeed, the development of agri-food systems or agricultural districts in Italy shows how appropriate industrialisation may overcome the deficiencies of a fragmented farm structure (see Chapter 2). The particular benefit of such agricultural districts 'is that of being able to maintain agricultural value-added within agriculture and indeed the rural economy as a whole' (Merlo and Manente, 1994, p. 144).

The most promising path for rural development may thus be to develop agri-food industries that add value to local products, which may be marketed as high quality items based on traditional production methods: 'A factor acting in favour of such rural location is the so-called "green consumerism" which tends to encourage high-quality agricultural produce, processed in rural areas, especially when the landscape and environment within which a product is produced adds to its final value' (Merlo and Manente, 1994, p. 145). If rural areas ceased to be agricultural, their perceived landscape value would probably fall, tourists would be less likely to visit them, and there would be fewer opportunities for the local sale or wider marketing of high-quality food products. Abandoning agriculture could be a dangerous strategy for rural areas. While other activities have much to contribute to their vitality, agriculture is likely to retain a central economic and social role in most such areas.

All except the most remote rural areas in Britain have seen a repopulation since the 1970s as they have become sites for hi-tech and service businesses (Winter, 1996, p. 304). However, many of the incomers have often been in the older age groups and have often bought goods and services outside the immediate locality (which is often unable to meet their specialised demands), thus doing little to stem the decline of local services. House prices have been forced up, to the detriment of local inhabitants, with younger people having to migrate to towns to find affordable housing. In England, 73 per cent of parishes have no bus service, 39 per cent have no shop, and 40 per cent have no post office, and the number of both shops and post offices is continuing to decline (Country Landowners' Association, 1994, para. 94).

The Country Landowners' Association has called for a shift of emphasis from the CAP to a more broadly-based European rural policy (ERP). This would be a framework rather than an interventionist policy, with the aim of facilitating sustainable development in rural areas. Its objectives would include the development of rural communities, the diversification of the economies of rural areas, and support for socioeconomic programmes where there is market failure (Country Landowners' Association, 1995). Fischler has certainly showed himself to be sympathetic to a greater emphasis on broader rural policy objectives in the CAP. The former deputy director general of DGVI, Sir Michael Franklin, has suggested that an integrated rural policy might imply a shift in the power centre of agricultural support away from the agriculture directorate and Council (*Agra Europe*, 4 October 1996, p. P/2). Following the 'Cork declaration' drawn up after a Commission sponsored conference in November 1996, it was announced that proposals for a common rural development policy would be brought forward in 1997. The contradictory nature of the Cork declaration, and the difficulty of funding such a policy suggested that the stated objective of placing sustainable rural development at the top of the EU agenda might be difficult to achieve.

CAP objectives

The objectives of the CAP were drawn up in a very different political climate. The food shortages experienced in Germany and elsewhere in the aftermath of the Second World War remained a vivid memory. Food security still seemed to be a relevant objective in a context of international tension. There was a concern that rural populations might be tempted to support right-wing movements and oppose European integration if their welfare was not safeguarded. The best

way to help rural areas appeared to be to support farmers. Environmental issues were scarcely thought about, and in any case the
pattern of farming was less threatening to the environment. Consumers were preoccupied with obtaining a sufficient quantity of food
rather than with its quality. Public health issues were regarded as
being important, but were seen as soluble through the systematic
encouragement of better hygiene and such practices as the pasteurisation of milk. The media-led food scares would have been incon-
ceivable in the 1950s.

Farming was seen as a natural, wholesome activity embodying
sturdy traditional values that were an important counter-balance to
the artificiality of city life: 'Bringing in the harvest' was an annual
standby of cinema newsreels in Britain in the 1950s. Neighbours
young and old would be seen happily working in the sunshine (no
fear of skin cancer), after which they would sit down to a hearty
supper, secure in the knowledge that they had helped to fill the
nation's bread-basket. All sentimental artifice, of course, but it was a
long time before the positive image of farming and the countryside
was eroded by the realities of modern farming systems, and it is still
strong in some member states, such as France.

Although the process of change has differed, not just from one
member state to another, but also within different regions of a single
country, farming has become a more high-input, technologically
sophisticated activity in which the farmer has to match his or her
production skills with business skills, including an understanding of
finance and marketing. Consumers have become increasingly concerned about the intensive pattern of farming that has developed.
They are worried about the safety of the food produced, the way in
which livestock is treated, and the impact of farming on the environment. For many, the BSE episode encapsulated these concerns,
producing a lack of trust in a scientifically-based agriculture.

Through all these economic, social and political changes, the treaty
objectives of the CAP have remained unchanged. Rieger seeks to
refute what he sees as superficial criticisms of the CAP by arguing
that it is a welfare state institution that has pursued a strategy of
defensive modernisation to integrate a disadvantaged and socially
isolated group (farmers) into national societies and polities (Rieger,
1996). Although his arguments offer a healthy corrective to the most
exaggerated criticisms of the CAP, there is a broad acceptance that a
point has been reached where 'enduring reform now needs a change
to the Agricultural provisions of the Treaty' (Land Use and Food

Policy Inter-Group, 1995, p. 4) The Land Use and Food Policy Inter-Group argues for an EU food policy that would take into account all the participants in the food chain including growers, suppliers, processors and consumers. They recommend that Article 39 of the Treaty of Rome should be redrafted to set out the following objectives of a common food policy: (a) to ensure a competitive and economically sustainable agri-food industry, utilising technology, capable of constantly supplying a wide and varied choice of foodstuffs to the consumer; (b) to ensure that all food products placed on the market are fit and proper for human consumption; (c) to ensure that basic food supplies reach the consumer at a reasonable price; (d) to ensure that animals intended for human consumption are reared and slaughtered in a humane manner that minimises measurable suffering; (e) to ensure that all products raised in the soil are raised and harvested in a manner that is environmentally sustainable; and (f) to achieve the above within five years of the entry into force of these provisions, so that thereafter there would be no more direct product subsidies in order not to distort the single market, and to promote the Union's export competitiveness.

As the Land Use and Food Policy Inter-Group recognises, it would be desirable to complement these food policy objectives by a policy that sought to maintain rural communities which they term a Land Policy. In their view, this could be dealt either by replacing article 38)4) of the Treaty, which deals with the establishment of a common agricultural policy, or under Articles 130b and 130c.

Amending the treaty in this way would serve as a formal recognition that the CAP had to be changed fundamentally. In practice, a continuing process of incremental change is more likely. The Inter Governmental Conference is not likely to modify the agricultural parts of the treaty, and indeed its main tasks lie elsewhere. Incremental change is more likely because, as this book has argued, the member states have different, but important, interests in the current policy which arise from the structure of their agricultural economies. The member states are not the only significant actors in the decision-making process, but they are in a position to prevent truly radical change.

There are nevertheless, some grounds for optimism. A succession of incremental changes could lead cumulatively to a very different policy, with the change of objectives occurring at the end of the process. Such an outcome would be less coherent and would take longer than one that was objective-led, but it is more politically realistic. There are six grounds for optimism that the process of reform might move more quickly in the future than in the past.

First, although the shape of the CAP often seems to be determined by an elaborate process of intergovernmental bargaining in which a succession of trade-offs produces suboptimal policy outcomes, the policy debate about the CAP does have a positive impact. Although the interests that benefit from the CAP are often able to hide behind its complexity, the arguments put forward by an 'advocacy coalition' of agricultural economists or others have brought about an increasing realisation, among informed opinion at last, that here is a policy that has outdated objectives, which in any case it fails to meet. The loose but visible network of agricultural policy reformers meets Sabatier's definition of an advocacy coalition in so far as it is made up of people from a variety of positions who share 'a set of basic values, causal assumptions, and problem perceptions – and who show a nontrivial degree of coordinated activity over time' (Sabatier, 1993, p. 25). If nothing else, they are reading the influential *Agra Europe* each week, a publication that takes a reform stance, which in part stems from a perspective close to that of agribusiness.

Second, it is evident that the onset of economic and monetary union is having an increasing impact on the CAP. The EU Budget Council decided in July 1996 that the farm budget for 1997 would be one billion ECU less than originally proposed, leading to a virtually unchanged total figure in 1997 compared with 1996. Modest though such a cut may appear to be, it 'is unprecedented in the development of the CAP. In the past, the agricultural budget was sacred and immune to any attempts to economise on EU spending' (*Agra Europe*, 26 July 1996, p. P/4). However, EMU is the central political objective of the EU, and its achievement is seen as being essential to its future success. If CAP spending has to be cut so that member states are able to reduce public expenditure and debt to meet the convergence criteria for the single currency, then it is increasingly evident that agricultural policy objectives will have to give way to achieving the more important goal of EMU.

Third, the exogenous pressures for reform are likely to intensify rather than reduce. The advocacy coalition has a long-term impact by changing the terms of the debate, but 'changes in the core aspects of a policy are usually the results of perturbations in noncognitive factors external to the subsystem' (Sabatier, 1993, p. 20). The latest US Farm Bill suggests that American agribusiness is seeking to pursue a policy, whether wisely or not, of seeking to act as the world's bread-basket through the export of basic commodities. Pressures for trade liberalisation from powerful interests within the United States are likely to increase, reinforced by the Cairns Group. Globalisation is a complex and contested phenomenon, and particularly in the case of agriculture, it is important not to treat it as a linear process which necessarily produces convergence in methods of production (Byé and Fonte, 1994; McMichael, 1994). Nevertheless, 'bringing agriculture under a GATT regime is profoundly symbolic of the move to legitimize world market integration because of agriculture's identification with place and nation' (McMichael, 1994, p. 285). Bringing agriculture fully within the GATT regime is the first step in a process with an unknown final outcome, but one which is likely to have an increasing impact on the CAP in the twenty-first century.

Fourth, there are increasing indications that Germany's position on the CAP is changing. This is partly a consequence of the structural changes in German agriculture brought about by unification, but it also reflects the priority that Germany attaches to bringing the CEECs within the EU. The achievement of this objective is not compatible with the CAP of the late 1990s. In addition, EMU is also a major factor, with budgetary cuts made to achieve convergence criteria putting pressure on agricultural spending. If spending on cherished social security objectives has to be cut, then spending on agriculture is put under closer scrutiny. When cuts in arable aid were proposed by the Commission in the aftermath of the BSE crisis, it seemed likely that 'Meeting the economic criteria for the single currency, with the help of unspent funds from the EU budget, is more important to Germany's political elite than the wealth of cereal farmers (*Agra Europe*, 2 August 1996, p. P/6).

The paper circulated by the German ministry of agriculture in June 1996 arguing that the CAP will need major changes if it is to survive the challenges of eastern enlargement and the next round of world trade liberalisation, represents a significant shift in the German position. Of course, it is not the end of the story: 'The paper urges Germany to take a positive role in the formulation of new policy to ensure its interests are properly represented' (*Agra Europe*, 21 June 1966, p. E/6). Radical farm policy reform would threaten the interests of Bavarian farmers, and Bavaria continues to exert considerable influence within German domestic politics. Nevertheless, the terms of the debate within Germany are changing, and this may in turn have some influence on France's position. If Germany and France shift their positions, then real reform is possible.

Fifth, public opinion within the EU is shifting, albeit at different speeds in Northern and Southern states, towards an agriculture that produces safer food in a more environmentally friendly way that takes better care of animals. Of course, one must be careful not to accept too readily the model of a post-Fordist agriculture in which high-quality, high-value-added food products are produced in an environmentally sustainable fashion by a kind of reinvented postmodernist peasantry. There is still plenty of demand from poorer consumers for standardised, cheap food products, which will be articulated by the supermarket chains. Even wealthier consumers sometimes seem to think that they can have an environmentally friendly agriculture and cheap food. Nevertheless, a democratic European Union that aspires to full legitimacy has to listen to the concerns about food policy expressed by many of its citizens.

Sixth, and this is likely to be a very long-run change, the rigid positions of the member states may be dissolved by the increasing influence exerted by regions, some of which cut across member-state boundaries. It has been emphasised throughout this book that each member state contains many different types of agriculture, and a point may be reached well into the twenty-first century when the farmers of south-east England, northern France and the Po valley recognise that they have interests in common which are stronger than their national interests, while those in Brittany will align themselves with farmers in the west of England. Given the xenophobia associated with the BSE affair in Britain, this may seem to be a utopian vision. Yet simultaneous processes of globalisation and localisation may one day undermine the national differences that seem so important in economic and political terms in the last years of the twentieth century.

In June 1996, Guy Legras, the Commission's Director-General for Agriculture, announced that the Commission would present outline proposals in the ensuing twelve months for a major package of policy reforms on the scale of the MacSharry proposals. This admission of the need for a 'reform of the reform' or a 'MacSharry II' seems in part to result from an acceptance on the part of the Commission that continuing productivity gains in agriculture are likely, thus undermining earlier reforms. A new reflections document is to be produced, covering such issues as the next round of multilateral trade negotiations and the impact of CEEC membership: 'The work is focusing particularly on how to deal with increased restrictions on subsidised exports, possibly by seeking a greater alignment of EU and world market prices, thereby eliminating the need for subsidies' (*Agra Europe*, 12 July 1996, p. P/4).

Further significant reform of the CAP is in the interests of the EU as a political entity. It is not a good use of resources to spend over half of its budget on a policy that does not really help to sustain rural life; allows large-scale fraud; increases food prices for consumers; and is environmentally damaging. It is difficult to have confidence in a set of institutions and political processes that produce such an outcome. However, as it matures, the EU may show an increasing capacity to learn from its errors and to develop a set of agricultural policies that are more relevant to the needs of the twenty-first century. Securing change in the CAP is often a slow and frustrating process, but too much impatience might undermine what is still in many ways a cornerstone of the EU. For Eurosceptics, the CAP epitomises all that is wrong with the EU; for those who believe in the European vision, it demonstrates how difficult it is to create a new international entity through a process of bargaining and mutual adjustment.

As the process of international economic integration known as globalisation starts to influence agriculture, one of the last reservoirs of fully autonomous national policies, there is a need for European co-operation to ensure that objectives other than those of a purely economic character are taken into account. Of course, there is a paradox in that the EU both facilitates the activities of the transnational corporations that are the main driving force behind globalisation, and also seeks to create a social Europe that takes care of the socially excluded. The tension between the need for a competitive economy and the common desire for a caring society can never be completely resolved. Nevertheless, part of Europe's mission must to be sustain and develop its rural areas and the people who live within them in a way that protects the environment and respects the rights of farm animals. Europe thus needs a common agricultural policy, but one with different objectives and mechanisms from the current policy. It must have it and one day it will have it.

Bibliography

Allanson, P., J. Murdoch, P. Lowe and G. Garrod (1994) 'The Rural Economy: An Evolutionary Perspective', Centre for Rural Economy Working Paper No. 1, University of Newcastle upon Tyne.

Atkin, M. (1993) *Snouts in the Trough* (Cambridge: Woodhead).

Baldock, D. and K. Mitchell (1995) *Cross-Compliance within the Common Agricultural Policy* (London: Institute for European Environmental Policy).

Barnes, R. C. (1995) 'Disorderly Dairying and Anglo Institutional Solutions: A Comparative Study of England and Canada, 1850–1939', Ph.D. thesis, University of Wisconsin-Madison.

Berkhout, P. and Meester, M. (1994) 'Dutch Agricultural Policy Objectives', in R. Kjeldahl and M. Tracy (eds) *Renationalisation of the Common Agricultural Policy?* (Tonbridge: Combined Book Services).

Bernstein, N. (1994) 'National Support: Impact and Prospects', in R. Kjeldahl and M. Tracy (eds) *Renationalisation of the Common Agricultural Policy?* (Tonbridge: Combined Book Services).

Bielders, F. (1966) 'Russia, Ukraine and CEECs', Agra Europe Outlook 96 conference, London.

Bojduniak, R. and I. Sturgess, (1995) 'Cereals and Oilseeds Products', in J. Strak and W. Morgan (eds), *The UK Food and Drink Industry* (Northborough: Euro PA and Associates).

Boyle, G. E., B. Kearney, T. McCarthy and M. Keane (no date) *The Competitiveness of Irish Agriculture* (Dublin: Allied Irish Bank and Farmers Journal).

Byé, P. and M. Fonte (1994) 'Is the Technical Model of Agriculture Changing Radically?', in P. McMichael (ed.) *The Global Restructuring of Agro-Food Systems* (Ithaca, NY: Cornell University Press).

Capo, E. (1995) 'Transformation and Development in Italian Rural Society', *Sociologia Ruralis*, vol. XXXV, pp. 297–308.

CAP Review Group (1995) *European Agriculture: The Case for Radical Reform* (London: Ministry of Agriculture, Fisheries and Food).

Charvet, J.-P. (1994) *La France agricole: en état de choc* (Paris: Editions Liris).

Châtenay, P. (1996) 'Outlook for Sugar', Agra Europe Outlook 96 conference, London.

Clunies-Ross, T. and G. Cox (1994) 'Challenging the Productivist Paradigm: Organic Farming and the Politics of Agricultural Change', in P. Lowe, T. Marsden and S. Whatmore (eds), *Regulating Agriculture* (London: David Fulton).

Collins, N. (1995) 'Agricultural Policy Networks of the Republic of Ireland and Northern Ireland', *Political Studies*, vol. 43, pp. 664–82.

Country Landowners' Association (1994) 'Focus on the CAP: A CLA Discussion Paper' (London: Country Landowners' Association).

Country Landowners' Association (1995) *A Rural Policy for Europe* (London: Country Landowners' Association).

Court of Auditors (1989) 'Special Report No. 1/89 on the Agrimonetary System Accompanied by the Replies of the Commission', *Official Journal of the European Communities*, 24 May, C128/1–C128/80.

Court of Auditors (1991) 'Special Report No. 4/91 on the Operation of the Common Organization of the Market in the Sugar and Isoglucose Sector together with the Replies of the Commission', *Official Journal of the European Communities*, 7 November, C290/1–C290/56.

Court of Auditors (1994) 'Special Report No. 3/94 on the Implementation of the Intervention Measures Provided for by the Organization of the Market in Beef and Veal together with the Commission's Replies', *Official Journal of the European Communities*, 14 December, C356/1–C356/41.

Cox, G., P. Lowe and M. Winter (1989) 'The Farm Crisis in Britain', in D. Goodman and M. Redclift (eds), *The International Farm Crisis* (London: Macmillan).

Cox, G., P. Lowe and M. Winter (1990) *The Voluntary Principle in Conservation* (Chichester: Packard).

Coyle, W. (1996) 'China and South East Asia', Agra Europe Outlook 96 conference, London.

Daugbjerg, C. (1996) 'Policy Networks and Agricultural Policy Reforms in Sweden and the European Community: Explaining Different Reform Outcomes', Paper presented at the annual conference of the Political Studies Association, Glasgow.

Delorme, H. (1994) 'French Agricultural Policy Objectives', in R. Kjeldahl and M. Tracy (eds), *Renationalisation of the Common Agricultural Policy?* (Tonbridge: Combined Book Services).

De Maria, B. (1996) 'Outlook for Cereals', Paper presented at Agra Europe Outlook 96 conference, London.

Doran-Schiratti, M. (1996) 'GATT Implementation: An Interim Assessment', Agra Europe Outlook 96 conference, London.

Dupont, C. and P. Sciarini (1994) 'Narrowing the Farm Gap. The Bargaining over Agricultural Policies in the Uruguay Round', Paper presented at the APSA meetings, New York.

Economist Intelligence Unit (1990) *Europe's Dairy Industry: Tackling the Single Market* (London: Economist Intelligence Unit).

Edelman, M. (1967) *The Symbolic Uses of Politics* (Urbana, Ill.: University of Illionois Press).

Elégoët, F. and J. Frouws (1990) *Strategies Agricoles: Les Quotas Laitiers en Bretagne, France, Hollande* (Rennes: Tud Ha Bro).

Estrada, E. M. (1995) 'Farmers' Unions and the Restructuring of European Agriculture, *Sociologia Ruralis*, vol. XXXV, pp. 348–65.

European Commission (1987) 'The Regional Impact of the Common Agricultural Policy in Spain and Portugal' (Brussels: Commission of the European Communities).

European Commission (1989) *The Agricultural Situation in the Community: 1988 Report* (Luxembourg: Office of Official Publications of the European Communities).

European Commission (1991) 'Communication of the Commission to the Council. The Development and Future of the CAP: Reflections Paper of the Commission', COM(91) 100 final, Brussels.

European Commission (1993a) 'Commission Communication to the Council. Development and Future of Wine Sector policy', COM(93) 380 final, Brussels.

European Commission (1993b) *Towards Sustainability* (Luxembourg: Office for Official Publications for the European Communities).

European Commission (1994a) *The Economics of the Common Agricultual Policy*, Reports and Studies No. 5, *European Economy* (Luxembourg: Office for Official Publications of the European Communities).

European Commission (1994b) *The Agricultural Situation in the Community: 1993 Report* (Luxembourg: Office for Official Publications of the European Communities).

European Commission (1995) *The Agricultural Situation in the European Union: 1994 Report* (Luxembourg: Office for Official Publications of the European Communities).

European Commission (1996) *The Agricultural Situation in the European Union: 1995 Report* (Luxembourg: Office for Official Publications of the European Communities).

European Council (1995) *Report of the Council on the Functioning of the Treaty of the European Union* (Brussels: European Union – Council).

European Parliament (1989) *Report drawn up on behalf of the Committee on Economic and Monetary Affairs and Industrial Policy on the Food Industry* (Luxembourg: Office for Official Publications of the European Communities).

European Parliament (1992a) *Report of the Committee on Agriculture, Fisheries and Rural Development on Beekeeping in the European Community: Problems and Requirements*, PE 156.232/fin.

European Parliament (1992b) *Report of the Committee on Agriculture, Fisheries and Rural Development on a Commission Proposal for a Council Regulation on the Common Organization of the Market in Bananas*, PE 202.495/fin/Part A.

European Parliament (1993) *Report of the Committee on Agriculture, Fisheries and Rural Development on Protection and Support for Bergamot Growing*, PE 205.455/fin.

European Parliament (1994) *Report of the Committee on Agriculture, Fisheries and Rural Development on an Assessment and Forecast of the Community's Dairy Policy*, PE 208.219/fin.

Farmers' Link (1995) *Just Green Bananas!* (Norwich: Farmers' Link).

Fearne, A. (1991) 'The History and Development of the CAP 1945–1985', in C. Ritson and D. Harvey (eds), *The Common Agricultural Policy and the World Economy* (Wallingford: C.A.B. International).

Fennell, R. (1979) *The Common Agricultural Policy of the European Community* (London: Granada).

Fischler, F. (1996) 'Keynote Address', Agra Europe Outlook 96 conference, London.

Ford, B.J. (1996) *BSE: the Facts* (London: Corgi Books).

Frouws, J. and J. van Tatenhove (1993) 'Agriculture, Environment and the State: The Development of Agro-Environmental Policy-Making in the Netherlands', *Sociologia Ruralis*, vol. XXXIII, pp. 220–39.

Frouws, J. and M. Ettema (1994) 'Specialized Farmers' Associations in The Netherlands', in D. Symes and A. Jansen (eds), *Agricultural Restructuring and Rural Change in Europe* (Wageningen: Wageningen Studies in Sociology).

Gale Johnson, D. (1991) *World Agriculture in Disarray* (2nd edn) (London: Macmillan).

Gardner, B. (1996) 'The Future of the CAP: Change and Stability 1996–2015', Agra Europe Outlook 96 conference, London.

Garrido, F. and E. Moyano (1996) 'Spain', in M. Whitby (ed.) *The European Environment and CAP Reform* (Wallingford: CAB International).

GATT (1993) *Trade Policy Review, Poland 1992 vol. I* (Geneva: General Agreement on Tariffs and Trade).

Goussios, D. (1995) 'The European and Local Context of Greek Farming', *Sociologia Ruralis*, vol. XXXV, pp. 322–34.

Goussios, D. and E. Zacopoulou (1990) 'The Co-operative and Union Movement in Greece', in F. Just (ed.), *Co-operatives and Farmers' Unions in Western Europe* (Esbjerg: South Jutland University Press).

Grant, W. (1981) 'The Politics of the Green Pound', *Journal of Common Market Studies*, vol. XIX, pp. 313–29.

Grant, W. (1991) *The Dairy Industry: An International Comparison* (Aldershot: Dartmouth).

Grant, W. and MacNamara, A. (1995) 'When Policy Communities Intersect: The Case of Agriculture and Banking', *Political Studies*, vol. 43, pp. 509–15.

Gray, O.W. (1989) 'Pressure Groups and their Influence on Agricultural Policy and its Reform in the European Community', Ph.D. thesis, University of Bath.

Greer, A. (1996) *Rural Politics in Northern Ireland* (Aldershot: Avebury).

Hall, P. (1986) *Governing the Economy* (Cambridge: Polity Press).

Hall, R. (1995) 'Europe's Top 100 Dairy Companies', *Milk Industry Journal*, pp. 12–13.

Harding, F. (1989) 'Dairy Products', in C.R.W. Spedding (ed.), *The Human Food Chain* (London: Elsevier).

Hartmann, M. (1996) 'Implications of EU East Englargement for the CAP', Paper presented at CREDIT conference, Nottingham.

Hathaway, D.E. and M.D. Ingco (1995) 'Agricultural Liberalization and the Uruguay Round', World Bank conference on The Uruguay Round and the Developing Economies, Washington, DC.

Heinze, R.G. and Voelzkow, H. (1993) 'Organizational Problems for the German Farmers' Association and Alternative Policy Options', *Sociologia Ruralis*, vol. XXXIII, pp. 25–41.

Hendriks, G. (1991) *Germany and European Integration. The Common Agricultural Policy: an Area of Conflict* (Oxford: Berg).

Hendriks, G. (1994) 'The National Politics of International Trade Reform: the Case of Germany', in P. Lowe, T. Marsden and S. Whatmore (eds), *Regulating Agriculture* (London: David Fulton).

Hendriks, G. (1995) 'German Agricultural Policy Objectives', in R. Kjeldahl and M. Tracy (eds), *Renationalisation of the Common Agricultural Policy?* (Tonbridge: Combined Book Services).

Hill, B. (1984) *The Common Agricultural Policy: Past, Present and Future* (London: Methuen).

Hill, B. and D. Ray (1987) *Economics for Agriculture* (London: Macmillan).

Hogg, D. (1996) 'Opening Address', Agra Europe Outlook 96 conference, London.

House of Lords (1988) Select Committee on the European Communities 18th Report 1987–88, *Review of the Sheepmeat Regime* (London: HMSO).

House of Lords (1994a) Select Committee on the European Communities 12th Report 1993–4, *Financial Control and Fraud in the Community* (London: HMSO).

House of Lords (1994b) Select Committee on the European Communities 10th Report 1993–4, *The Implications for Agriculture of the Europe Agreements: Volume II – Evidence* (London: HMSO).

House of Lords (1996) Select Committee on the European Communities 12th Report 1995–6, *Enlargement and CAP Reform* (London: HMSO).

Hussey, G. (1995) *Ireland Today: Anatomy of a Changing State* (Harmondsworth: Penguin).

IDA (1991) *A Future in Food* (Dublin: Industrial Development Authority).

Ingco, M. D. (1995) 'Agricultural Trade Liberalization in the Uruguay Round: One Step Forward, One Step Back?', World Bank conference on the Uruguay Round and the Developing Economies, Washington, DC.

Ingersent, K. A., A. J. Rayner and R. C. Hine (eds), (1994) *Agriculture in the Uruguay Round* (London: Macmillan).

Jachnik, P. (1996) 'Outlook for Dairy', Agra Europe Outlook 96 conference, London.

Jenkins, R. (1989) *European Diary 1977–81* (London: Collins).

Johnson, D. G. (1995) *Less Than Meets the Eye: the Modest Impact of CAP Reform* (London: Centre for Policy Studies).

Josling, T. (1993) 'Agricultural Policy Reform in the USA and the EC', in A. J. Rayner and D. Colman (eds), *Current Issues in Agricultural Economics* (London: Macmillan).

Josling, T. and S. Tangermann (1995) *Toward a CAP for the Next Century* (London: European Policy Forum.

Josling, T. E., S. Tangermann and T. K. Warley (forthcoming) *Agriculture in the GATT* (London: Macmillan).

Just, F. (1990) 'Butter, Bacon and Organisational Power in Danish Agriculture', in F. Just (ed.), *Co-operatives and Farmers' Unions in Western Europe* (Esbjerg: South Jutland University Press).

Katzenstein, P. (1985) *Small States in World Markets* (Ithaca, NY: Cornell University Press).

Keeler, J. T. S. (1987) *The Politics of Neocorporatism in France* (New York: Oxford University Press).

Keeler, J. T. S. (1996) 'Agricultural Power in the European Community: Explaining the Fate of CAP and GATT Negotiations', *Comparative Politics*, vol. 28, pp. 127–49.

Kjeldahl, R. and M. Tracy (eds), *Renationalisation of the Common Agricultural Policy?* (Tonbridge: Combined Book Services).

Kjeldahl, R. (1994) 'Introduction: Reforming the Reform', in R. Kjeldahl and M. Tracy (eds), *Renationalising the Common Agricultural Policy?* (Tonbridge: Combined Book Services).

Kol, J. and B. Kuijpers (1996) 'The Costs for Consumers and Taxpayers of the Common Agricultural Policy of the European Union: the Case of the Netherlands' (Rotterdam: Erasmus Centre for European Integration Studies).

Kowalski, A. (1991) 'Agriculture', in C. Blazycouer and R. Rapacki (eds), *Poland in the 1990s* (London: Pinter).

Land Use and Food Policy Inter-Group (1995) *The Secret Garden* (Brussels: Land Use and Food Policy Inter-Group of the European Parliament).

Le Heron, R. (1993) *Globalized Agriculture* (Oxford: Pergamon Press).

Libby, R. T. (1992) *Protecting Markets: US Policy and the World Grain Trade* (Ithaca, NY: Cornell University Press).

Lowe, D. (1996) 'The Development Policy of the European Union and the Mid-Term Review of the Lomé Partnership', in N. Nugent (ed.), *The European Union 1995: Annual Review of Activities* (Oxford: Basil Blackwell).

Lowe, P., T. Marsden and S. Whatmore (1994) 'Changing Regulatory Orders: The Analysis of the Economic Governance of Agriculture', in P. Lowe, T. Marsden and S. Whatmore (eds), *Regulating Agriculture* (London: David Fulton).

Mackel, C. (1977) 'The Development, Role and Effects of Green Money in a Period of Economic Instability', *North of Scotland College of Agriculture Bulletin*, no. 13.

Malhan, N. (1996) 'The Implications of Unification for Germany's Role in the European Union', Ph.D. thesis, University of Warwick.

Marks, L. (1993) 'Biotechnology', in P. Johnson (ed.), *European Industries* (Aldershot: Edward Elgar).

Marsden, T., S. Whatmore and R. Munton (1990) 'The Role of Banking Capital and Credit Relations in British Food Production', in T. Marsden and J. Little (eds), *Political, Social and Economic Perspectives on the International Food System* (Aldershot: Avebury).

Marsden, T., S. Whatmore, R. Munton and J. Little (1986) 'The Restructing Process and Economic Centrality in Capitalist Agriculture', *Journal of Rural Studies*, vol. 2, pp. 271–80.

Marsden, T. K. and S. Whatmore (1994) 'Finance Capital and Food System Restructuring: National Incorporation of Global Dynamics', in P. McMichael (ed.), *The Global Restructuring of Food Systems* (Ithaca, NY: Cornell University Press.

Marsh, J. and S. Tangermann (1996) *Preparing Europe's Rural Economy for the 21st Century* (Brussels: Land Use and Food Policy Inter-Group of the European Parliament).

McMichael P. (1994) 'Global Restructuring: Some Lines of Enquiry', in P. McMichael (ed.), *The Global Restrucuturing of Agro-Food Systems* (Ithaca, NY: Cornell University Press).

Merlo, M. and M. Manente (1994) 'Consequences of Common Agricultural Policy Reform for Rural Development and the Environment', in *European Economy Reports and Studies*, no. 5.

Micheletti, M. (1987) 'Organization and Representation of Farmers' Interests in Sweden', *Sociologia Ruralis*, vol. XXVII, pp. 166–80.

Ministerio de Agricultura (1993) *The Spanish Agrofood Sector* (Madrid: Ministero de Agricultura).

Moyer, H. W. and T. E. Josling (1990) *Agricultural Policy Reform: Politics and Process in the EC and USA* (Hemel Hempstead: Harvester Wheatsheaf).

Munk, K. J. (1993) 'The Rationale for the Common Agricultural Policy and other EC Sectoral Policies', *European Economy, Reports and Studies*, no. 5, pp. 295–314.

National Consumer Council (1988) *Consumers and the Common Agricultural Policy* (London: HMSO).

National Consumer Council (1995) *Agricultural Policy in the European Union* (London: National Consumer Council).

Neville, W. and F. Mordaunt (1993) *A Guide to the Reformed Common Agricultural Policy* (London: Estates Gazette).

Neville-Rolfe, E. (1984) *The Politics of Agriculture in the European Community* (London: Policy Studies Institute).

Newby, H. (1978) 'The Rural Sociology of Advanced Capitalist Societies', in H. Newby (ed.), *International Perspectives in Rural Sociology* (Chichester: John Wiley).

Newby, H. (1979) *Green and Pleasant Land?* (Harmondsworth: Penguin).

Nugent, N. (1991) *The Government and Politics of the European Community*, (2nd edition) (London: Macmillan).

Ockenden, J. and Franklin, M. (1995) *European Agriculture: Making the CAP Fit the Future* (London: Pinter).

OECD (1989) *Economic Survey 1988/9: Portugal* (Paris: Organisation for Economic Co-operation and Development).

OECD (1992a) *Biotechnology, Agriculture and Food* (Paris: Organisation for Economic Co-operation and Development).

OECD (1992b) *Economic Surveys 1991/2: Austria* (Paris: Organisation for Economic Co-operation and Development).

OECD (1992c) *The Tomato Market in OECD Countries* (Paris: Organisation for Economic Co-operation and Development).

OECD (1994a) *Agricultural Policies, Markets and Trade: Monitoring and Outlook 1994* (Paris: Organisation for Economic Co-operation and Development).

OECD (1994b) *Farm Employment and Economic Adjustment in OECD Countries* (Paris: Organisation for Economic Co-operation and Development).

OECD (1994c) *Review of Agricultural Policies: Hungary* (Paris: Organisation for Economic Co-operation and Development).

OECD (1995a) *Agricultural Policies, Markets and Trade: Monitoring and Outlook, 1995* (Paris: Organisation for Economic Co-operation and Development).

OECD (1995b) *Agricultural Policies, Markets and Trade in the Central and East European Countries* (Paris: Organisation for Economic Co-operation and Development).

OECD (1995c) *The Uruguay Round: A Preliminary Evaluation of the Impacts of the Agreement on Agriculture in the OECD Countries* (Paris: Organisation for Economic Co-operation and Development).

O'Neill, P. (1993) 'Big Five Lift Profits', *Co-op*, May, pp. 16–19.

Page, E. C. and Wouters, L. (1995) 'The Europeanization of the National Bureaucracies?', in J. Pierre (ed.), *Bureaucracy in the Modern State* (Aldershot: Edward Elgar).

Pedersen, J. D. (1993) 'The EC and the Developing Countries: Still Partners?', in O. Norgaard, T. Pedersen and N. Petersen (eds), *The European Community in World Politics* (London: Pinter).

Pérez-Diaz, V. (1983) 'The New Agriculturalists', unpublished TS, University of Madrid.

Petit, M., M. de Benedictis, D. Britton, M. de Groot, W. Henrichsmeyer and F. Leshi (1987) *Agricultural Policy Formation in the European Community: The Birth of Milk Quotas and CAP Reform* (Amsterdam: Elsevier).

Phillips, P. W. (1990) *Wheat, Europe and the GATT* (London: Pinter).

Pinder, J. (1991) *European Community: the Building of a Union* (Oxford University Press).

Pollert, A. (1993) *The Single European Market: Multinationals, Merger and Concentration in the Food Processing Industry* (Coventry: University of Warwick European Public Policy Institute).

Povellato, A. (1996) 'Italy', in M. Whitby (ed.), *The European Environment and CAP Reform* (Wallingford: CAB Books).

Preeg, E. H. (1995) *Traders in a Brave New World* (University of Chicago Press).

Répassy, H. and D. Symes (1993) 'Perspectives on Agrarian Reform in East–Central Europe', *Sociologia Ruralis*, vol. XXXIII, pp. 81–91.

Residuary Milk Marketing Board (1994) *EC Dairy Facts and Figures* (Thames Ditton: Residuary Milk Marketing Board).

Rieger, E. (1996) 'The Common Agricultural Policy', in H. Wallace and W. Wallace (eds), *Policy-making in the European Union*, (3rd edn) (Oxford University Press).

RSPB (1995) 'A Review of the 1992 CAP Arable Reforms' (Sandy, Beds: Royal Society for the Protection of Birds).

Sabatier, P. A. (1995) 'Policy Change over a Decade or More', in P. Sabatier and H. Jenkins-Smith (eds), *Policy Change and Learning an Advocacy Coalition Approach* (Boulder, Col.: Westview Press).

Schmitt, G. (1995) 'Why is the Agriculture of Advanced Western Economies Still Organized by Family Farms? Will this Continue to be so in the Future?', in G. H. Peters (ed.), *Agricultural Economics* (Aldershot: Edward Elgar).

Schwinne, E. (1993) 'The Deutschmark, Green Rate Changes and the German Position', conference on Crisis in the Agrimonetary System?', London.

Secretariat-General of the Commission (1968) *Memorandum on the Reform of Agriculture* (Brussels: European Commission).

Seymour, S., G. Cox and P. Lowe (1992) 'Nitrates in Water: the Politics of the Polluter Pays Principle', *Sociologia Ruralis*, vol. XXXII, pp. 82–103.

Smith, M. J. (1988) 'Consumers and British Agricultural Policy: a Case of Long-Term Exclusion', *Essex Papers in Politics and Government*, no. 48, University of Essex.

Stewart, T. P. (ed.), (1993) *The GATT Uruguay Round: A Negotiating History*, (3 vols) (Deventer: Kluwer).

Swinbank, A. (1978) *The British Interest and the Green Pound* (Reading: Centre for Agricultural Strategy).

Swinbank, A. (1989) 'The Common Agricultural Policy and the Politics of European Decision Making', *Journal of Common Market Studies*, vol. XXVII, pp. 303–22.

Swinbank, A. (1992) 'A Future for Green "Money"?' Annual conference of the Agricultural Economics Society, Aberdeen.

Swinbank, A. (1993a) 'CAP Reform, 1992', *Journal of Common Market Studies*, vol. 31, pp. 359–72.

Swinbank, A. (1993b) 'The EC's New Agrimonetary System', University of Reading, Department of Agricultural Economics and Management, Discussion Paper 93/04.

Swinbank, A. (1996a) 'The CAP Decision-Making Process' in C. Ritson and D. Harvey (eds), 'The Common Agricultural Policy', MS (Wallingford: CAB International).

Swinbank, A. (1996b) 'The Problem with Green Money', Agra Europe Outlook 96 conference, London.

Swinbank, A. and Tanner, C. (1996) *Farm Policy and Trade Conflict: the Uruguay Round and Common Agricultural Policy Reform* (Ann Arbor, Mich.: University of Michigan Press).

Tangermann, S. (1992) 'European Integration and the Common Agricultural Policy', in C. E. Barfield and M. Perlman (eds), *Industry, Services and Agriculture* (Washington DC: The AEI Press).

Tangermann, S. (1996) 'CAP Reform: What Next?', Paper presented at CREDIT conference, Nottingham.

Thomson, K. J. (1996) 'The CAP and the WTO after the Uruguay Round Agriculture Agreement' CREDIT conference, Nottingham.

Tracy, M. (1989) *Government and Agriculture in Western Europe 1880–1988*, (3rd edn) (Hemel Hempstead: Harvester Wheatsheaf).

Tracy, M. (1994) 'Summary of Major Policy Issues', in R. Kjeldahl and M. Tracy (eds), *Renationalisation of the Common Agricultural Policy?* (Tonbridge: Combined Book Services).

Tracy, M. (1995) 'The Commission's "Agricultural Strategy Paper": A Commentary', Agricultural Economics Society conference, London.

Traxler, F. (1985) 'Prerequisites, Problem-Solving Capacity and Limits of Neo-Corporatist Regulation: A Case Study of Private Interest Governance and Economic Performance in Austria', in W. Streeck and P. C. Schmitter (eds), *Private Interest Government* (London: Sage).

University of Cambridge (1994) *Report on Farming in the Eastern Counties of England* (Cambridge: Agricultural Economics Unit, Department of Land Economy).

Vroom, B. de (1987) 'The Food Industry and Quality Regulation', in W. Grant (ed.), *Business Interests, Organizational Development and Private Interest Government* (Berlin: de Gruyter).

Waarden, F. van (1987) 'Sector Structure, Interests and Associative Action in the Food Processing Industry', in W. Grant (ed.), *Business Interests, Organizational Development and Private Interest Government* (Berlin: de Gruyter).

Weale, A., G. Pridham, A. Williams and M. Porter (1996) 'Environmental Administration in Six European States: Secular Convergence or National Distinctiveness?', *Public Administration*, vol. 74, pp. 255–74.

Wilkinson, A. (1994) 'Renationalisation: An Evolving Debate', in R. Kjeldahl and M. Tracy (eds), *Renationalisation of the Common Agricultural Policy?* (Tonbridge: Combined Book Services).

Winter, M. (1995) *Networks of Knowledge* (Godalming: World Wide Fund for Nature).

Winter, M. (1996) *Rural Politics* (London: Routledge).

Winters, L. A. (1993) 'The Political Economy of Industrial Countries' Agricultural Policies', in A. J. Rayner and D. Colman (eds), *Current Issues in Agricultural Economics* (London: Macmillan).

Index